Customer Relationship Management

Customer Relationship Management

KAVITA SINGH

Orange Boooks International
NEW DELHI-110002

ISBN : 978-93-83263-51-6

Published in 2018 in India by

Orange Boooks International

Contact Us
113A, Prakasha Scout,
Ansari Road, Daryaganj,
New Delhi - 110 002
INDIA
Phone:- 011-43046297,
011-43522777
Email:- Info@obipd.com

Preface

Customer Relationship Management (CRM) is a comprehensive textbook designed to meet the needs of postgraduate management students specializing in marketing. It explains the concepts and application of CRM through numerous examples, exhibits, and cases.

Customer relationship management is a broadly recognized, widely-implemented strategy for managing a company's interactions with customers, clients and sales prospects. It involves using technology to organize, automate, and synchronize business processes—principally sales activities, but also those for marketing, customer service, and technical support. The overall goals are to find, attract, and win new clients, nurture and retain those the company already has, entice former clients back into the fold, and reduce the costs of marketing and client service. Customer relationship management denotes a company-wide business strategy embracing all client-facing departments and even beyond. When an implementation is effective, people, processes, and technology work together to increase profitability, and reduce operational costs.

To characterize a marketing system, it must first be defined. The concept of a market has several meanings. It is often seen as a place or location where people meet to buy and sell goods. Conceptually, a market involves the exchange of goods and services for money or on a barter basis with or without spatial connotations. Marketing includes all the activities that are involved in moving products from producers to consumers.

Customer Relationship Management (CRM) is fundamental to building a customer-centric organisation. CRM system links together the customer data into single and logical customer repository. CRM in banking is a key element of differentiation that allows a bank to develop its customer base and sales capacity. The goal of CRM is to manage all aspects of customer interactions in a manner that enables banks to maximise profitability from every customer. Increasing competition, deregulation, and the internet have all contributed to the increase in customer power. Technology has reduced barriers to entry and exit for the customers, making it easier to switch banks or brokers without feeling the pinch in the wallet. Retaining customers is a major concern for banking institutions which underscores the importance of customer relationship management (CRM).

Customers, faced with an increasing array of banking products and services, are expecting more from banks in terms of customised offerings, attractive returns, ease of access and transparency in dealings. By using knowledge of the customer, banks can turn customer relationship into a key competitive advantage. Banks can develop customer relationships across a broad spectrum of touch points ?branches, kiosks, ATMs, internet, electronic banking, smart cards, call centres and phone banking. The full integration of these systems, their associated business processes, and the methods for which information is extracted and used, forms the basis for CRM.

This is a reference book. All the matter is just compiled and edited in nature, taken from the various sources which are in public domain.

The book will suit to the needs of students, teachers, scholars and general readers.

—*Editor*

Contents

1

Introduction

Customer Relationship Management (CRM) is fundamental to building a customer-centric organisation. CRM system links together the customer data into single and logical customer repository. CRM in banking is a key element of differentiation that allows a bank to develop its customer base and sales capacity. The goal of CRM is to manage all aspects of customer interactions in a manner that enables banks to maximise profitability from every customer. Increasing competition, deregulation, and the internet have all contributed to the increase in customer power. Technology has reduced barriers to entry and exit for the customers, making it easier to switch banks or brokers without feeling the pinch in the wallet. Retaining customers is a major concern for banking institutions which underscores the importance of customer relationship management (CRM).

Customers, faced with an increasing array of banking products and services, are expecting more from banks in terms of customised offerings, attractive returns, ease of access and transparency in dealings. By using *knowledge of the customer*, banks can turn customer relationship into a key competitive advantage. Banks can develop customer relationships across a broad spectrum of touch points ?branches, kiosks, ATMs, internet, electronic banking, smart cards, call centres and phone banking. The full integration of these systems, their associated business processes, and the methods for which information is extracted and used, forms the basis for CRM.

CUSTOMER LIFECYCLE MANAGEMENT

Customer Lifecycle Management, or CLM is the measurement of multiple customer related metrics, which, when analysed for a period of time, indicate performance of a business. The overall scope of the CLM implementation process encompasses all domains or departments of an organization, which generally brings all sources of static and dynamic data, marketing processes, and value added services to a unified decision supporting platform through iterative phases of customer acquisition, retention, cross and up-selling, and lapsed customer win-back.

Some detailed CLM models further breakdown these phases into acquisition, introduction to products, profiling of customers, growth of customer base, cultivation of loyalty among customers, and termination of customer relationship.

According to a DM Review magazine article by Claudia Imhoff, et al., "The purpose of the customer life cycle is to define and communicate the stages through which a customer progresses when considering, purchasing and using products, and the associated business processes a company uses to move the customer through the customer life cycle."

B2B

Business-to-business (B2B) describes commerce transactions between businesses, such as between a manufacturer and a wholesaler, or between a wholesaler and a retailer. Contrasting terms are business-to-consumer (B2C) and business-to-government (B2G).

The volume of B2B (Business-to-Business) transactions is much higher than the volume of B2C transactions. The primary reason for this is that in a typical supply chain there will be many B2B transactions involving sub components or raw materials, and only one B2C transaction, specifically sale of the finished product to the end customer. For example, an automobile manufacturer makes several B2B transactions such as buying tires, glass for windscreens, and rubber hoses for its vehicles. The final transaction, a finished vehicle sold to the consumer, is a single (B2C) transaction.

B2B is also used in the context of communication and collaboration. Many businesses are now using social media to connect with their consumers (B2C); however, they are now using similar tools within the business so employees can connect with one another. When communication is taking place amongst employees, this can be referred to as "B2B" communication.

Etymology

The term "business-to-business" was originally coined to describe the electronic communications between businesses or enterprises in order to distinguish it from the communications between businesses and consumers (B2C). It eventually came to be used in marketing as well, initially describing only industrial or capital goods marketing. Today it is widely used to describe all products and services used by enterprises. Many professional institutions and the trade publications focus much more on B2C than B2B, although most sales and marketing personnel are in the B2B sector.

B2C

Business-to-consumer (B2C, sometimes also called Business-to-Customer) describes activities of businesses serving end consumers with products and/or services.

An example of a B2C transaction would be a person buying a pair of shoes from a retailer. The transactions that led to the shoes being available for purchase, that is the purchase of the leather, laces, rubber, etc. However, the sale of the shoe from the shoemaker to the retailer would be considered a (B2B) transaction.

Types of Business to Consumer

While the term e-commerce refers to all online transactions, B2C stands for "business-to-consumer" and applies to any business or organization that sells its products or services to consumers over the Internet for its own use. When most people think of B2C e-commerce, they think of Amazon, the online bookseller that launched its site in 1995 and quickly took on the nation's major retailers. In addition to online retailers, B2C has grown to include services such as online banking, travel services, online auctions, health information and real estate sites. Peer-to-peer sites such as Craigslist also fall under the B2C category.

B2C e-commerce went through some tough times, particularly after the technology-heavy Nasdaq crumbled in 2000. In the ensuing dotcom carnage, hundreds of e-commerce sites shut their virtual doors and some experts predicted years of struggle for online retail ventures. Since then, however, shoppers have continued to flock to the web in increasing numbers. In fact, North American consumers adopted e-commerce so much that despite growing fears about identity theft, they spent $172 billion shopping online in 2005, up from $38.8 billion in 2000.

By 2010, consumers are expected to spend $329 billion each year online, according to Forrester Research. What's more, the percentage of U.S. households shopping online is expected to grow from 39 percent this year to 48 percent in 2010.

In October 2010, an extension of B2C, B21 was] According to marketingterms "B2C businesses played a large role in the rapid development of the commercial Internet in the late 20th century. Large sums of venture capital flowed to consumers in the form of free online services and discounted shopping, spurring adoption of the new medium."

Business to Consumer e-consumer quickly developed as an alternative way for companies to sell more products to a larger market.B2C e-commerce provided not only multiple advantages to a company but also to the consumers.

The main advantages for both the business and consumer are that by opening their market up to B2C e-commerce trade they are reducing transactions costs. Businesses usually ship their products to a number of stores to make them visible to the consumer. However, by using B2C commerce they can instead showcase all of their products on the internet which reduces the cost of transaction. B2C also allows their customers to better access information about different product and sellers which broadens the selection available to their customers. Business to consumer ecommerce is valuable to the economy because it creates a more unique way for businesses and consumers to interact.

Unique Attributes

- *Negotiation:* Selling to another business involves haggling over prices, delivery and product specifications. Not so with most consumer sales. That makes it easier for retailers to put a catalog online, and it's why the first B2C applications were for buying finished goods or commodities that are simple to describe and price.
- *Integration:* Retailers don't have to integrate with their customers' systems. Companies selling to other businesses, however, need to make sure they can communicate without human intervention.

CUSTOMER RELATIONSHIP LEVELS AND TOOLS

Companies can build customer relationships at many levels—economic, social, technical, and legal—depending on the nature of the target market. At one extreme, a company with many low-margin customers may seek to develop bam relationships with them.

For example, Procter & Gamble does not phone all of its Tide customers to get to know them personally and express its appreciation for their business. Instead, P&G creates relationships through brand-building advertising, sales promotions, a 1-800 customer response number, and its Tide Clothesline Web site. At the other extreme, in markets with few customer! and high margins, sellers want to create partnerships with key customers. For example, P&G customer teams work closely with Wal-Mart, Safeway, and other large retailers. Boeing works closely with American Airlines, Delta, and other airlines in designing its airplanes and ensuring that Boeing airplanes fully satisfy their requirements. In between these two extreme situations, other levels of relationship marketing are appropriate.

Today, more and more companies are developing customer loyalty and retention programs. Beyond offering consistently high value and satisfaction, marketers can use a number of specific marketing tools to develop stronger bonds with consumers. First, a company might build value and satisfaction by adding financial benefits to the customer relationship. For example, many companies now offer frequency marketing programs that reward customers who buy frequency or in large amounts. Airlines offer frequent flier programs, hotels give room upgrades to their frequent guests, and supermarkets give patronage refunds.

Other companies sponsor club marketing programs that offer members special discounts and other benefits. For example: Swiss watchmaker, Swatch, uses its club to cater to collectors, who on average buy nine of the company's quirky watches every year. Club members can buy exclusives, such as the "Garden Turf" watch, a clear watch with an Astroturf band. They also receive the World Journal, a magazine filled with Swatch-centric news from the four Corners of the globe-Swatch counts on enthusiastic word of mouth from club members as a boost to business. "Our members are like walking billboards," says the manager of Swatch's club, Trish O'Callaghan. "They love, live, and breathe our product. They are ambassadors for Swatch."

Upon submitting a 525 fee to the Volkswagen Club, members receive the first issue of a club magazine, Volkwagen World, a T-shirt, a road atlas and decal, a phone card, and discount offers on travel and recreation. Members can also take advantage of discounts on parts and service from local dealers, and, as a particularly nifty touch, members can apply for a club Visa card with a picture of their own V W on the front.

Thanks in part to its magic club aimed at children. Spain's Telepizza now claims a 65 percent share of the Spanish pizza market compared to less than 20 percent for Pizza Hut. As the largest membership club in Spain, with 3 million children enrolled, the magic club offers children small prizes, usually simple magic tricks, with every order.

Harley-Davidson sponsors the Harley Owners Group (HOG), which now numbers 330,000 members, about a third of all Harley owners. The first-time buyer of a Harley-Davidson motorcycle gets a free one-year membership with annual renewal costing $40. HOG benefits include a magazine (Hog Tales),a copy of the H. O. C. Touring Handbook, a complete H.O.G. World Alias, an emergency pickup service, a specially designed insurance program, theft reward service, discount hotel rates, and a Fly

& Ride program enabling members to rent Harleys while on vacation. A second approach is to add social benefits as well as financial benefits.

Here the company increases its social bonds with customers by learning individual customers' needs and wants and then personalizing its products and services. For example, to build better relationships with its customers, in the summer of 1994 and again in 1999 Saturn invited all of its owners to 3 "Saturn Homecoming" at its manufacturing facility in Spring Hill, Tennessee. The two-day affair included family events, plant tours, entertainment, and physical challenge activities designed to build trust and a team spirit. Says Saturn's manager of corporate communications, "The Homecoming parry is another way of building ....relationships, and it shows that we treat our customers differently than any other car company." More than 60,000 people attended the most recent homecoming, traveling from as far as Alaska and Taiwan, with another 150,000 celebrating the occasion at the dealerships where they bought their cars.

A third approach to building customer relationships is to add structural lies as well as financial and social benefits. For example, a business marketer might supply customers with special equipment or computer linkages that help them manage their orders, payroll, or inventory. McKesson Corporation, a leading pharmaceutical wholesaler, has invested millions of dollars in its electronic data interchange (EDI) system to help small pharmacies manage their inventory, their order entry, and their shelf space. FedEx offers Web links to its customers to keep them from defecting to competitors such as UPS. Customers can use the Web site to link with FedEx's computers, arrange shipments, and check the status of their FedEx packages.

Relationship marketing means that marketers must focus on managing their customers as well as their products. At the same time, they don't want relationships with every customer. In fact, there are undesirable customers for every company. Ultimately, marketing involves attracting, keeping, and growing profitable customers. Thus, in addition to assessing the value that it delivers to customers, a firm should actively measure the value of individual customers to the firm. Once it has identified profitable customers, it can create attractive offers and special handling to bind these customers to the company for a lifetime. But what should the company do with unprofitable customers If it can't turn them into profitable ones, it may even want to "tire" customers that are too unreasonable or that cost more to serve than they are worth.

A useful type of analysis for assessing the value of a customer to a firm. Customers make up the columns of the figure and products or services make up the rows. Each cell contains a symbol for the profitability of selling a given product or service to a given customer. Customer C1 is very profitable—he or she buys three profit-making products, products P1P2 and P3 Customer C2 yields mixed profitability, buying one profitable product and one unprofitable product. Customer C3 generates losses by purchasing one profitable product and two unprofitable ones ("loss leaders"). What can the company do about consumers like C3 First, the company should consider raising the prices of its less profitable products or eliminating them. Second, the company also can try to cross-sell its profit-making products to its unprofitable customers. If these actions cause customers like C3 to defect, it may be for the good. In fact, the company might benefit by encouraging its unprofitable customers to switch to competitors.

TECHNOLOGY AND CUSTOMER RELATIONSHIPS MANAGEMENT IN BANKING INDUSTRY

Changing customer expectations, advances in technology and globalization of the economy are the new dimensions that have brought growing pressures on banks in terms of CRM. It is imperative that to a detailed study is undertaken to find out the existing ways of doing business by banks, their present marketing tech and to formulate enhanced CRM for the better performance of banking industry. The study results will be helpful in improving the effectiveness of internal marketing and to find out whether customization or standardization will be suitable for the present scenario in banking sector.

There is evidence of this trend in every industry. In the financial industry, banks have embraced customer relationship marketing. They offer packaged checking, loan, mortgage and investment account solutions based on usage patterns. Customers that bank on the Internet, via telephone, debit card and ATM might pay more for excess check usage and less or nothing at all in monthly fees. People who commonly use traditional teller services for their banking needs and rarely or never bank via telephone or online are offered solutions that provide low-priced or unlimited check writing with a more substantial monthly fee or a high per-transaction cost.

Organizations must nurture their client relationships to ensure customer satisfaction and subsequent loyalty. While this might sound like considerably more work, it is much more costly long term to focus solely on winning customers than it is to concentrate on keeping them. In the end, the cost of doing business is less because your customers are reached more successfully. Companies are able to target the right customer with the most appropriate solution, ensuring the most profitable promotions and highest propensity to buy.

Review of Literature

Parasuraman A.,(2000) made a study on "superior customer service and marketing Excellence: Two sides of the same success coin". The first half of the article studied the nature and determination of high quality customer service and the second half of the article made a study as to why superior customer service and marketing excellence are two faces of the same success coin. The researches discussed the meaning and measurement of service quality and offers managerial guidelines for delivering superior service to customer. He argued for broadening the scope of marketing to include the delivery of customer service as an integral component and a judicious blend of conventional marketing and superior customer service is the best receipe for sustained market success.

Parimal Vyas(2000) made a study on "Measurement of customer satisfaction: A study of banking services". This paper attempted at studying empirically customer satisfaction with the services provided by different banks and also analysed the responses of customer towards the actual time taken by banks to complete the banking transaction. The finding of the study revealed that nationalised banks and co-operative banks need to improve on reducing the overall time taken to complete banking transaction, comparatively, the private and foreign banks took much less time for completing their transactions.

Nationalised and co-operative banks need to increase the use of information technology and CRM to deliver standardized customer specific banks service to its targeted customer.

Anjana Grewal (2000) in her article "winning strategies and processes for effective CRM in banking and financial services", presented a case study on relationship management practices developed in a leading foreign bank in India in the early nineties. It was a practical paper and provided insight into what made it happen, the developed model outlined ten stages for effective customer relationship practices in financial services. These span across defining customer relationship, understanding transaction behaviour and business volumes for different customer. Developing a customer profitability model, creating the organization structure to support relationship management practices, developing training programs, relationship pricing continuously evaluating the role of relationship managers with emerging technology are the new trends expected of the relationship role.

Sharlesh and Mohan(2000) carried out a study to gain an insight into one current status of CRM. In Indian services firms and their relationship management practices and programs being implemented by them. The research revealed that aspects such as business processes, information technology, employee empowerment, quality assurance and customer knowledge strategies should be made more customer-centric.

Aravind Brahme(2000) in his article "customer complaints" has stated that customer complaints are a universal phenomenon and a service industry like banking is no exception. Handling of complaints should be considered as a core activity and viewed as one of the key functions. He draws a clear distinction between verbal and written complaints and also the way to deal with both of them. The study elaborates on as to why organisations lose customer and states that 68% of the customers are lost due to short comings in customer service. A suggestion regarding the complaint handling cell or unit is made and characteristics of a complaint system have been enlisted by the author. He has proposed organizing of workshops on complaints handling for the bank staff to develop an awareness and positive approach.

Parimal Vyas(2004) made a study on a "Measurement of customer satisfaction on IT adoption in banking services". This study was an empirical study based on descriptive research design to measure customer satisfaction considering the prevalent state of IT adoption among selected branch of nationalized banks, private banks, co-operative bank and foreign banks located at baroda. The findings of the study revealed that there was an effective implementation of E-Banking services in the case of private banks and foreign bank whereas nationalised bank were found to have a lessor degree of computerization.

CUSTOMER RELATIONSHIP MANAGEMENT: THE CONCEPT

Customer Relationship Management is the establishment, development, maintenance and optimization of long-term mutually valuable relationships between consumers and the organizations. Successful customer relationship management focuses on understanding the needs and desires of the customers and is achieved by placing these needs at the heart of the business by integrating them with the organization's strategy, people, technology and business processes.

At the heart of a perfect, CRM strategy is the creation of mutual value for all the parties involved in the business process. It is about creating a sustainable competitive advantage by being the best at understanding, communicating, and delivering, and developing existing customer relationships in addition to creating and keeping new customers. So the concept of product life cycle is giving way to the concept of customer life cycle focusing on the development of products and services that anticipate the future need of the existing customers and creating additional services that extend existing customer relationships beyond transactions.

Need of Crm in the Banking Industry

Over time, retail bank customers tend to increase their holding of the other products from across the range of financial products/services available.

* Long-term customers are more likely to become a referral source.
* The longer a relationship continues, the better a bank can understand the customer and his/her needs & preferences, and so greater the opportunity to tailor products and services and cross-sell the product/ service range.
* Customers in long-term relationships are more comfortable with the service, the organization, methods and procedures. This helps reduce operating cost and costs arising out of customer error.

With increased number of banks, products and services and practically nil switching costs, customers are easily switching banks whenever they find better services and products. Banks are finding it tough to get new customers, and more importantly, retain existing customers. According to a research by Reichheld and Sasser in the Harvard Business Review, 5% increase in customer retention can increase profitability by 35% in banking business, 50% in insurance and brokerage, and 125% in the consumer credit card market. Therefore, banks are now stressing on retaining customers and increasing market share.

TECHNOLOGY AND CRM IN BANKS

Customer Relationship Management (CRM) in the Indian banking system is fundamental to building a customer-centric organization. CRM systems link customer data into a single and logical customer repository. CRM in banking is a key element that allows a bank to develop its customer base and sales capacity. The goal of CRM is to manage all aspects of customer interactions in a manner that enables banks to maximize profitability from every customer. Increasing competition, deregulation, and the internet have all contributed to the increase in customer power. Customers, faced with an increasing array of banking products and services, are expecting more from banks in terms of customized offerings, attractive returns, ease of access, and transparency in dealings. Retaining customers is a major concern for banking institutions which underscores the importance of CRM. Banks can turn customer relationship into a key competitive advantage through strategic development across a broad spectrum.

The key to successfully making this switch in marketing focus is altering the way in which organizations analyse their customer data. Most of the data organizations need in order to yield integrated, accurate customer information comes directly from the customers themselves: their demographics, their purchasing patterns, their likes and dislikes, their means and methods of purchasing, their buying history.

The good news is most organizations are likely to have most of this data. The bad news is that most of this information is in bits and pieces and lives in disparate *data* sources across an organization. To compound the problem, those systems do not speak the same language; and many organizations have no means of efficiently consolidating and analysing the data into meaningful decision support information. This may cause organizations to think that from a marketing or customer relationship management perspective, they are back at square one. That is not the case. Knowing that the data is within reach is the first step to the solution. Next, it must be found, run through the data quality process and integrated based on business rules – then it can be analysed.

Undoubtedly, an organization that is not using information technology to understand and serve its customers better will be out-performed, out-sold, out-smarted and probably out of business before the end of the next decade. Competition within a global marketplace dictates that companies distinguish themselves from the competition through their customer relationships. It is impossible for employees to provide the level of service customers expect if information about them is scattered throughout an organization or is just plain unavailable. Good customer information architecture can effectively integrate data from many sources (e.g., financial, claims, customer and call Centre systems).

For example, In Banking systems – credit card, instalment loan, investments, trust account, mortgage, etc. – are isolated within each division, how can that institution leverage its customer information? The financial institution with fragmented customer information is bombarding customers with redundant, confusing propositions that often don't apply to their individual situations. Today's customers want to be able to glance at their entire financial portfolio and see how they can optimize their financial future. The financial industry has responded to this with consolidated monthly statements and e-commerce solutions that give clients real time access to their portfolios. Furthermore, financial institutions that enable customers' access to personal account information, loan payment and money managing services online will have a clear advantage over their competitors who do not offer sophisticated, e-commerce solutions.

Delivery channels provide sophisticated analysis tools and customer interfaces. When the dust settles, the clear market leaders will be the organizations taking advantage of the Internet age by implementing e-commerce solutions on top of robust analytical solutions that are supported by data warehousing technology.

Decision support systems are used for analysis of customer information. Decision support systems (supported by the data warehouse) are the tools that enable decision-makers to analyse their data. These systems are typically functionally specific (i.e., product performance analysis, risk analysis, call pattern analysis, etc.).

Developing and implementing an enterprise customer relationship management solution, facilitates business communication by collecting and combining customer-driven data into an easily accessible operational data store and data warehouse that makes information available to the enterprise and, potentially, to customers accessing organizations via the Internet. The financial services industry has been a leading adopter of leveraging the vast amounts of customer information locked in legacy systems.

Financial institutions have various goals and objectives. Some organizations want to maximize their cross-selling opportunities, understand customer buying patterns and demographics, and analyse loan performance. Others want to better increase the effectiveness of their customer service and conduct risk analysis. Mergers and acquisitions often present the need to integrate financial, claims, customer and application data from companies that have merged. Some companies want to assess their credit risk, better understand market segmentation and more effectively detect fraud. Some organizations' main goal is to service their customers better.

For example, they want to conduct credit line analysis so they can offer better consolidation rates and/or raise or lower credit lines. Other organizations want to streamline and maximize their marketing efforts. All of these business issues can be solved and objectives can be reached by using and analysing information appropriately. Although the initial investment in this technology is expensive, companies must focus on the long-term benefits.

BENEFITS OF CRM

A CRM system may be chosen because it is thought to provide the following advantages:

- Quality and efficiency
- Decrease in overall costs
- Decision support
- Enterprise agility
- Customer Attention.

Challenges

Successful development, implementation, use and support of customer relationship management systems can provide a significant advantage to the user, but often, there are obstacles that obstruct the user from using the system to its full potential. Instances of a CRM attempting to contain a large, complex group of data can become cumbersome and difficult to understand for an ill-trained user. Additionally, an interface that is difficult to navigate or understand can hinder the CRM's effectiveness, causing users to pick and choose which areas of the system to be used, while others may be pushed aside. This fragmented implementation can cause inherent challenges, as only certain parts are used and the system is not fully functional. The increased use of customer relationship management software has also led to an industry-wide shift in evaluating the role of the developer in designing and maintaining its software. Companies are urged to consider the overall impact of a viable CRM software suite and the potential for good or harm in its use.

Complexity

Tools and workflows can be complex, especially for large businesses. Previously these tools were generally limited to contact management: monitoring and recording interactions and communications. Software solutions then expanded to embrace deal tracking, territories, opportunities, and the sales pipeline itself. Next came the advent of tools for other client-interface business functions, as described below. These tools have been, and still are, offered as on-premises software that companies purchase and run on their own IT infrastructure.

Poor Usability

One of the largest challenges that customer relationship management systems face is poor usability. With a difficult interface for a user to navigate, implementation can be fragmented or not entirely complete. The importance of usability in a system has developed over time. Customers are likely not as patient to work through malfunctions or gaps in user safety, and there is an expectation that the usability of systems should be somewhat intuitive: "it helps make the machine an extension of the way I think — not how it wants to me think."

An intuitive design can prove most effective in developing the content and layout of a customer relationship management system. Two 2008 case studies show that the layout of a system provides a strong correlation to the ease of use for a system and that it proved more beneficial for the design to focus on presenting information in a way that reflected the most important goals and tasks of the user, rather than the structure of the organization. This "ease of service" is paramount for developing a system that is usable.

In many cases, the growth of capabilities and complexities of systems has hampered the usability of a customer relationship management system. An overly complex computer system can result in an equally complex and non-friendly user interface, thus not allowing the system to work as fully intended. This bloated software can appear sluggish and/or overwhelming to the user, keeping the system from full use and potential. A series of 1998 research indicates that each item added to an information display can significantly affect the overall experience the user.

Fragmentation

Often, poor usability can lead to implementations that are fragmented — isolated initiatives by individual departments to address their own needs. Systems that start disunited usually stay that way: siloed thinking and decision processes frequently lead to separate and incompatible systems, and dysfunctional processes.

A fragmented implementation can negate any financial benefit associated with a customer relationship management system, as companies choose not to use all the associated features factored when justifying the investment. Instead, it is important that support for the CRM system is companywide. The challenge of fragmented implementations may be mitigated with improvements in late-generation CRM systems.

Business Reputation

Business reputation has become a growing challenge. The outcome of internal fragmentation that is observed and commented upon by customers is now visible to the rest of the world in the era of the social customer;

in the past, only employees or partners were aware of it. Addressing the fragmentation requires a shift in philosophy and mindset in an organization so that everyone considers the impact to the customer of policy, decisions and actions. Human response at all levels of the organization can affect the customer experience for good or ill. Even one unhappy customer can deliver a body blow to a business.

Some developments and shifts have made companies more conscious of the life-cycle of a customer relationship management system. Companies now consider the possibility of brand loyalty and persistence of its users to purchase updates, upgrades and future editions of software.

Additionally, CRM systems face the challenge of producing viable financial profits, with a 2002 study suggesting that less than half of CRM projects are expected to provide a significant return on investment. Poor usability and low usage rates lead many companies to indicate that it was difficult to justify investment in the software without the potential for more tangible gains.

Security Concerns

A large challenge faced by developers and users is found in striking a balance between ease of use in the CRM interface and suitable and acceptable security measures and features. Corporations investing in CRM software do so expecting a relative ease of use while also requiring that customer and other sensitive data remain secure. This balance can be difficult, as many believe that improvements in security come at the expense of system usability.

Research and study show the importance of designing and developing technology that balances a positive user interface with security features that meet industry and corporate standards. A 2002 study shows, however, that security and usability can coexist harmoniously. In many ways, a secure CRM system can become more usable.

Researchers have argued that, in most cases, security breaches are the result of user-error (such as unintentionally downloading and executing a computer virus). In these events, the computer system acted as it should in identifying a file and then, following the user's orders to execute the file, exposed the computer and network to a harmful virus. Researchers argue that a more usable system creates less confusion and lessens the amount of potentially harmful errors, in turn creating a more secure and stable CRM system.

Technical writers can play a large role in developing customer relationship management systems that are secure and easy to use. A series of 2008 research shows that CRM systems, among others, need to be more open to flexibility of technical writers, allowing these professionals to become content builders. These professionals can then gather information and use it at their preference, developing a system that allows users to easily access desired information and is secure and trusted by its users.

TYPES/VARIATIONS

Sales Force Automation

Sales force automation (SFA) involves using software to streamline all phases of the sales process, minimizing the time that sales representatives need to spend on each phase. This allows a business to use fewer sales representatives to manage their clients. At the heart of SFA is a contact management system for tracking and recording every stage in the sales process for each prospective client, from initial contact to final disposition. Many SFA applications also include insights into opportunities, territories, sales forecasts and workflow automation, quote generation, and product knowledge. Modules for Web 2.0 e-commerce and pricing are new, emerging interests in SFA.

Marketing

CRM systems for marketing help the enterprise identify and target potential clients and generate leads for the sales team. A key marketing capability is tracking and measuring multichannel campaigns, including email, search, social media, telephone and direct mail. Metrics monitored include clicks, responses, leads, deals, and revenue. Alternatively, Prospect Relationship Management (PRM) solutions offer to track customer behaviour and nurture them from first contact to sale, often cutting out the active sales process altogether. In a web-focused marketing CRM solution, organizations create and track specific web activities that help develop the client relationship. These activities may include such activities as free downloads, online video content, and online web presentations.

CUSTOMER SERVICE AND SUPPORT

Recognizing that service is an important factor in attracting and retaining customers, organizations are increasingly turning to technology to help them improve their clients' experience while aiming to increase efficiency and minimize costs. Even so, a 2009 study revealed that only 39% of corporate executives believe their employees have the right tools and authority to solve client problems.

Appointment

Creating and scheduling appointments with customers is a central activity of most customer oriented businesses. Sales, customer support, and service personnel regularly spend a portion of their time getting in touch with customers and prospects through a variety of means to agree on a time and place for meeting for a sales conversation or to deliver customer service. Appointment CRM is a relatively new CRM platform category in which an automated system is used to offer a suite of suitable appointment times to a customer via e-mail or through a web site. An automated process is used to schedule and confirm the appointment, and place it on the appropriate person's calendar. Appointment CRM systems can be an origination point for a sales lead and are generally integrated with sales and marketing CRM systems to capture and store the interaction.

Analytics

Relevant analytics capabilities are often interwoven into applications for sales, marketing, and service. These features can be complemented and augmented with links to separate, purpose-built applications for analytics and business intelligence. Sales analytics let companies monitor and understand client actions and preferences, through sales forecasting and data quality. Marketing applications generally come with predictive analytics to improve segmentation and targeting, and features for measuring the effectiveness of online, offline, and search marketing campaigns. Web analytics have evolved significantly from their starting point of merely tracking mouse clicks on Web sites. By evaluating "buy signals," marketers can see which prospects are most likely to transact and also identify those who are bogged down in a sales process and need assistance. Marketing and finance personnel also use analytics to assess the value of multifaceted programs as a whole.

These types of analytics are increasing in popularity as companies demand greater visibility into the performance of call centres and other service and support channels, in order to correct problems before they affect satisfaction levels. Support-focused applications typically include dashboards similar to those for sales, plus capabilities to measure and analyse response times, service quality, agent performance, and the frequency of various issues.

Integrated/Collaborative

Departments within enterprises — especially large enterprises — tend to function with little collaboration. More recently, the development and adoption of these tools and services have fostered greater fluidity and cooperation among sales, service, and marketing. This finds expression in the concept of collaborative systems that use technology to build bridges between departments. For example, feedback from a technical support centre can enlighten marketers about specific services and product features clients are asking for. Reps, in their turn, want to be able to pursue these opportunities without the burden of re-entering records and contact data into a separate SFA system.

Small Business

For small business, basic client service can be accomplished by a contact manager system: an integrated solution that lets organizations and individuals efficiently track and record interactions, including emails, documents, jobs, faxes, scheduling, and more. These tools usually focus on accounts rather than on individual contacts. They also generally include opportunity insight for tracking sales pipelines plus added functionality for marketing and service. As with larger enterprises, small businesses are finding value in online solutions, especially for mobile and telecommuting workers.

Social Media

Social media sites like Twitter, LinkedIn and Facebook are amplifying the voice of people in the marketplace and are having profound and far-reaching effects on the ways in which people buy. Customers can now research companies online and then ask for recommendations through social media channels, making their buying decision without contacting the company.

People also use social media to share opinions and experiences on companies, products and services. As social media is not as widely moderated or censored as mainstream media, individuals can say anything they want about a company or brand, positive or negative.

Increasingly, companies are looking to gain access to these conversations and take part in the dialogue. More than a few systems are now integrating to social networking sites.

Social media promoters cite a number of business advantages, such as using online communities as a source of high-quality leads and a vehicle for crowd sourcing solutions to client-support problems. Companies can also leverage client stated habits and preferences to "hyper-target" their sales and marketing communications. Some analysts take the view that business-to-business marketers should proceed cautiously when weaving social media into their business processes. These observers recommend careful market research to determine if and where the phenomenon can provide measurable benefits for client interactions, sales and support. It is stated that people feel their interactions are peer-to-peer between them and their contacts, and resent company involvement, sometimes responding with negatives about that company.

NON-PROFIT AND MEMBERSHIP-BASED

Systems for non-profit and membership-based organizations help track constituents and their involvement in the organization. Capabilities typically include tracking the following: fund-raising, demographics, membership levels, membership directories, volunteering and communications with individuals. Many include tools for identifying potential donors based on previous donations and participation. In light of the growth of social networking tools, there may be some overlap between social/community driven tools and non-profit/membership tools.

Strategy

For larger-scale enterprises, a complete and detailed plan is required to obtain the funding, resources, and companywide support that can make the initiative of choosing and implementing a system successfully. Benefits must be defined, risks assessed, and cost quantified in three general areas:

- *Processes:* Though these systems have many technological components, business processes lie at its core. It can be seen as a more client-centric way of doing business, enabled by technology that consolidates and intelligently distributes pertinent information about clients, sales, marketing effectiveness, responsiveness, and market trends. Therefore, a company must analyse its business workflows and processes before choosing a technology platform; some will likely need re-engineering to better serve the overall goal of winning and satisfying clients. Moreover, planners need to determine the types of client information that are most relevant, and how best to employ them.
- *People*: For an initiative to be effective, an organization must convince its staff that the new technology and workflows will benefit employees as well as clients. Senior executives need to be strong and visible advocates who can clearly state and support the case for change. Collaboration, teamwork, and two-way communication should be encouraged across hierarchical boundaries, especially with respect to process improvement.

- *Technology:* In evaluating technology, key factors include alignment with the company's business process strategy and goals, including the ability to deliver the right data to the right employees and sufficient ease of adoption and use. Platform selection is best undertaken by a carefully chosen group of executives who understand the business processes to be automated as well as the software issues. Depending upon the size of the company and the breadth of data, choosing an application can take anywhere from a few weeks to a year or more.

Implementation—Implementation Issues

Increases in revenue, higher rates of client satisfaction, and significant savings in operating costs are some of the benefits to an enterprise. Proponents emphasize that technology should be implemented only in the context of careful strategic and operational planning. Implementations almost invariably fall short when one or more facets of this prescription are ignored:

- *Poor planning:* Initiatives can easily fail when efforts are limited to choosing and deploying software, without an accompanying rationale, context, and support for the workforce. In other instances, enterprises simply automate flawed client-facing processes rather than redesign them according to best practices.
- *Poor integration:* For many companies, integrations are piecemeal initiatives that address a glaring need: improving a particular client-facing process or two or automating a favoured sales or client support channel. Such "point solutions" offer little or no integration or alignment with a company's overall strategy. They offer a less than complete client view and often lead to unsatisfactory user experiences.
- *Toward a solution:* overcoming siloed thinking. Experts advise organizations to recognize the immense value of integrating their client-facing operations. In this view, internally-focused, department-centric views should be discarded in favour of reorienting processes toward information-sharing across marketing, sales, and service. For example, sales representatives need to know about current issues and relevant marketing promotions before attempting to cross-sell to a specific client. Marketing staff should be able to leverage client information from sales and service to better target campaigns and offers. And support agents require quick and complete access to a client's sales and service history.

Adoption Issues

Historically, the landscape is littered with instances of low adoption rates. Many of the challenges listed above offer a glimpse into some of the obstacles that corporations implementing a CRM suite face; in many cases time, resources and staffing do not allow for the troubleshooting necessary to tackle an issue and the system is shelved or sidestepped instead.

Statistics

In 2003, a Gartner report estimated that more than $1 billion had been spent on software that was not being used. More recent research indicates that the problem, while perhaps less severe, is a long way from being solved. According to *CSO Insights*, less than 40 percent of 1,275 participating companies had end-user adoption rates above 90 percent. Additionally, many corporations only use CRM systems on a partial or fragmented basis, thus missing opportunities for effective marketing and efficiency.

In a 2007 survey from the U.K., four-fifths of senior executives reported that their biggest challenge is getting their staff to use the systems they had installed. Further, 43 percent of respondents said they use less than half the functionality of their existing system; 72 percent indicated they would trade functionality for ease of use; 51 percent cited data synchronization as a major issue; and 67 percent said that finding time to evaluate systems was a major problem. With expenditures expected to exceed $11 billion in 2010, enterprises need to address and overcome persistent adoption challenges.

The amount of time needed for the development and implementation of a customer relationship management system can prove costly to the implementation as well. Research indicates that implementation timelines that are greater than 90 days in length run an increased risk in the CRM system failing to yield successful results.

Increasing Usage and Adoption Rates

Specialists offer these recommendations for boosting adoptions rates and coaxing users to blend these tools into their daily workflow:

- Choose a system that is easy to use: Not all solutions are created equal; some vendors offer applications that are more user-friendly — a factor that should be as important to the decision as is functionality.
- *Choose appropriate capabilities:* Employees need to know that the time they invest in learning and in using the new system will not

be wasted, indeed that it will yield "personal" advantages; otherwise, they will ignore or circumvent the system.

- *Provide training:* Changing the way people work is no small task; to be successful, some familiarization training and help-desk support are usually required, even with today's more usable systems.
- *Lead by example:* Upper management must use the new application themselves, thereby showing employees that the top leaders fully support the application or else it will skew the ultimate course of the initiative toward failure, by risking a greatly reduced rate of adoption by employees.

Additionally, researchers found the following themes were common in systems that users evaluated favourably. These positive evaluations led to the increased use and more thorough implementation of the CRM system. Further recommendations include

- *"Breadcrumb Trail":* This offers the user a path, usually at the top of a web or CRM page, to return to the starting point of navigation. This can prove useful for users who might find themselves lost or unsure how they got to the current screen in the CRM.
- *Readily available search engine boxes:* Research shows that users are quick to seek immediate results through the use of a search engine box. A CRM that uses a search box will keep assistance and immediate results quickly within the reach of a user.
- *Help Option Menu:* An outlet for quick assistance or frequently asked questions can provide users with a lifeline that makes the customer relationship management software easier to use. Researchers suggest making this resource a large component of the CRM during the development stage.

A larger theme is found in that the responsiveness, intuitive design and overall usability of a system can influence the users' opinions and preferences of systems.

Researchers noted a strong correlation between the design and layout of a user interface and the perceived level of trust from the user. The researchers found that users felt more comfortable on a system evaluated as usable and applied that comfort and trust into increased use and adoption.

Help Menus

One of the largest issues surrounding the implementation and adoption of a CRM comes in the perceived lack of technical and user support in using the system. Individual users — and large corporations — find themselves equally stymied by a system that is not easily understood. Technical support in the form of a qualified and comprehensive help menu can provide significant improvement in implementation when providing focused, context-specific information.

Data show that CRM users are oftentimes unwilling to consult a help menu if it is not easily accessible and immediate in providing assistance. A 1998 case study found that users would consult the help menu for an average of two or three screens, abandoning the assistance if desired results weren't found by that time.

Researchers believe that help menus can provide assistance to users through introducing additional screenshots and other visual and interactive aids. A 2004 case study concluded that the proper use of screenshots can significantly support a user's "developing a mental model of the program" and help in "identifying and locating window elements and objects." This research concluded that screen shots allowed users to "learn more, make fewer mistakes, and learn in a shorter time frame," which can certainly assist in increasing the time frame for full implementation of a CRM system with limited technical or human support.

Experts have identified five characteristics to make a help menu effective:

- "context-specific" — the help menu contains only the information relevant to the topic that is being discussed or sought
- "useful" — in conjunction with being context-specific, the help menu must be comprehensive in including all of the information that the user seeks
- "obvious to invoke" — the user must have no trouble in locating the help menu or how to gain access to its contents
- "non-intrusive" — the help menu must not interfere with the user's primary path of work and must maintain a distance that allows for its use only when requested
- "easily available" — the information of the help menu must be accessible with little or few steps required

Development

Thoughtful and thorough development can avoid many of the challenges and obstacles faced in using and implementing a customer relationship management system. With shifts in competition and the increasing reliance by corporations to use a CRM system, development of software has become more important than ever. Technical communicators can play a significant role in developing software that is usable and easy to navigate.

Clarity

One of the largest issues in developing a usable customer relationship management system comes in the form of clear and concise presentation. Developers are urged to consider the importance of creating software that is easy to understand and without unnecessary confusion, thus allowing a user to navigate the system with ease and confidence.

Strong writing skills can prove extremely beneficial for software development and creation. A 1998 case study showed that software engineering majors who successfully completed a technical writing course created capstone experience projects that were more mindful of end user design than the projects completed by their peers. The case study yielded significant results:

- Students who completed the technical writing course submitted capstone projects that contained more vivid and explicit detail in writing than their peers who did not complete the course. Researchers note that the students appeared to weigh multiple implications on the potential user, and explained their decisions more thoroughly than their peers.
- Those participating in the writing course sought out test users more frequently to add a perspective outside their own as developer. Students appeared sensitive of the user's ability to understand the developed software.
- The faculty member overseeing the capstone submissions felt that students who did not enrol in the technical writing class were at a significant disadvantage when compared to their peers who did register for the course.

In the case study, researchers argue for the inclusion of technical writers in the development process of software systems. These professionals can offer insight into usability in communication for software projects. Technical writing can help build a unified resource for successful documentation, training and execution of customer relationship management systems.

Test Users

In many circumstances, test users play a significant role in developing software. These users offer software developers an outside perspective of the project, oftentimes helping developers gain insight into potential areas of trouble that might have been overlooked or passed over because of familiarity with the system.

Test users can also provide feedback from a targeted audience: a software development team creating a customer relationship management software system for higher education can have a user with a similar profile explore the technology, offering opportunities to cater the further development of the system. Test users help developers discover which areas of the software perform well, and which areas require further attention.

Research notes that test users can prove to be most effective in providing developers a structured overview of the software creation. These users can provide a fresh perspective that can reflect on the state of the CRM development without the typically narrow or invested focus of a software developer.

A 2007 study suggests some important steps are needed in creating a quality and effective test environment for software development. In this case study, researchers observed a Danish software company in the midst of new creating new software with usability in mind. The study found these four observations most appropriate:

- The developers must make a conscious effort and commitment to the test user. Researchers note that the company had dedicated specific research space and staff focused exclusively on usability.
- Usability efforts must carry equal concern in the eyes of developers as other technology-related concerns in the creation stage. The study found that test users became discouraged when items flagged as needing attention were marked as lower priority by the software developers.
- Realistic expectations from both test users and software developers help maintain a productive environment. Researchers note that developers began to limit seeking input from test users after the test users suggested remedies the developers felt were improbable, leading the developers to believe consulting the test users would only prove to be more work.
- Developers must make themselves available to test users and colleagues alike throughout the creation process of a software system.

The researchers note that some of the best instances of usability adjustments can be made through casual conversation, and that oftentimes usability is bypassed by developers because these individuals never think to consult test users. Allowing users to test developing products can have its limits in effectiveness, as the culture of the industry and desired outcomes can affect the effect on CRM creation, as a 2008 case study suggests that the responsiveness of test users can vary dramatically depending on the industry and field of the user.

Research suggests that test users can rate the importance or severity of potential software issues in a significantly different fashion than software developers. Similarly so, researchers note the potential for costly delay if developers spend too much time attempting to coerce hesitant test users from participating.

Additionally, involving too many test users can prove cumbersome and delay the development of a CRM system. Additional research notes that test users may be able to identify an area that proves challenging in a software system, but might have difficulty explaining the outcome. A related 2007 case study noted that test users were able to describe roughly a third of the usability problems. Further, the language used by test users in many circumstances proves to be quite general and lacking the specific nature needed by developers to enact real change.

Privacy and Data Security System

One of the primary functions of these tools is to collect information about clients, thus a company must consider the desire for privacy and data security, as well as the legislative and cultural norms. Some clients prefer assurances that their data will not be shared with third parties without their prior consent and that safeguards are in place to prevent illegal access by third parties.

Related Trends

Many CRM vendors offer Web-based tools (cloud computing) and software as a service (SaaS), which are accessed via a secure Internet connection and displayed in a Web browser. These applications are sold as subscriptions, with customers not needing to invest in purchasing and maintaining IT hardware, and subscription fees are a fraction of the cost of purchasing software outright.

The era of the "social customer" refers to the use of social media (Twitter, Facebook, LinkedIn, Yelp, customer reviews in Amazon etc.) by customers in ways that allow other potential customers to glimpse real world experience of current customers with the seller's products and services. This shift increases the power of customers to make purchase decisions that are informed by other parties sometimes outside of the control of the seller or seller's network.

In response, CRM philosophy and strategy has shifted to encompass social networks and user communities, podcasting, and personalization in addition to internally generated marketing, advertising and webpage design. With the spread of self-initiated customer reviews, the user experience of a product or service requires increased attention to design and simplicity, as customer expectations have risen. CRM as a philosophy and strategy is growing to encompass these broader components of the customer relationship, so that businesses may anticipate and innovate to better serve customers, referred to as "Social CRM".

Another related development is Vendor Relationship Management, or VRM, which is the customer-side counterpart of CRM: tools and services that equip customers to be both independent of vendors and better able to engage with them. VRM development has grown out of efforts by Project VRM at Harvard's Berkman Centre for Internet & Society and Identity Commons' Internet Identity Workshops, as well as by a growing number of startups and established companies. VRM was the subject of a cover story in the May 2010 issue of *CRM* Magazine.

In a 2001 research note, META Group (now Gartner) analyst Doug Laney first proposed, defined and coined the term *Extended Relationship Management.* He defined XRM as the principle and practice of applying CRM disciplines and technologies to other core enterprise constituents, primarily partners, employees and suppliers...as well as other secondary allies including government, press, and industry consortia.

2

Customer Value and Service Orientation

Understanding the business begins with a clear understanding of customer value. Providing a superior customer value requires an understanding of service orientation. Against this backdrop, the rest proceeds to follow the logic that sound decisions and actions cannot be made and performed without a solid understanding of the customer.

You cannot claim to be customer focused if you don't have the appropriate information on the customer. What kinds of customer data are important and why? How do we collect, interpret, and use this data? Where are the opportunities for gathering customer information? Information on all customer preferences, attitudes, and activities associated with the acquisition and use of the product provides a deeper understanding of the customer. This part develops the various methods and approaches to ensuring that the firm is adequately prepared to make customer-focused decisions.

Customer information should drive the design and delivery of customer value. What is involved in conceiving and designing a customer-focused product offering or service delivery? How would a firm go about tracking whether it is maximizing the returns from its value-creating assets? In this part are about effective and efficient value creation and delivery.

Who are the right customers and how can the firm ensure their loyalty to the firm and its products? This part covers topics such as service quality and guaranteeing quality service. When the product fails the customer, what does the firm need to do to recover from that failure in the context of customer service? What must firms do to proactively manage customer defections?

How does the firm create and maintain a customer-focused culture— a culture that is so focused on the customer that all decisions and actions of all personnel and systems in place create superior value for the customer at a reasonable profit? This final part provides the framework to analyze and manage the firm's value systems to be customer focused.

The principal concepts can be stated as a truism: Businesses cannot succeed in the long term unless they are focused on its customers so as to provide them with superior service. This is how firms attain and maintain a competitive advantage and therefore provide superior customer value at sustainable profits.

Thus, the two fundamental and closely related concepts evident here are "customer focus" and "service orientation." After reading this book, you will be able to engage yourself and the firm in a service-oriented mode of designing and delivering customer-focused value to maintain profitable relationships with the right customers. You will appreciate what is required to sustain a competitive advantage for sustainable profits by:

- Adopting a customer-focused and service-oriented frame of mind
- Understanding the business by understanding customer value
- Capitalizing on the opportunities and use of customer information
- Designing and delivering profitable customer value
- Focusing on the right customer and managing that relationship
- Establishing a customer-focused and service-oriented culture in the firm

Customer-focused firms are the product of customer-focused employees and processes. Customer-focused employees are the responsibility of the executives of the firm. As an executive, you will find that when you stop and think of the ideas and concepts, you will have begun to engage in the intellectual exercise leading to a customer-focused and service-oriented frame of mind. You will be able to specify what the firm should actually be doing to be customer focused.

CUSTOMER VALUE AND SERVICE ORIENTATION

Customers buy solutions, not products. Every firm needs to understand what it is providing the customer in terms of customer value, not by focusing on the product but by focusing on the customer. In doing so, the firm is able to assess whether it is providing superior customer value and whether it has a sustainable competitive advantage. Competitive advantage cannot be sustained unless it can be protected from competitor matching. Any aspect of the product can be matched by the competition. What is most difficult for the competition to match is how the firm approaches and treats the customer. The firm *serves* the customer by providing product enhancements in the form of service. When other firms can provide the same service, the differentiator is in the service orientation of the firm.

Customer Value

Many firms focus on the product rather than on the customer. When the focus is on the customer, the business is defined in terms of customer value, not in terms of product. The product is viewed as a customer solution and experience. That is, for any firm, the most fundamental definition of its business.

Try this one. What business is Amazon in? That you can buy just about anything on Amazon may not be too much of an exaggeration. The company abandoned or at least cut back on its strategy of buying up companies, as it did with Drugstore.com in 1999. It now handles retail for such established brands as Toys 'R' Us, Target, and Circuit City. Amazon shocked everyone in early 2002, when they announced their first operations profit of $59 million and a net profit of $5 million in the previous quarter. What value does Amazon provide its customer?

Customers don't buy products. They buy solutions. If firms are focused on the customer, they ought to see themselves in the role of providing solutions, not products. The information technology sector has popularized the term "solutions providers, " with labels such as application service providers (ASPs, as they are called) or technology solutions providers. These labels may be appropriate at the very general level and allow people to gloss over and take for granted the real meaning of the term *solutions.* The label has no real meaning as a concept unless it can be translated into customer value terms. Customers buy value in the solutions. Thus, customer value defines the primary purpose of any business.

This presents an approach to conducting a critical analysis of this fundamental question of "defining the business of a firm." In doing so, it defines "customer value" and redefines "products" in the customer-focused perspective. Finally, this briefly indicates the fruits of a customer-focused organization providing superior customer value.

Management guru Peter Drucker said in his 1954 book, *The Practice of Management,* "to know what a business is we have to start with its purpose." He goes on to say: "There is only one valid definition of business purpose: *to create a customer.*" Drucker reiterates this concept in a number of different ways, always emphasizing that "it is the customer who determines what a business is." It is not important what the business thinks it is producing.

The customer determines the value of what the business produces based on what the customer thinks he or she is buying. Such a perspective places the final result in focus—what the product *does* for the customer. Thus, the purpose of a business is what it creates for the customer. The first and foremost question for any firm to ask is, what business are we in? How many firms diligently confront this question? And, when they do encounter this question, whose perspective do they take?

Taking the customer's perspective to answer this fundamental question forces a number of thought processes that benefit the firm in different ways. In fact, businesses will find that approaching the question of *what business are we in?* in so fundamental a manner not only allows the firm to understand its existing customers, but will also help open up new market potential. It forces the analysis of value-creating assets, including the firm's skills and knowledge sets. The question also opens up the analysis of who the competition is. When firms strive to beat rivals, they typically end up competing within the confines of existing business.

Firms sometimes do not realize that they compete with firms in other industries. They are able to see this if they articulate their business from the customer's perspective. When customers consider their options in meeting a need, they don't limit themselves to one industry. Without realizing it as such, their solutions may involve different industries. Firms are forced to redefine their competitive landscape when they take the customer's perspective because they will find themselves competing outside their well-defined spaces. Kim and Mauborgne call it competing in a "market space.

They urge firms to expand their view of their business by looking "across substitute industries, across strategic groups, across buyer groups, across complementary product and service offerings, across the functional-emotional orientation of an industry and even across time." They argue this point with examples of how Home Depot cultivated the do-it-yourself market from homeowners using contractors, how Intuit saw that people managing personal finances using a pencil and paper calculation actually competed with their software, how overnight package delivery firms FedEx and UPS competed with telephones and fax machines, and how Southwest Airlines competed with driving. This argument illustrates the definition of a business from the perspective of the customer. Not only does it underscore the value that the customer places on what the firm delivers, but it also reveals that the customer's perspective redefines the business.

Well-known Harvard scholar Ted Levitt expanded on Drucker's thesis of defining a business from a customer's perspective when he popularized the concept "marketing myopia, " where firms and entire industries (such as buggy-whip makers) could perish when inwardly focused. He used the example of railroads as an industry that suffered from marketing myopia because it did not see itself in the business of transportation, but rather in the railroad business. Contrast this with a firm like the Williams Companies, one of the world's largest pipeline builders. Until a few years ago, it built steel pipes to move oil and natural gas. Today, it also builds fiber-optic pipes for the big cable companies. Clearly, Williams did not see itself as being in the oil and gas business, but as being in the business of serving big companies that needed to move material (or data) through pipes. Would Williams have seen this opportunity if it had been focused on competing within the oil and gas industry?

To expand your opportunities, you need to look beyond the product horizon and into the customer's space. For example, if a family was looking for something to do on a Saturday, consider their options: have some friends over for dinner, go out for dinner, go to a nearby mall, go to the movies, go to a play or a show, go bowling, go to a miniature golf course, go for a drive to the lake or the beach—and many other options. Now, look at these options in terms of all of the different industries that are competing with each other. If you were a firm in any one of these industries, you could be defining your business the same way as any of the other industries, depending on who your typical customer is. The customer's perspective broadens your own view of your product.

Taking the customer's perspective helps firms identify what they are about—their mission and their values. They are better able to understand their strengths and sources of competitive advantage. Firms are better positioned and more effective in allocating resources and efforts, both strategically and operationally. They are better situated to understand what would be considered superior customer value.

Products as Solutions

Where do you even begin when you want to define your business? Let us consider the basics. What *do* businesses sell, at the most general level? In what terms will your response be made? Do you see services and goods as solutions to a customer problem—a need to be met? Customer needs are problems searching for solutions and firms are providers of solutions to customer problems. When seen this way, firms draw focus away from products and orient themselves to the customer with the sole purpose of delivering solutions to problems. The business is defined in terms of customer solutions. Firms suffering from a product focus define their product by its capabilities in terms of product features and promptly lose sight of the customer. The solutions-to-problems approach emphasizes the customer rather than the product. It emphasizes product benefits rather than product features.

Firms must align processes, people, and their entire culture to serving the customer rather than on making and selling products. In customer-focused firms, processes are designed with customers in mind. The output of the processes, the product, is defined by the customer need it serves. In serving the customer, firms offer a combination of benefits or values. Are all products, therefore, a service to the customer? In a sense, yes! The solution represents the value that the firm is providing customers by serving their needs.

Firms' activities produce solutions as value bundles that we call products. All products involve a mix of value producing components—tangibles and intangibles—in value bundles. The proportion of tangibles and intangibles in the entity that the customer takes title to prompts the artificial distinction between services and products. This unfortunate dichotomy detracts from the necessary customer focus in the conception of the product. Regardless of whether the total product is predominantly a packaged good or a service, in a business-to-business (B2B) or business-to-consumers (B2C) context, all solutions to customer problems can be seen as bundles of benefits or value bundles designed to deliver value by meeting customer problems or needs. This book adopts the approach that all products are a mix of physical goods and services in some proportion.

Some solutions employ more tangibles (physical goods) than intangibles (services) in meeting customer needs, while others may provide an intangible (service) involving physical objects. The important question is, what is that total solution from the customer's perspective? It is more important to understand what the value bundle *does* for the customer than what the bundle *is*. To identify the value bundle, one needs to identify and understand the customer.

Identifying the Customer

To understand the customer is to understand your business. To understand the customer's perspective is basic to defining a business. The first obvious question is, who is the customer? If the firm defines the customer too narrowly or without context, any subsequent analysis is flawed. Firms either focus on their end users as packaged-goods firms tend to do, or as in the case of industrial firms, the focus is on the immediate customer. Both cases reflect a narrow view and a lack of understanding of the context. To determine who the customer is, the question to ask is, how does what we produce or provide add value to the client's value creating process?

Most important, what do customers see as the value we are providing to their value creation process? This point is central to what we know as the "value chain" concept. An understanding of customers requires an understanding of the customers' value chain that includes the set of their value consumption activities. If the value created by the immediate customer creates value for a subsequent customer, that customer is also an indirect customer of the firm. We really need to identify the customer as a first step to determine whose perspective we should take and to understand the customer value that we are providing.

Performing the analysis of the customer sometimes forces the redefining of the customer. For Bright Horizons, a workplace child care and early education service company, it made a huge difference in how they went about their business when they viewed employers, and not parents, as their primary customers. The company could now tap into the financial and other resources of corporations and gain access to a much wider pool of parents. The value they were providing to the employer became the focus of the company. Chase Manhattan, for example, figured that its child care centre was yielding 110 percent return on investment through reduced absenteeism. Similarly, Merck found that its employee retention rate among those who were young parents went up dramatically.

The customer-focused perspective blurs the boundaries between entities in the value chain. Take the case of Aramark Corp., a firm that caters special events and runs cafeterias for big corporate clients. Nancy Naatz, resident district manager for business services for Aramark, has an office in the premises of her customer, Sears, in Chicago. Since Ms. Naatz is on location at her client's company, she is able to observe and interact with the local vendors Aramark has contracted to supply and serve Sears. Ms. Naatz is able to understand Sears executives' and employees' nutritional needs and interact with the vendors to ensure that the appropriate choices are made available. In this case, Aramark matches the food vendors' solution with the needs of the Sears employees who are the real customers.

So, who is the customer? The perspective of *which* customer I inspect and analyze, so as to help determine the business of my business, is the question. This question also raises the fundamental marketing decision of what or who our target market should be. It is a logical place to start before making any marketing or operations decision. Of all the potential customers that make up the market, which particular type of customer is most appropriate for our solution? The analysis involves segmentation, and the decision involved is one of targeting.

We are able then to determine which particular type of customer from the universe of all customers for this product would find most value in what our value-creating assets can produce. We thus segment the market and target those segments for whom our value-creating assets can provide differentiation and a cost advantage. To know who the customer is necessitates an understanding of the typical customer in that segment at a general or aggregate level.

Traditionally, customer profiles have come out of the segmentation exercise. Segmentation variables in the B2C context have included demographic, psychographic, and behavioural variables. For customer-focused management we need information on all of the characteristics of the need or problem or use-situation that the customer is involved in, encompassing all of the activities of the customer that the product is a part of. Consequently, the question, who is the customer? You want to know how the customer purchases and uses the product.

Similarly, the profile of the customer in a B2B context involves understanding the business of the organizational customer. For either the B2C or the B2B context, an understanding of the customers requires analysis of their use-situations, and the contexts within which a product helps them in what they do. Of what value are you to them? Now we begin to hint at the notion of what customer value really is. The answers lie in the *consumption* of the product, not in its production.

Customer Value

Customer value is what the customer thinks he or she is getting in return for what the customer has to part with, reflecting an implicit comparison akin to "give and receive." It has been described as the quotient of quality over price. Understanding the customer is about understanding customer value. Customer value is a complex concept and measuring it is complicated. But in the exercise of trying to understand customer value, the manager benefits from a better understanding of the customer and of the opportunities for a superior solution. Here are some characteristics of customer value that any manager should examine in an analysis of the firm and its activities: Customer value

- Is what the customer believes that a product or service provides in a certain use situation.
- Is an implicit comparison between what the customer receives from the provider and what the customer provides in time, effort, and

money. The frame of reference is not just the price tag on the product, but also the ease and convenience in the acquisition and use of the product and the whole interactive experience the customer has with the firm.

- Is the customer's rather than the provider's perspective. It has to do with customer perceptions of the product and the firm, and not the provider's perspective of what the firm is delivering.
- Is dynamic, in that it can change over time before, during, and after the purchase, use, over repeated use of the product, and during all the various stages in the relationship with the providing firm.
- Can vary over different use situations. Your automobile may provide less or more value in transporting a group of kids to the ballpark compared to taking the spouse to the boss's house for a party.
- Can be shaped by attitudes, opinions, and behaviours of others, such as friends, family, media, the providing firm, and other competitors in the industry as well as in substitute industries.
- Determines customer satisfaction and the likelihood of brand or firm loyalty. This cause-effect relationship could be affected by comparisons with competitors and other substitutes.
- Is hard to measure and keep track of. Customers may find it hard to articulate all the different dimensions of customer value and firms may find it a rather onerous task to keep track of all the manifestations of customer value.

Your Value to the Customer

In order to determine what business a firm is in, therefore, the fundamental and imperative exercise is to understand customer value. Let us begin the analysis with the question, what exactly does customer value consist of? It is not easy to determine what the customer is getting as value from a product or service. To understand customer value, you really need to get into the customer's way of thinking about products. In a recent *Harvard Business Review* article, Chase and Dasu urge the use of behavioural science to get into the head of the customer, to understand their total experience with the product or service. Only then can you grasp all the components of customer value.

Examining the components and determinants of customer value is a critical step in the analysis. It requires analysis of the benefits as well as costs to the customer. The benefits seen are evident in the perceptions of the product performance. Perceptions of product performance are framed in the context of customer expectations. The expectations are shaped by past experience with the product and by messages about the product received from a variety of sources such as friends and family as well as from the marketer.

From an analytical perspective, product performance comes from functional (core) benefits and supplemental benefits. Functional benefits arise from the core attributes of the product. For instance, you buy a set of golf clubs. How the golf clubs affect your game is a core and functional benefit, as in the primary benefit from the product. The prestige of the brand image, the product return policy, and other customer service features would translate into supplemental benefits. Every customer value analysis requires that we identify and examine core and supplemental benefits.

Similarly, we need to identify the costs to the customer—both monetary and non-monetary costs. Monetary costs include costs incurred in the acquisition, use, and disposition of the solution. Non-monetary costs could include the time and effort in acquiring and benefiting from the solution and the opportunity costs where the product failed. Tom Wright, Buy.com's vice president of operations called his company's old way of handling returns "almost embarrassing." To return a product that a customer bought from Buy.com, the customer had to telephone Buy.com to generate a return authorization, which led to a shipping label from the package delivery firm (UPS) to be mailed to the customer, who then used that label to send the product back to Buy.com. It was weeks before the customer got credit for the product return! Imagine the non-monetary cost of aggravation to that customer.

Many firms that focus on acquiring customers do not retain customers because of their shallow understanding of customer value. Customer value includes interactions with the firm before, during, and after the consumption of the product. Smart firms are focusing on the whole customer and defining their business in terms of market spaces. The market space is the actual set of customer solutions defined by the consumption activities to which the firm caters.

In recognizing that customer value is dynamic, we need to place this analysis in the context of different use situations and how they are changed over time by various influences. Customers' concepts of what to expect from a provider change with each consumption experience. They learn from their own experiences with the product as well as vicariously from others. Competitor offerings and marketing messages continually shape their expectations. Therefore, implicit in the assessments made by the customer is a comparison with expectations based on the alternative—that is, the competition. Customer value analyses can be performed at a qualitative level and with some difficulty can be quantified as well. Data-driven representations of monetary worth of what a firm does for a customer are what Anderson and Narus called "customer value models." Such models are useful in assessing the customer value of your product and comparing it with the competition to determine whether you are providing superior customer value or not. The next fundamental question is, Can you provide this superior customer value at a sustainable profit by commanding revenues to cover costs and profits?

Mutual Value of Customer and Firm

Just as the customer value analysis requires an examination of the benefits versus the costs, the firm makes a similar analysis to determine its profit potential. In providing the customer value, what does the firm get in return? How do the monetary and nonmonetary benefits from the customer compare with what it cost the firm to provide that solution to that customer? Can we sustain these profits in the long term? A firm creates value for itself by creating value for the customer. In many ways, the value of a firm is reflected in the profits it provides its investors and the value of the customer to the firm is reflected in the profits that the customer provides the firm. The greater the values of the customer to the firm, the greater are the profits.

This means that the surplus from the revenues after costs is greater if you can attract and retain profitable customers in the long run. Part IV in this book covers the valuation of the customer by the firm. Firms can attract and retain customers if they can provide superior value. It could boil down to, can we command a premium on our solution? If you can, it turns out that the margins are not in the commoditized part of the product, it is in the services provided by the firm. The margins increase when you are able to extend your role in the customer's space. This may come in the form of "cross-selling" or "up-selling." It may be the case that the total solution provides such value to the customer that the customer is better off with you than with the competition.

As the firm gets more valuable to the customer, the customer gets more valuable to the firm. The value from a customer is derived not only from purchases. Customers can become advocates for the firm, the benefits of which are frequently less understood. The value of the customer in terms of purchases and referrals over the lifetime of the customer should be an imperative calculation for firms who are focused on the customer. It appears that in the final analysis, it is the customer-focused firm that can provide a complete solution through a service orientation that succeeds in providing superior customer value and in return enjoys sustainable profits. So, how is it that a firm is able to provide superior customer value? What gives them a sustainable competitive advantage, such that the firm has sustainable profits?

CUSTOMER VALUE OPPORTUNITIES

An understanding of the role that the firm's product plays in the customer's value chain could open up value-creating opportunities. A customer-focused firm has a detailed picture of the customer's consumption domain. When a firm views value consumption activities, it can see if there are other value creating opportunities that it can leverage from its assets. The watchmaker Swatch, for example, offers wrist watches with the technology that allows them to function as electronic passes at ski resorts in Switzerland or for public transportation in Finland.

Wrist gadgets can now serve not only the function of telling time, but also making phone calls, playing music and videos, browsing the Internet, or sending email. This example defies categorization of product. What is the product? It is a wallet or a pocketbook, as well as a telephone, a personal stereo, a personal VCR, and an Internet communications device! The exercise of determining what revenue opportunities Swatch's value-creating assets would offer forces a complete redefinition of the product.

The (product) solution is conceived to take advantage of opportunities to meet the needs in the customer's life with the assets that the firm has. Swatch has found a way to provide value to a recreational activity—skiing—and a functional activity—public transportation. It is contributing to the "customer access" components of the ski resort's and public transportation's product. By enabling customer access, information technology provides a whole range of supplementary benefits to a variety of products.

Contrast this with the example of a firm that does not understand the value of complementary product components and the customer's value chain. A customer came out of a movie theater in Kendall Square, Cambridge, and experienced a 40-minute ordeal trying to leave the theater's parking lot. She spent 30 minutes standing in line in frigid weather to pay the $2.50 parking fee and a further 15 minutes to exit the parking lot. When complaining to the management of the movie theater, she asked if she could pay the parking fee as she bought the movie ticket. She was told that the parking lot was owned by a different company and the theater would not take responsibility for the customer's bad experience at the parking lot.

In contrast, the airline SAS has been known to provide an annual dinner to taxicab drivers in Stockholm because the SAS management wants the drivers to treat passengers on the way to and from the airport with professional courtesy and respect. Clearly, firms that are customer-focused conceive their product differently from other firms, because of their intimate knowledge of the customer's consumption activities.

Information about the customer's consumption cycle, therefore, is a key prerequisite to exploring the opportunities that might be tapped. An understanding of how the customer actually benefits from the solution and the information of how, when, where, and with whom the customer consumes the product should provide some interesting revelations of what the firm is doing and can be doing in the composition of the total product solution for customers.

Thus, Procter & Gamble sends its researchers to homes to observe how people actually use laundry detergent. When Samsung was trying to break into the microwave business in the late 1970s and early 1980s, their design engineers observed homemakers shopping for microwaves at the retail store. You can stay ahead of the curve by offering value through supplementary product that your customer information tells you customers will be willing to pay for.

Even if the value-producing feature or activity cannot be priced separately, you may be able to command a premium for your superior customer value. Being customer-focused is critical in identifying opportunities for establishing superiority in customer value.

Conceiving and Designing

All decisions about the product and, therefore, the value-creating activities of the firm are based on an understanding of the value-consumption activities of its customers. What are the decisions and what are the issues to be considered in determining the total product by a firm? The three major decisions constituting the product strategy are: the product concept, the operations design, and the value creation and delivery process. The *product concept* defines the customer to be served and what value is to be provided. The *operations design* defines the productive assets of the firm required to create and deliver that value for that customer.

Together, the product concept and the operations design define the scope and configuration of the productive assets that can be leveraged to produce the specific customer value that maximizes profits to the firm. The *value creation and delivery process* executes the product concept with the operations design. In developing the product strategy, the firm makes a fundamental decision in answering the question of how the product will be positioned among all potential solutions to the customer's need.

This positioning question poses an asset- and market-based decision that comprises two perspectives.

- The *market-based perspective* looks outward at the market and asks what customer needs can be most profitably served by the firm.
- The *asset-based perspective* looks inward, at the firm's assets, and asks what assets of the firm can be most profitably leveraged by the firm.

The market-based perspective drives the product concept and the asset-based perspective drives the operations design. Thus, the initial step in developing product strategy involves two critical analyses. The product concept requires analyses of the various segments in the marketspace, while the operations design requires analyses of the firm's productive factors. These two sets of analyses are essential to determining what value-creating activities the firm should engage in to generate the maximum revenue from its assets.

The Market-Based Perspective

A market analysis to determine what would be the most profitable segment mix for a configuration of the productive assets of the firm is the foundation for product strategy. First you need to identify the segments and the solutions that are currently available to the segments. The target market selection or the selected market segments to be served can be based on the profitability and size of each segment that the firm's assets are best positioned to serve.

Here, a formal comparison of all the current solutions from the customer's perspective is necessary. Based on this analysis, the firm is able to determine what it can provide better than the alternative available to the appropriate target market, thus framing the firm's competitive advantage. Only after such customer needs analysis is it possible to specify what would be the desired customer value in the product offering.

The intended customer value in the product offering can now be translated into a detailed picture of the product concept—what the core and supplementary product ought to be.

Remember that the customer value also reflects the customer's implicit assessment of the firm's solution compared to competitive offerings and, indeed, all solutions that are available to customers in the segment. To ensure that the product concept can effectively be superior customer value, the core product should combine the imperatives that have become commodities in the product category with the appropriate features in the supplementary product to reflect superiority in customer value. Thus, the product concept embodies the product differentiation and the superiority in customer value.

The Asset-Based Perspective

The operations design decision rests on how best the assets of the firm can be most profitably leveraged and follows a sequence of questions that pertain to the productive assets and capabilities of the firm and how they should be deployed: What people, facilities, equipment assets are needed to create and deliver the product? Which employees' skills and knowledge would be needed? When and where would specific human capital be needed and for how much time? Similar questions are asked about the facilities and equipment of the firm. Of course, when the asset or resource is not available within the firm, it seeks suppliers or outsources that part of the value creation. Ultimately, the question is what competitive advantage the firm is capable of and how the assets needed should be configured.

Value Creation and Delivery Process

The process decisions are about determining the specific activities of the value creation and delivery. The process of making the product and delivering it to the customer must be detailed. The value creation and delivery activities required are set in a specific sequence. The firm must deliberate on the structure, content, and process of creating and delivering the product to the customer.

No product differentiation from supplementary product can be seen in isolation. If the total benefits from the product are not worth the costs that the customer incurs in acquiring and using the product, the product is likely to fail. The more carefully the firm designs the process with the customer in mind, the more likely the process ensures ease, convenience and quality for the customer. Thus, the customer-focused firm designs the creation and delivery process with the customer's perception of benefits and costs in the value consumption process.

Ensuring Customer-focused Value Creation

Firms must also recognize that since customer value is dynamic, they need to continually monitor and improve this customer value. Ignorance of the need to innovate to sustain competitive advantage is a common mistake committed by the complacent firm. The argument is sometimes made that the firm's priority of customer focus minimizes the attention to innovation. Customer focus and innovation are not contradictory, an either/or strategic decision. Indeed, to be customer-focused would mean that the firm is continually looking for new ways and solutions to meet customer needs—and to be aware that customer needs evolve as well.

Visualize what the firm needs to do to ensure that it is creating and delivering customer-focused value that can be sustained. To sustain superiority in customer value the firm must ensure that management continually assess its market and its assets to ensure that the choice of customer and the value being created and delivered by the firm maximizes the profit goals of the firm.

How well is the customer value in the product concept translated to the operations design and the value creation and delivery process? Is the superiority in customer value being executed. The answer lies in the customer's judgment. Customer-focused firms will let the customer decide whether the firm's value creation and delivery is customer-focused.

Continual customer satisfaction assessment information needs to be available for the customer-focused firm to improve by changing the product concept, the operations design, and the value creation and delivery process, or to continually reassess whether its assets and capabilities are being leveraged to realize the maximum profit potential. To ensure customer-focused value creation and delivery, firms must assess customers' perceptions of the benefits they receive as well as the costs incurred by them.

As an ongoing assessment of customer value, firms must continually assess customer needs and customer satisfaction. As customer needs change, the value bundle needs to be reviewed in terms of its product concept, operations design and delivery. An assessment of customer satisfaction presents an opportunity to improve customer value. The smart firm will continually monitor customer satisfaction to understand what customers perceive as the benefits they are getting from product compared to the costs that they incur.

Based on customer satisfaction, does the value bundle need to be modified and redesigned? Are the assets and capabilities of the firm being leveraged for maximum sustainable profits? If the expected customer value cannot be delivered with the existing value-creating assets, then the firm has two choices. Either it acquires or outsources the required value-creating assets and capabilities, or it determines that the target market decision needs revisiting. These questions are posed as a frame for a customer-focused analysis of the value creation and delivery of the firm.

Managing Customer Interactions

The process of delivering value is a tricky and detail-rich exercise; it requires careful planning, using techniques such as blueprinting to visualize the entire customer experience. From the customer perspective, some service encounters are critical incidents requiring more attention than others. All service encounters must be staged for a customer-focused experience just as in the production of theater.

Why does Kimberly-Clark manage the discount retailer Costco's inventory of its diapers? The firm has a salesperson live near the Costco headquarters, and a data analyst responsible for overseeing stock at 155 Costco stores in the western United States. Similarly, Procter & Gamble stations 250 people near Wal-mart's headquarters in Bentonville, Arkansas. Large retailers are asking suppliers to more actively manage the movement of products from factory to retail store shelves. P&G estimates that stock-outs amount to 11 percent of an average retailer's annual sales.

When firms like Kimberly-Clark pay more attention to how its immediate customers—the retailers—create value to their customers, they demonstrate that they are being customer focused. In fact, the Kimberly-Clark salesperson passed on information on how customers place packages in their shopping cart that played into package design for diapers. Wayne Sanders, chairman and CEO of Kimberly-Clark, attributes this change to the information age.

Prior to the industrial revolution, a service orientation and the individual-to-individual interaction was the predominant mode of competitiveness. Assembly-line production distanced the firm from the customer due to the sheer number of customers and the physical distance between the customers and the firm brought about by the wonders of modern transportation. Manufacturing goods became the engine of individual and collective (national) economic growth.

Mechanization far outpaced services and replaced producer-customer interaction, relying instead on intermediary institutions to provide a specialized set of competencies that the producing firm lacked. Businesses lost sight of the customer. Now, information technology has brought this full circle, back to the customer.

We call it the information age because what has changed in our time is that new technology has revolutionized the way information is handled. Another equally significant revolution is the change in the customer's domain. Customers not only have access to more information on products and service offerings, they also have the ability to interact with the providers of products and services in ways not previously possible. Providers can also present enhancements to customer experiences from the functionalities presented by technology. Service providers must, however, also manage customer participation when they utilize technology.

When firms take advantage of online marketplaces, it might be necessary to make changes in organizational structure so that value creation and delivery processes are adjusted to the addition of the online delivery. Two key technologies underlie this information age technology phenomenon: the Internet and wireless communications.

What customer access to these technologies has done is to bring customer interactions to a new level and to the front and centre in how a firm deals with the customer. These interactions are essentially service encounters with the customer.

Much has been said about the service encounter—customer interactions with the firm. In a way, all customer relationship management (CRM) solutions are basically technology support to ensure that the firm maximizes returns from customers by enabling customer-focused interactions. The service encounter is truly "where the rubber hits the road"—where the prospects of customer loyalty are materialized or lost. It is where promises made in advertising are honored or reneged on, and where expectations of customers are disappointed or met. It is where all the assets of the firm need to be brought to bear.

Service encounters with the customers are also laden with the challenges of a product that is produced and consumed in real time, where failures are bound to happen. When the firm designs the value creation process with the customer in mind, it will be prepared for all predictable eventualities. When the service fails, smart firms have smart processes, that recover and learn from the failure. They have service recovery and knowledge management processes in place.

As firms compete more and more on services, the management of the customer interaction becomes critical to ensure superiority in customer value. As the core product is a commodity, and most facilitating services approach the commodity state, the competitiveness comes from how the customer is treated by the firm at each and every encounter.

This discusses a method for designing the value delivery process with special attention paid to the service encounter and the critical incidents in the value creation and delivery process. A framework for designing the service encounter based on the theatrical metaphor is offered as a way to examine the customer focus of value creation and delivery.

The Ingredients of Customer Interactions

Analyzing customer interactions can be very rewarding. Amazon constantly tracks the reasons for every customer contact. It has made numerous changes to its value creation and delivery process based on customer input. The customer service function at Amazon is considered a research lab for ways to improve the Amazon customer experience. We can turn to the unique characteristics of services to obtain a clear understanding of what is involved in a customer interaction. Something intangible is always exchanged in the interaction (intangibility). Without a customer, there is no interaction and the separation of production and consumption is irrelevant (inseparability).

To conduct the interaction, the firm has the resources and infrastructure in place that "perish" when not utilized (perishability). Each interaction is unique (variability). From these characteristics, emerge situations that are challenges and opportunities typical to the service firm. We need to keep these in mind as we design the process of creating and delivering customer value. At the most general level, all customer interactions occur in a certain place (or space), at a certain time, for a certain duration, between certain entities, in a certain manner for a certain purpose.

Consider these as ingredients in a customer interaction and categorize them into elements of structure, content, and process. When the customer interaction is mapped onto the consumption activity cycle, the objective of the interaction becomes the driving force behind the design of the interaction in terms of its structure, content, and process.

- *Structure* relates to who or what entities are involved in the interaction.
- *Content* relates to the subject, the task, and its significance in the interaction.
- *Process* relates to the sequence of steps in the interaction.

The primary decisions that would configure the structure of the interaction involve the nature of the interaction—what entity should represent the firm, should the interaction be face-to-face or not, what technology can be utilized, where should it occur, and so forth. As a complementary question about the customer: What entities from the customer's domain are involved in the interaction? Similarly, decisions determining the content of the interaction should centre around the task and include what information should be required in the interaction, what should transpire between the parties, and what value should be created and consumed in the interaction.

Decisions about process would include a script of the interaction and the roles of both parties in the interaction. Any of these decisions must be based on the information that the firm has about the customer's consumption cycle and on preferences regarding these dimensions of the interaction. For example, technology may provide the firm with scale economies, but the customer may want to disengage from the script and interact with a person instead. Ultimately, the important question is what value is being created in the interaction.

DELIVERING SUPERIOR CUSTOMER VALUE

What characterizes firms that can provide *superior* customer value? To answer this question, we have ample evidence from research on such firms. Every firm in any industry provides some customer value. The firm that provides superior customer value is the one that has a sustainable competitive advantage. Firms compete with each other on differentiable aspects of the total solution. If we can conceptualize that every product has parts that are commodities and parts that differentiate it from others, superior value is in the augmented product, not in the conceptual core.

For example, all airlines provide transportation from point A to point B. But the total solution includes aspects other than the physical transportation of the person itself, such as amenities on the airplane. A firm must seek opportunities to differentiate itself from the competition in ways that are meaningful and relevant to the customer. How do firms find opportunities to differentiate themselves in a way that it is sustainable?

Consider how CDW creates superior customer value. CDW is the leading B2B e-commerce firm selling technology equipment to small and medium-sized firms. Wall Street analysts claim that the firm uses a "clicks and people" strategy. Supposedly, their competitive advantage is superior customer service and lower customer acquisition costs. The firm's Web site is tailored to each specific customer as a "custom extranet." How are they able to sustain this competitive advantage? Their own chief financial officer, Harry Harczak, notes that retaining people is key. In his experience, the productivity difference between an employee who has been at the firm six months versus one there three years is a factor of six. CDW values employee commitment.

What are the generalizable characteristics of firms that create superior customer value? A team of Harvard Business School researchers set out to discover exactly this and concluded that successful firms such as BancOne, Intuit, Southwest Airlines, ServiceMaster, USAA, Taco Bell, and MCI made employees and customers paramount. These researchers modeled the findings from their case studies into a framework they called "the service profit chain." Their cases provided data to establish powerful relationships between profitability, customer loyalty, and employee satisfaction, loyalty, and productivity. Evident in the whole model is the focus on the customer and the service orientation of satisfied employees, and the implications on investors and other stakeholders of the firm.

As firms focus on customer needs and become service oriented to deliver satisfaction, there are favourable ripple effects throughout the firm. Consistent delivery of customer satisfaction persuades customers to be loyal because perceived risk in buying a product from that firm is substantially reduced. When providers of solutions to customer needs are able to consistently deliver expected value, customers are more likely to be consistently satisfied. By way of their continued patronage, they become more valuable to the firm. When customers are loyal to the provider by choice, it is also in their best interest to support the provider because the prosperity and longevity of the provider is beneficial to the customer. Similarly, with regard to employees, research has shown that when employee satisfaction is high employees are more likely to be loyal to the company. When employee loyalty is high, employees are likely to be more productive and to be providing quality products and service.

Neither employees nor customers are likely to be loyal unless their expectations are met and they are satisfied. Therefore, customer satisfaction and employee satisfaction are inherently tied to each other, in that, when employees are loyal to the firm, they provide superior performances driving customer loyalty. When employees are productive and customer loyalty is high, the firm is successful and can command a premium.

With increased profitability and growth prospects, investors are attracted to the firm, which in turn makes more resources available to the firm. With more resources available to the firm, capital is available to continuously improve value-creating assets (people and processes) and to produce consistently superior customer value in its products and service. This sequence of events, presented as the "loyalty circle", contributes to profitability and growth and requires that people and processes are aligned to deliver superior customer value. Delivering superior value should be a relentless endeavor for the firm.

DELIVERING CUSTOMER VALUE AND SATISFACTION

Marketers alone cannot deliver superior customer value and satisfaction. Although it plays a leading role, marketing can be only a partner in attracting, keeping, and growing customers. Relationship marketing requires that marketers must work closely with other company departments to form an effective value chain that serves the customer. Moreover, the company can be effective only to the extent that it works effectively with its marketing system partners to form a competitively superior value-delivery network. We now take a closer look at the concepts of a company value chain and value-delivery network.

Company Value Chain. Each company department can be thought of as a link in the company's value chain. That is, each department carries out value-creating activities to design, produce, market, deliver, and support the firm's products. The film's success depends not only on how well each department performs its work, but also on how well the activities of various departments are coordinated.

For example, we learned previously that the goal of Ritz-Carlton Hotels is to deliver "a truly memorable experience." Marketers make up an important link in the Ritz-Carlton value chain that creates this experience. They conduct research to learn about customer needs, design services to meet these needs, advertise to inform guests about services and locations, and perform other value-creating activities.

However, other departments must also perform well in order to make the Ritz-Carlton experience a reality. For example, the Ritz-Carlton housekeeping and maintenance staffs make certain that everything at the Ritz-Carlton looks and works just right, meeting customers' exacting standards for room cleanliness and functioning. The human resources department hires people-oriented employees, trains them carefully, and motivates them to ferret out and attend to even the slightest customer want. Ritz-Carlton employees treat customers as individuals, not as nameless, faceless members of a mass market. Whenever possible, they refer to guests by name and give each guest a warm welcome every day. Finally, the information systems department maintains an extensive customer database, which holds more than 500,000 individual customer preferences, accessible by all hotels in the worldwide Ritz chain. A frequent guest who requests a specific type of room at the Ritz in San Francisco will be delighted to find a similar room assigned when he or she checks into the Atlanta Ritz months later, arranged just the way that he or she likes it.

A company's value chain is only as strong as its weakest link. Success depends on how well each department performs its work of adding value for customers and on how well the activities of different departments are coordinated. At Ritz-Carlton, if customer-contact people are poorly selected or trained, or if rooms are anything less than spotless, marketers cannot fulfil their promise of a truly memorable experience. Customer Value-Delivery Network. In its search for competitive advantage, the firm needs to look beyond its own value chain and into the value chains of its suppliers, distributors, and ultimately customers.

Consider McDonald's. People do not swarm to the world's 24,500 McDonald's restaurants only because they love the chains hamburgers. In fact, according to one national survey, consumers rank McDonald's behind Burger King and Wendy's in taste preference." Still, McDonald's commands over a 16 percent share of the nation's fast-food business and over 40 percent of the burger segment. Consumers flock to the McDonald's system, not just to its food products. Throughout the world, McDonald's finely tuned system delivers a high standard of what the company calls QSCV—quality service, cleanliness, and value. McDonald's is effective only to the extent that it successfully partners with its franchisees, suppliers, and others to jointly deliver exceptionally high customer value.

More companies today are "partnering" with the other members of the supply chain to improve the performance of the customer value-delivery network. For example, Honda has designed a program for working closely with its suppliers to help them reduce their costs and improve quality. When Honda chose Donnelly Corporation to supply all of the mirrors for its U.S.-made cars, it sent engineers swarming over Donnelly's plants, looking for ways to improve its products and operations. This helped Donnelly reduce its costs by 2 percent in the first year. As a result of its improved performance, Donnelly's sales to Honda have grown from $5 million annually Co more than $60 million in less than 10 years. In turn, Honda has gained an efficient, low-cost supplier of quality components. As a result of Honda's partnerships with Donnelly and other suppliers, Honda customers receive greater value in the form of lower-cost, higher-quality cars.

Increasingly in today's marketplace, competition no longer takes place between individual competitors. Rather, it takes place between the entire value-delivery networks created by these competitors. Thus, Honda's performance against another automaker —say Toyota—depends on the quality of Honda's overall value-delivery network versus Toyota's. Companies no longer compete—their entire marketing networks do.

MANAGERIAL OPPORTUNITIES AND CHALLENGES

The implications of the fundamental characteristics of services suggest that managers need to examine how they would adapt their business processes to take advantage of the opportunities and to address the challenges. The following is a discussion of some of the key managerial challenges and opportunities.

Reducing Customers' Perceived Risk

With products that contain a significant proportion of intangibles and where the core product is a service, managers of services need to continuously monitor and understand the risk customers feel when they purchase the service. What is the nature of the risk? How do you lower this risk? Professional services providers such as lawyers and doctors have certifications prominently displayed on their walls. Consulting firms provide lists of clients, mutual funds companies show off their performance charts. What would be most appropriate for you to do to reduce customer perceived risk? To determine this you begin by understanding what those risk levers might be. What is the source of the anxiety that customers feel? To what would you attribute the risk that they feel?

Only when this is clearly understood can you think about the possible ways you might reduce their perceived risk. To understand the risk, you need to break down the service into the features that contribute value toward the total solution.

Which service features produce benefits, and how can the risk associated with each feature-benefit connection be reduced? The degree to which the customer feels assured that expectations of these benefits will be met would depend on how you can instill confidence in the customer that you have the ability to deliver on those expectations. Christopher Hart is credited with the concept of service guarantees that works to reduce perceived risk. L.L. Bean's famed "100per cent satisfaction guaranteed" goes back to 1912, when the founder was marketing the Maine hunting shoe. Service providers who understand their customers' perceived risk seek to address it.

Customization versus Standardization

One of the powerful implications of the fundamental characteristics of services is that they are not produced ahead of time. The service is designed, created, and delivered to customer specifications. While customization is possible, some standardized parameters are also necessary to derive economies of scale. There is opportunity to standardize as well as to customize. Where there is low margin from a service component and the volume provides the profits, perhaps ways to standardize the production process would be appropriate. On the other hand, if there is opportunity for high margin, customization and low volume is the way to go.

Consider the difference between automated telephone-based customer service and a fee sometimes charged for customers who want individual attention. Professional or knowledge based services are generally customized and are high-margin, whereas dry cleaning services are low-margin services and require considerable standardization and the required volume. The opportunity is to increase margins by providing customized experiences and the challenge is in standardizing the process to reduce costs and maintain consistent quality.

Quality Consistency

A related issue to the opportunity to customize is the accompanying challenge posed by the variability of the product. Since services are produced in real time, and they have a high degree of variability, the challenge is to ensure a consistent quality in the service.

Managers must assess the sources of variation. Sources of the variability are typically associated with the people delivering the service. Every interaction with the customer provides or facilitates some aspect of the product bundle, and therefore the quality of the product is dependent on each and every interaction between the service provider and the customer. Therefore, selecting, training, and motivating frontline personnel become very critical.

For example, service firms such as Walt Disney amusement parks and the Ritz-Carlton hotels have a specific profile in mind when they hire people for the front line. These firms provide extensive service training for their frontline employees, and they motivate employees to provide customer satisfaction. FedEx rewards employees who take care of customers in service failures. Empowered frontline personnel are more likely to deliver quality service.

Demand and Capacity Management

Since services are perishable, productive factors that are in place may be idle at low demand times and stretched to capacity at high demand times. The demand is fluctuating, and it might be impossible or at best a serious challenge to stretch or contract capacity. Therefore, smoothing demand and managing capacity become a constant endeavor for the managers of services. The key to managing this challenge is to understand the demand patterns and to figure out the flexibilities in your capacity. To the extent that the demand patterns can be predicted with a good understanding of customer behaviour, service providers can manage demand as well as capacity. Pricing is commonly used in smoothing demand.

Early bird specials, matinee prices, lower fares if you stay over Saturdays are all different ways by which service firms use pricing to manage demand. Reservations and appointments are another way for service managers to smooth demand. Different segments and markets are served at different times and prices to fill capacity. Hotels depend to a great extent on the lucrative conferences and meetings market to ensure capacity utilization.

Such capacity-constrained services rely more on managing demand than on managing capacity primarily because it is harder to adjust capacity. Product mix adjustments are another way of managing capacity, whereas the more versatile the value-creating assets are in producing different services with the same productive factors, the better the capacity management opportunities. For example, ski resorts turn into hiking or whitewater rafting facilities in the summer. Staffing and scheduling are typical capacity-side management options that the service firm employs. Creative use of value producing assets is critical for efficient and effective management of a firm's capacity.

Managing the Customer

Since the customer is part of the process and some degree of interaction with the customer is necessary and inevitable, managers of services must find ways to educate customers on their roles. If the customer fails in playing the appropriate coproducer role, it could ruin the process and the outcome quality. A clear understanding of the steps in the process and how, where, and when customers interact with the process is a must. Doctors, nurses, and pharmacists provide directions and instructions for patient roles. Banks and other financial institutions have specific protocols for various financial transactions.

A key question to ask is how the customer should participate in the process and whether you have the appropriate instructions for your customer. Differences in customer willingness and ability to participate in the production of the process force the issue of segmentation on the service delivery process. Thus, restaurants have self-service, take-out, or drive-through options. Automatic teller machines are an early example of self-service in banking services. Hotels have express check-in and check-out facilities. Airlines have electronic ticketing options. Self-service checkout facilities have become a standard option at grocery stores in the United States and elsewhere.

It is clear as we think about these issues that not all services are alike. While all services face all these challenges to some degree, the challenges manifest themselves differently in different services. In fact, the management solutions presented are more applicable in some and inappropriate or impossible in others. There is a systematic way of addressing these differences among services by examining characteristics that differentiate services from one another. A service that shares characteristics with another service exhibits similar challenges and opportunities.

Category Characteristics Of A Specific Service

In employing the service orientation, every manager needs to understand that there are different types of services in every product, each with its own manifestations of the fundamental characteristics of services. The nature of these manifestations in different services implies different situations for the customer and the manager. While all services are fundamentally intangible, inseparable, perishable, and variable, services differ from each other along dimensions peculiar to their category. These category characteristics provide the manager with an insight into the specific situations that they have to deal with in their particular service category.

Christopher Lovelock demonstrated that this sort of categorizing is necessary and powerful as a means of understanding the managerial situations specific to each type of service. Service managers should look toward other services that share similar characteristics and expect to find similar challenges and transferable solutions to those challenges. Consider for example that hospitals provide executive-style rooms for the businessperson who is a patient. They learned this from hotels that have executive-style suites for the businessperson. Now consider the service characteristics that are shared between hospitals and hotels.

In both cases, the customer comes to the factory and frequently requires an overnight stay. In both situations, the executive is likely to be away from an office with all its business support for an extended period of time. Both services are similar in the type of customer interactions, even though they are in two completely different service sectors. An analysis represents the benefits of learning from the successes of services that share certain specific service characteristics.

Managers of services can understand the specific challenges and opportunities presented by the characteristics of their product and corresponding situations by examining a number of characteristics that profile a service category. Here are a few characteristics to examine:

- Tangible or intangible act
- Person or thing as recipient of the act

- Type of interaction between provider and customer
- Service delivered by people or equipment
- Extent of customization or standardization

What are the tangible and intangible acts involved in the services that you are providing? Is the service act delivered on a person or a thing? For example, if you are an entertainment electronics repair and service provider, you perform tangible acts on a DVD player and intangible acts with the customer as you obtain information on what problems the customer has experienced with the DVD player. Now, examine the nature of the acts and the impact on the customer. When you are working on the DVD player, the customer needs not be present and the process that you employ need not be visible to the customer. However, you do interact with the customer at a number of points, from the initial customer call to the final interaction at delivery or pickup of the DVD player.

Similarly, you might analyze your service about the nature of interaction of with the customer. Is it face-to-face or arm's length, via telephone or the Internet? Do you visit the customer or does the customer visit your premises? How much technology is involved in the interface with the customer? Sometimes the customer does not even interact with a person. How much standardization is built into the service? Are there options provided to customers who require a customized interaction? What benefits does this analysis provide the manager?

The challenges and opportunities discussed earlier as fundamental are common to all service managers. By understanding the characteristics of their specific category of services, the manager can find ways to take advantage of the opportunities and address the challenges of their specific situation. Additionally, in understanding how the fundamental characteristic of intangibility manifests itself in their particular situation, managers can understand customers' perceived risk and use the tangibles in the customer experience to reduce the risk that customers perceive.

By understanding the nature of the interaction, managers are in a better place to manage the roles of customers and recognize opportunities for customization and standardization to improve the customer experience and, therefore, customer value. What is most interesting is that you may find that service businesses in a different industry sharing certain characteristics may offer you innovative ideas to meet these challenges and capitalize on opportunities to better serve customers in your business.

In order to understand how the required service-oriented frame of mind needs to be handled in the customer-focused firm, the firm analyzes the various services with which it augments the product. Each service is analyzed from a fundamental and category perspective. The fundamental nature of services requires an analysis of the implications of the intangible, inseparable, perishable, and variable nature of services for managerial action.

The analysis of category characteristics specific to each type of service should deal with how these consequences of these characteristics manifest themselves in that situation. The customer-focused analysis should cover the nature and the recipient of the act, the nature of the interaction, and the fluctuation of the demand.

RECOGNISING THE CULTURE WITHIN DIFFERENT ORGANISATIONS

In a B2B environment it is vital that organisations understand their customers 'corporate' culture. In the B2C marketplace the organisation needs to seek acceptance of its culture from its cus-tomer base. Knowing exactly how your client company wishes to orchestrate its business will enable you to offer what is perceived by them as excellent customer service. Without this knowledge the service that you offer will, at best, be mediocre; at worst not even be recognised. As we have already discussed, the recognition of a corporate culture within industry is not always an easy task, rather paradoxically it is often easier for somebody outside of the organisation to identify. Defining a corporate culture is a difficult analysis to make, and yet everyone will understand it when exposed to it.

Let us examine the successful high-street retailer, John Lewis Partnership. For many years the John Lewis Partnership refused to open on Saturday afternoons; furthermore it was the only chain that would not accept transactions via credit card. Yet the company prospered with premises in London's prestigious Oxford Street. Its customers understood its corporate culture. The 'partnership' element means that all of those working within the organisation are 'partners'; they have a share of the profits and a vested interest in the organisation's performance. As customers grew more sophisticated, so their demands changed. We were living in a plastic society, everybody has credit or debit cards and cash is very much a last resort. The John Lewis Partnership had to relent; they had to start accepting credit cards. Although this was against their corporate culture, they recognised their customers' needs, adopted part of the customers' culture and adapted the business processes to ensure that they satisfied their customers' needs.

At the outset of the Internet explosion, the general message to customers was that they should be able to shop at any time, be customers at any time; therefore the closing of a store on a Saturday afternoon was not seen as best possible customer service. So, the John Lewis Partnership relented yet again and opened on a Saturday all day. In doing this they have not diminished the culture within the organisation; everyone is still a partner and customer service levels have rocketed. The amount of people using the partnership and its sister organisation, Waitrose, the grocery retail arm, is in an upward arc of which any organisation would be proud. Recognising its own culture and adapting it to offer a better customer service has served the purpose for that particular organisation. It is a lesson that can be learned and adopted by many other organisations.

MARRYING A CULTURE OF PROFIT TO A SERVICE EXCELLENCE ETHIC

Every business is in existence to make a profit. In order to make a profit, every business must have customers. Marrying the culture of profit to the service excellence ethic is something that must evolve; it is not something that can be manufactured. Many organisations still see the service excellence ethic as being a cost element and a drain on financial resources. This need not be true provided the pursuance of customer service excellence has followed a structured path. Customer service excellence will lead to greater profit. Customers will stay longer, will remain loyal and will utilise your services, adding to your margins. The longer customers stay, the more they spend with you, and the greater the profit. So, it is important to take many of the best practice issues in this book and others, implement them in a structured way, and let them evolve into a service offering that enables the organisation to profit at the same time.

The profit culture can exist alongside service excellence, and already does successfully for many organisations. They may make strange bedfellows but service and profit really are a 'match made in heaven'. The first step to achieving this match is for the organ-isation to accept that it is in existence to make a profit and not to be frightened to highlight that fact in external and internal com-munications.

Being proud of being in existence to make profit is an import-ant step to ensuring that the cultures marry as time progresses. Investors, shareholders and other stakeholders will be satisfied that the company is able to discuss its motives openly and transparently even when these motives are profit-driven. With the exception of a few specifically ethically driven subjects, the majority of consumers are unlikely to baulk at an organisation because it wants to make a profit. We have established that customers are becoming more sophisticated, and they understand that a business has overheads and must make a profit. Finding a way of measuring the customer service excellence payback is an important element to marrying that part of the business to the rest of the enterprise. A customer service director would unquestionably aid this pro-cess. Any organisational dinosaurs evaluating customer service as a cost centre rather than a profit centre will ensure that the marriage hits the rocks. Measuring the value of customer service and pub-lishing the findings internally will help to ensure that profit and service continue to grow.

UNDERGOING A CULTURAL CHANGE

Resistance to change, in any situation, is a force that should not be underestimated. When the magnitude of the change is some-thing as subtle yet powerful as corporate culture, then the resistance can almost be overwhelming. To undergo this type of change effectively without too much pain is a difficult process, and one that must be managed acutely from the outset to com-pletion. Introducing change demands explanation of why the change is necessary. 'Why change?' must first be answered in the boardroom to define what needs changing. These revelations must then be communicated through the entire enterprise. Everyone must be aware of why they are undertaking this change process.

Having communicated the motives downstream, it is then that the reticence will start to grow. The organisation must be prepared and able to answer the fears of all those affected by the change in corporate direction. The challenges that are then faced will be varied and many, and within the overall rollout of the culture change there must be provision made for a long consul-tation period. Fears in the labour market will ensure that every-one is concerned about possible redundancies. Downstream staff and some middle management will look for underlying cynical reasons for the changes taking place. Putting the message across to your staff that the organisation is undergoing a cultural change will concern them as to whether they will still be working for the same 'type' of organisation. Again it's important to put across what the endgame is likely to be and what results the organisation is looking to achieve.

Particular challenges are faced when new personnel at the very top of the hierarchy are introduced. A new CEO or vice-president will often send ripples throughout the organisation or enterprise. The outgoing incumbent will be a known entity and the entire workforce will have a particular view of that person. The incoming executive will be an unknown quantity, and the only know-ledge anyone within the organisation will have is of his previous record. If the new incumbent has worked with an organization that has made redundancies, or restructured or downsized signific-antly, the fear factor among the workforce will escalate.

To manage this, it is important to have a transparent and open approach and for the new 'head honcho' to be accessible to as many of the workforce as possible. During open dialogue with staff, it is important to get them to buy in to the process. This is best achieved by identifying the strongest pockets of resistance and avoiding or excluding them from certain processes at this stage. Concentrate on the most willing sectors within the organisation. Often this is the service personnel. Enlist them as psuedo-customers and get them to sell your message to the rest of your employees. Achieve total buy-in from your supporters, let them reap the benefits and sing the praises of the new regime. Let them discuss with other people from other departments how the new regime affects them and their working practices, and let them effectively give the good news message. Because this sector of employees is already empowered and used to taking on board other people's (customers') grievances, they are the likely candid-ates for assessing individual needs best, and therefore putting across the message of the cultural change in many different ways to ensure maximum effect. There will inevitably be some die-hard opponents who are unwilling to come along for the ride; not everyone behaves to set patterns. To maximise the speed with which cultural change can happen, you may need to let go of some of your human resources if they are not willing to buy in.

CHANGE MANAGEMENT ISSUES

Managing change has several challenges and being an intangible process is a difficult task to master. When change is managed well, it is almost imperceptible. Change will always require manage-ment of specific issues, some of which are:

1 Resistance to change
2 Fear of change
3 Fear of underlying motives
4 Fear of job losses
5 Fear of losing out
6 Insecurities
7 Personalities
8 Change of routine
9 Learning new tasks
10. Financial penalties

Take those ten elements that need managing and multiply by the number of employees in your workforce and the magnitude of the problem comes sharply into focus. Managing change effect-ively is as much about managing personalities as it is about man-aging processes.

The best way to achieve successful management of all the issues is to take each particular item in isolation and continue to deal with that issue until the majority of people who are affected by it concur with your views. The temptation, too often, is to identify all of the potential problems and try to deal with them simultaneously.

The difficulty with this method is that if you were to deal with all ten issues in one communication, certain sectors of your staff would put different emphasis on each of the points. They may look at the order in which they were presented or the amount of space given to each particular issue and apportion a corresponding amount of importance to each.

Soon, it would be leveled that the organisation was not concerned with fear of redundancy issues because it was 'ninth on the list'; far better to deal on an issue-by-issue basis. Recognise when it is time to move on; there is absolutely nothing to be gained by covering old ground when the workforce has accepted the proposed changes. Give yourself a reasonable timeframe and stick to it.

TOP-DOWN APPROACH TO SERVICE CULTURE

An empowered service department will feel that it, and it alone, deals with customer issues. However, in order to reach that stage, there must exist a top-down approach to that service culture. Someone in the boardroom must sponsor the entire process and take customer service issues to a higher level.

In many ways this takes us full circle to the customer service director as discussed in Chapter 2. Someone at board level who is committed to the service ethic as well as the conventional business processes is a vital link to offering excellent customer service. Differentiation through service will be the key driver for business as we progress through the first decade of a new millennium.

A customer service director will also be ideally placed to assess the challenges of customer unions as they emerge and react to service challenges as they present themselves. The customer service director will also be in a position to drive forward the value of the brand; either to umbrella organisations for customer unions or to just maintain the brand values and the culture that is inherent in it. To try to manage this from any-where below board level will inevitably undermine the initiative because of the board's lack of buy-in and scepticism. If the board appoints a customer service director to ensure that the customer is a central part of the business, then they will be more willing to act on the advice of that director.

It is important that the service director is seen to be champion-ing the causes of the service personnel, and not just seen as a strategist. Service personnel on the ground must feel empowered and must feel that someone in the boardroom is supporting their decisions and their choices. It is important that customer service does not get diluted and become all things to all men and that it is clearly understood precisely what customer service really means to the organisation. Customer service should never be an alternative phrase for a 'sales person' or for 'an engineer' or other part of the business. Customer service must mean serving the customer – pure and simple.

3

Customer Focused Management

Businesses fail when the fundamental question—what business are we in?—is either ignored or misunderstood. To answer this question appropriately, businesses have to be customer focused. What does being customer focused mean? Why is it that customer-focused firms achieve a sustainable competitive advantage? What does customer-focused management involve?

A January 2001 issue of the *Wall Street Journal* featured an article titled: "Can these dot-coms be saved?" The dot-com malaise was becoming widespread. The message in the article was simple, the question straightforward, but the answers were not readily evident. A closer look reveals that the answers are implicit in the questions within the article. "Is Priceline's vaunted name-your-own-price model good for anything but plane tickets?" "If traditional catalog retailers can make money selling clothing why can't a Web site like Bluefly?" "Can Webvan's net-fueled automation turn profits delivering cornflakes?" All three of these Internet examples represent a very typical situation that most if not all dot-coms, including that mainstay, Yahoo!, had been facing. The problem was endemic to the dot-com business. The technology was powerful, but in each case, the appropriate revenue model remained elusive.

The question on everyone's mind was: Where are the profits? And, when the profits arrive, would they be sustainable? The answer is in the question. If you asked the right questions, you could find the right answers. A Francis Bacon quote comes to mind: "A prudent question is one-half of wisdom." As the dot-com frenzy reached epidemic proportions, the right questions were not being asked, and the right answers were not available. All this may (yet again) seem simplistic, but many of the dot-com failures were at least partly attributable to a lack of due diligence. The analyses about sustainable profitability must be preceded by the fundamental question of what business the firm is in. Unfortunately, the times were such that the promises of information technology overshadowed the fundamentals and good judgment on the part of many among us.

The business you are in

To make a profit in any business, you need to be able to sell for more than it costs you to produce. This is a basic prerequisite for any business, really. A viable business must produce enough revenues to cover costs and have surplus as profit. Ironically, the dot-com phenomenon brought the term "business or revenue model" to common parlance. The business or revenue model is a model that depicts how a business will generate revenue and what it will cost to do that.

The more important question may be, is the model sustainable in the long term? Sustainable profits come from sustainable competitive advantage, which in turn comes from consistently creating and delivering superior value. The concept of that superior value is essentially the business of your business. To really understand how you are going to make a profit, you have to first examine a more fundamental question: *"What business are you in?"*

- Priceline.com started with buying unsold airline seats at a heavy discount and allowing passengers to bid for them online. This is still its core business. Priceline experimented with selling gasoline and groceries and had to give these up. So, what business is priceline.com in? General retailer or broker of airline seats? Airline seats are perishable in that, if the seats are not sold before the plane takes off, the assets in the form of unsold seats perish. Priceline.com auctioning these seats off is a win-win situation for airlines as well as for passengers who are looking for cheap tickets and are willing to make last-minute travel plans. Why is it a "win" for airlines, and why is it a "win" for which type of customer? If this is priceline's business model, does it translate to gasoline and groceries?
- Can Bluefly compete with traditional catalog clothing retailers on price? Is Bluefly really in a different business? If not, it is in direct competition with established catalog retailers such as L.L. Bean and Land's End. Can these catalog retailers not offer a Web site retail front just as easily as Bluefly? Can Bluefly provide superior value compared to these established retailers, at a sustainable profit? If Bluefly is in a different business, what is it?
- Web grocers like Webvan are out of business. Why? Most likely, their analysis of the business model was flawed. Are they in the grocery business or in the delivery business? Can they sell what

they produce/provide for more than what it costs them to produce it? And can they deliver better customer value than the competition? Who or what is the competition? Ultimately, the question is: Can they provide sustainable superior customer value at sustainable profit?

With very few exceptions, such as the Internet auction firm eBay, the job-hunting site Monster.com, and the online bank NetBank, just about every dot-com firm was not profitable when they issued their IPOs in the mid to late 1990s. In 2001, Priceline.com turned its first profitable quarter. Eight months after that article in the *Wall Street Journal* about saving the dot-coms, a more direct article in the same business-oriented newspaper provided a peek at the real cause of dot-com troubles: "Latest dot-com fad is a bit old-fashioned: It's called profitability."

A handful of dot-com firms including online travel sites Expedia and Travelocity, online brokerage Ameritrade, real estate listing site Homestore.com, and online ticketing site Ticketmaster were beginning to show promise of steady profits. Most Internet firms struggled with the fundamental questions or, worse, had not even dealt with them. Many relied on advertising dollars to support profits. In the mid to late 1990s about 600 dot-coms, including such short-lived but well-known Internet brand names such as Webvan and eToys, failed. The business models at many firms appear to have been flawed.

Many of them offered free content and banked on revenues from advertising on their Web sites. Facing severe drops in advertising revenues in a slow economy, most dot-coms began charging for content in a desperate bid to attain profitability. The focus had reverted to the fundamentals of doing business: What customer value are you creating and can you make a profit doing it?

Barry Diller of USA Networks, who has been successful in lining up cash-producing Internet firms, put it bluntly: "You have to deliver a better product to your customer, not just offer an Internet retail option for the sake of dabbling in some new technology." Better product than what? Better than previously available and better than the competition. Mr. Diller was actually referring to superior customer value. The experienced business leader never loses sight of the fundamentals.

Peter Crist, vice chairman of the executive recruiting firm Korn/Ferry International, should know about management talent. He was quoted in the *Wall Street Journal* as saying, "There's a whole generation of people in their 50s and 60s, who started a business and focused on the fundamentals that we're losing." Case in point is Heartland Express CEO Russell Gerdin, who spends a lot of time on details—details of the costs and revenues of his operations, route-by-route, on a day-to-day basis. Gerdin never sways from his focus: short-haul business, where he has a competitive advantage over the "big guys."

How firms go about determining what it takes to provide superior customer value at a sustainable profit is the fundamental issue for any business. If you miss the fundamentals, you will fail in just about any endeavor, in the business world or in any other walk of life. This book is just as much about fundamentals as it is about obtaining and sustaining a competitive advantage. You cannot attain that sustainable competitive advantage unless you have mastered the fundamentals of creating and delivering superior customer value.

As discussed, the analyses confronting the fundamental question of "what business are we in?" must begin with a clear understanding of who the customer is and what customer value is being provided. Is this customer value superior to the customer's alternative? Firms must ensure that they can provide this customer value in the long term at a reasonable profit. To be able to *sustain* the profits, the firm needs to provide this customer value better than the competition. Continuously providing superior customer value leads to sustainable profits from a sustainable competitive advantage.

To make *sustainable* profits, firms must be able to continue to provide customer value at a cost lower than what the customer is willing to pay. What the customer is willing to pay is commensurate with the perceived value of the solution. If factors of production are equally accessible to all firms, what makes perceived value of one better than another?

The answer, clearly, must lie in something that is not available to all. What is unique to a firm may very well be the strength of its customer focus. When firms are focused on the customer, they understand what customer value is. A clear understanding of customer value gives the firm a clear view of its competitive status among the customer's choice of solutions.

CUSTOMER INFORMATION

Firms cannot claim a customer focus or attempt to satisfy customers unless they have customer knowledge—that is, a deep understanding of the needs of the customer. With all the brouhaha regarding the growing importance of customer relationship management (CRM), too many hotel companies are still vexed when it comes down to delivering on a service promise. For hotel companies looking to differentiate themselves from the competition, exceeding guest expectations is paramount since it leads to building loyalty. In this complex era, it is crucial to truly understand and anticipate guest desires in order to fulfill that service promise.

But just how to do it effectively has been an elusive and vague notion not fully grasped by many hoteliers. Customer-focused firms really understand their customers by proactively acquiring information on the entire consumption process, especially the consumption activities of the customer. Such information must be processed and used to guide each and every interaction with that customer. This information can be used not only to make changes and improvements in the value-creation and delivery processes of a firm but also in managing relationships with the right customers.

Managerial decisions and actions cannot be customer oriented when customer data is lacking. Do we know enough about the customer's consumption activities to enable us to create and deliver customer-focused value and manage relationships with the customer? Hotel companies need to be in the customer intimacy business. They have to focus on delivering what the customer wants. You have to have some product leadership to deliver on customer intimacy but you have to focus on the relationship above all else. All goals should be focused on customers rather than the product or operations. And getting those loyal relationships are paramount to the property or brand's success. 10 percent of all hotel guests account for 44 percent of all hotel nights.

To get those loyal customers, it's crucial a hotel employ a culture of managing the "total customer experience" and also embrace a culture of managing "moments of truth" when that experience is on the line. Also, property leadership should demand a culture that puts the customer at the "centre of your world."

While a hotelier doesn't have direct control over what someone says after they walk out, it's very possible to control the guest experience in such a way that they leave with only positive thoughts. Customer intimacy is essential for success in today's world. "If people don't feel welcome and have an emotional connection, their loyalty will be in question."

It's also a matter of creating emotional loyalty rather than functional loyalty. Whereas functional loyalty comes into play if a hotel is conveniently located near an airport, for example, emotional loyalty transcends pure need and promotes frequent stays because the experience moves beyond the brand attributes to an attachment to the guest's psyche.

As Lew Platt, former CEO of Hewlett Packard, is widely quoted as saying: "If HP knew what HP knows, we would be three times as profitable."

With the increasing ubiquity of information technology, there is an increasing focus on information—in a way, simply because it is there. Most managers understand the crucial role that good information plays in decision making. And here is a seemingly radical proposition: most data is underutilized in business. If you don't know what data is important, you may not recognize it when you see it. When there is an opportunity to obtain what may be valuable data, you will not access or gather, process, or utilize it.

Careful observation would reveal that as a norm, firms don't capitalize on opportunities to gather critical customer data. One reason may be that firms focus on the sort of data that is needed for a specific decision, such as in the development of a new product or an advertising campaign, especially in the B2C context, where there are no direct interactions with the customer. In the B2B context, where there is direct interaction with the customer, there is a greater amount of customer information being utilized for decision making. This is partly because formalized systems are in place to document customer information.

The customer being a business is very likely to have formalized purchasing procedures. Information-age technology has very naturally developed in the B2B case earlier and faster than in the B2C case. In the B2C business, where there is direct interaction with the customer, this technology is opening new thinking about customer data. A basic question is, what information is needed and for what purpose?

To manage the customer relationship, it's crucial to have deeper customer intelligence and then use that information to make each stay more memorable. For example, it is better to match up what your hotel does with each individual's lifestyle and give them something unique based on that lifestyle to reinforce the relationship. One suggestion made is to give, for example, a customer who stays 20 times a year and uses the gym regularly, a gym membership in their home town. That way, every time they go to the gym they will think of that hotel. It is a much better way to build loyalty then just giving them more points on their loyalty programme.

The Total Customer Experience. Customers want:

- A positive, enjoyable and unique experience from the beginning until the end of their experience
- They desire an emotional connection that, once made, often ensures long-term loyalty
- They must be valued for a lifelong contribution versus a one-time contribution to revenues

- Customers desire the perception that they are in control - ensure your customer-facing processes are engineered for how customers buy, when they buy and what they buy
- Customers want choice
- And they want this across all channels

The convergence of numerous information technologies in the gathering, storing, processing, disseminating, accessing, and using data has revolutionized the most generic of all business tasks—making informed business decisions. Communication, storage, and computational technologies have made this possible. Firms have found ways to deploy these technologies toward of increasing productivity. When the promise of technology is not delivered, as in many CRM and ERP projects, the focus has turned to how and why this data is useful for a business to support the investment in information technology.

One of the primary information systems of a firm is the customer information system. Customer-focused firms have used their information technology to develop smart customer information systems and broaden the scope of this business function. The role of the Chief Knowledge Officer, a title that was unheard of just a few years ago, is to manage the creation, discovery, and dissemination of knowledge in firms.

In the context of managing the knowledge resident with the firm about its business, customer information is one of the key pieces of the knowledge this person manages. The status given to this function is reflected in the seniority of the position and indicates the commitment of the firm to managing customer information that can be used to improve the value created and delivered by the firm.

The key issues discussed are: what kinds of customer information are needed to perform as a customer-focused firm, what information is required to usefully profile a customer, and how such a customer profile helps a firm understand the customer.

Need of Customer Information

The customer's desire to be known, confidence in service consistency, convenience, a feeling of welcoming and belonging and a comfort level where they know if there is a problem it will get handled right away. Of course, true loyalty goes beyond the physical hotel. These days loyalty is built with every single customer communication as well.

One way hotel companies communicate to customers is via emails. However, many companies are not communicating to their guests based on established preferences. For example, hotel brands will still offer ski vacations to die hard sun worshippers. At the hotel, many hotels are at the point where they are collecting information but are simply not tapping into that information to improve a guest stay. This can actually disenfranchise the guest since they have gone tot her trouble of providing their desires which are not being executed.

It's better to not gather the information, or say when it will actually be used. "It is more harmful to ask for that information and then not use it,In earlier, we saw that delivering superior customer value is a prerequisite for sustainable competitive advantage and that to be able to deliver superior customer value, a firm requires a good understanding of what customers value.

A good understanding of customer value presupposes good customer information. You cannot claim a customer focus, or seriously attempt to satisfy your customers, unless you understand their needs. An effective customer information system ensures that the appropriate knowledge of the customer is available for customer-focused decisions and actions. Without customer information, for example, it would be impossible to customize customer experiences, let alone manage customer relationships.

Knowledge of the customer is about being intimate with the customer. Customer intimacy is not just a cliché. Customer intimacy is a value discipline for firms that value and use an intimate knowledge of their customers to determine precisely which types of customers to serve and then align all their value-creation processes to create and deliver solutions to their specific type of customer. In a competitive landscape where competing products with little defensible product differentiation are becoming commodities, customization is one very powerful way to de-commoditize a product and build customer relationships.

Customization, as a term, is used broadly here to denote making changes in value creation and delivery such that the customer value is adjusted to each customer when and where appropriate. To know when and where customization is appropriate, you need to know your customer. Customer-focused firms pay attention to their customers. They listen to their customers. They really know their customers. The more knowledge the firm has about its customers, the more poised and able the firm is to deliver superior customer value.

Ritz-Carlton is known for its ability to personalize its service encounters with its frequent guests by maintaining a detailed preference profile at the individual customer level. With smart customer information systems,

Ritz-Carlton's frontline employees are empowered to address guests by their first names and with knowledge of the guest's specific preferences. CLASS (Customer Loyalty Anticipation and Satisfaction) is an example of the information technology backbone to the Ritz-Carlton's guest relationships management programme.

Nadia Kyzer knows that having a database system is not enough, saying: "If our employees didn't put the information to real concrete use, the system would be worthless." Many firms use their knowledge of the customer to tailor their products and messages, or to promote new services to their customers.

For example, on the Internet, firms use knowledge gained from cookies to model patterns of customer behaviour on their Web sites so as to target promotions deemed appropriate for that customer. But good customer information management goes beyond targeting messages and promotions. QVC, the television-based retailer, uses a "daily activity report" to capture, monitor, and respond to customer perceptions of quality. Indeed, customer information should drive all business processes of the firm, including anticipating and meeting customer needs, creating and delivering services, and anticipating and recovering from service failure. Customer-focused firms must have good customer information to support the decisions and activities of the firm.

Customer-focused decisions affecting customer value require information on customers' needs, their product preference criteria leading to brand choice or loyalty and their perceptions and behaviour with regard to the product. This is true not only in the acquisition and use, but also in the disposition of products. Since service firms interact with the customer during consumption of the product there is ample opportunity to obtain and respond to customer information.

For example, New England's largest bank, FleetBoston, recently instituted the "customer experience crusade." The firm hired new staff to be stationed in the lobbies of its large-volume banks to serve as "meeter-greeters" assisting customers with their banking problems. Ostensibly, the attempt was to reverse the lousy service reputation FleetBoston had acquired due to its preoccupation with challenges following its merger with BankBoston.

With the knowledge gained from the activities of these customer service agents, the bank could be learning a lot about customer experiences and about how its customers actually use a number of the bank's services. This knowledge could then be used to drive all decisions about structuring and delivering the bank's services.

Good customer information is an asset of the firm. Logically, anything that contributes to sustainable competitive advantage is an asset to the firm. Since information on customers is useful in better matching a firm's products as solutions to customer needs, customer information is an asset that contributes to sustainable competitive advantage. For example, retailing has become so fiercely competitive that customer information assets are now seen as a competitive advantage.

Customer loyalty programmes in retailing are an attempt to link customer information to transaction data. Customer databases with purchase histories showing shopping preferences can be used in customercentric business decisions. Customer information is so valuable that firms who share customer information have to be careful about ownership of the database. At the end of a joint project, for example, Wells Fargo bank and Microsoft went to court to determine who owned a customer database that was created as part of that joint venture.

A good example of the power of customer information is on the Internet. Personalized Web pages use customer information "on-thefly" to customize the online customer experience. It is common knowledge now that firms have data that tells them who is visiting, how long they are staying on the site, and where on the site visitors are spending their time. Firms have knowledge of customer behaviour on their Web site with information on where visitors were entering the Web site (beyond the home page) and leaving the Web site, what keywords or links brought them to the site, and so on. All this is possible with data-warehousing and data-mining techniques.

In the Internet age, entire new services, such as online investment brokerage firms, have sprung up with value propositions enabled by technology-powered databases of customer information. In the brave new investment world, such new business models have forced traditional investment brokerage houses to incorporate these added value propositions to their existing businesses.

Other new financial service models have emerged. For example, a number of online firms offer instant mortgage or credit application and approval. Much of this is possible because rules-based algorithms created from studying databases allow firms first to offer conditional approval then then to be able to verify the credit risk because financial institutions have well-developed databases of an individual's financial history with them.

While the technology is available to do more with information, it is unfortunate that the kinds of information that most firms obtain on a regular basis are usually limited to transactional data—such as what was purchased, when, and for how much. With this information, firms are able to use recency, frequency, and monetary data and conduct what is called RFM analysis. Patterns of relationships between the variables are used to determine the best prospects among the customers in the database—those that might be high-propensity targets for a promotion. Transactional data is important, but not adequate to make customer-focused decisions.

In addition to being able to individualize interactions with the customer, with customer information that goes beyond transactional data a firm can derive knowledge to guide anything from cost-saving measures in operations to new product decisions. To really understand the customer, firms need information on a multitude of dimensions other than just transactions around their other actual consumption activities.

Kinds of Customer Information

Customer-focused decisions and actions require customer information at two levels. At the aggregate level, customer information is about the market—or more specifically, about the typical customer in the segment(s)—and at the individual level, it is about a specific customer. When the number of customers for a firm is large and there is no opportunity to directly interact with the customer, it does not make economic sense to get down to the level of individual customer-specific profiles.

For example, Procter & Gamble may not be able to interact with each and every Crest toothpaste user. In such a situation, the customer profile is aggregated and constructed at the market segment level. On the other hand, for firms that directly interact with the customer, it makes sense to profile specific individual customers. For example, General Electric interacts with individual customers of kitchen appliances who contract customer service agreements. GE can use their knowledge of each individual customer to target service contract renewal offers or offers for replacement products when the normal life of the appliance has passed.

In general, it should become apparent that the more the aggregation, the less specific and accurate the information on individual customers. The level of aggregation of the information will also determine whether that information is useful for individualized or segment-level decisions, processes, and activities. As the level of aggregation of customer information increases, the level of aggregation of the customer solution increases and the firm is working at the segment level. With lower levels of aggregation, the firm is working at the individual customer level.

Customer information, whether at the market segment level and/or at the individual level, provides a profile of the customer that guides a customer-focused firm's decisions and actions. A customer profile should be based on two broad categories of information: *Background profile* is general customer information not directly related to the product and is not product-specific; and *consumption profile* is directly related to the product and is product-specific, in that it is about behaviour related to the consumption of the specific product.

Defining Customer Identity

The background profile helps to identify the customer and to understand the customer's product-related behaviour. Firms have been diligent about gathering demographic and psychographic data to establish the background profiles of customers in the B2C market. Customer-focused firms use this background profile to understand product-related consumption behaviour. Such information is managed on an ongoing basis. In the B2C context, "who the customer is" can be profiled along the dimensions of demographic, psychographic, and consumption behaviour.

Of these three dimensions, the demographic and psychographic dimensions provide the background profile. Similarly, the background profile of the B2B customer needs to be in terms of their size, type of industry, their corporate culture, and other characteristics used to identify the firm.

In the B2C context, customers purchase and consume solutions for individual or household use. Consumers' consumption of products are determined to a great deal by their backgrounds. Their personality, family, economic, social, ethnic, and cultural profile influence the way they think, feel, and behave at home, with their friends and social circles and in society in general.

This background profile helps us understand their consumption profile and the customer value they seek in specific product solutions for their needs in the context of their activities. Similarly, in the B2B context, the background profile of customers helps us understand their consumption profile and the customer value they seek in product solutions in the context of their value chain activities.

Business customers purchase and consume solutions for their own business activities. The type of industry they operate in, what value they create, their size, the skills and knowledge sets of their employees, and the "personality" of their firm (their corporate culture) affect the way firms think, feel, and behave in the marketplace with all their stakeholders, especially with their suppliers and their customers.

The Consumption Profile

Whereas the background profile serves to identify the customer, to truly understand customer value one needs systematic information on the purchase and use of the product by the customer. This information is crucial to get a complete picture of benefits and costs to the customer. A consumption profile comprises information that provides a comprehensive view of the customer's knowledge, attitude, and behaviour with respect to a specific need and associated solutions. The consumption profile containing information on product-related behaviour helps profile a customer in terms of the how the product is acquired, consumed, and disposed. Such a framework allows the provider of the solution to get into the "customer activity cycle, " as Sandra Vandermerwe calls it.

Consumer behaviour models frequently divide a customer's consumption experience or customer activity cycle into the three stages of preconsumption, consumption, and postconsumption. In essence, when the customer recognizes a need to be filled, the customer

1. Processes the options and selects a solution to meet that need,
2. Engages in procuring and utilizing that solution, and
3. Evaluates the effectiveness of that solution.

The valence of the evaluation of the experience with the solution provider then determines the predisposition of the customer toward that solution provider for subsequent consumption cycles. A positive predisposition may materialize in the form of repurchase, brand loyalty, and favourable word-of-mouth behaviour. All of the customer activities in each of the three stages of consumption should be the focus of the firm's attention.

In some consumption contexts, these stages are not as distinct as in others. For example, in most B2B and high-involvement contexts, the three stages and their respective decisions and activities are quite pronounced, while in low-involvement consumption contexts these stages are not as pronounced and deliberate. Regardless of whether the customer is highly involved with the consumption context or not, the information available to the firm regarding the customer's behaviour (purchase, use, and disposition) should help align the firm's decisions and actions in all three stages of consumption.

It is important to note here the differences in the consumption of tangible-dominant products and intangible-dominant products vis-àvis the firm's production activities. In the case of tangible-dominant products, the firm produces the product and then the customer consumes, or purchases and uses it. Whereas, with intangible-dominant products, the consumption process is temporally overlaid on the production process.

The Preconsumption Stage

Customer behaviour during this stage of the consumption cycle falls into three broad and sequential sets of activities: experiencing the need for a solution to a problem, identifying and analyzing the options to the problem, and deciding on a specific solution or way of meeting the need. For interactions with the customer during the preconsumption stage to be customer-focused, firms need to understand the perceptions, attitudes, and activities of customers as they go through their purchase decisions. Firms need to understand what customers expect from the solutions provider during this phase.

Since a product is a means to an end, to really know how the firm is doing with its products it is necessary to understand what the ends are. It becomes necessary to find out what role the firm's product plays in its use for the customer. It is also important to understand what those product roles might be in different usage situations. Often the customer's preferred solution can vary from one situation to another and yet the provider may not pay attention to that important change in the value that the customer is expecting from each customer experience.

The customer engages in accessing and assessing the relevant information on the ways in which a need can be met. Based on the information available to them, customers identify the various options and sort through information to determine the merits of each option. A number of complex issues about the customer experience in this stage are relevant for the firm. Where do customers get the information on the options—from what channels and in what form is the information sought? What are the firms, brands, or solution providers that are evoked in the customer's mind? What are the criteria that the customer uses to evaluate the choice of providers of solutions? What are their expectations from the solution? How do customers benefit from the products and services?

When Nike introduced its slip-on sneaker Presto, teens could select designs for their shoes, attach matching music to them, and email them as music videos to friends. Nike was engaging itself in the preconsumption activities of the teen shopper. The firm acted on its understanding of how teens make and follow fads and fashion to introduce a new and innovative footwear design. If you can understand and reach into the customer's preconsumption activities, you can identify and attract the most appropriate customer for your firm's solution. Customer acquisition efforts can be more precise. Customers make their choice after weighing all options against their criteria. Firms must learn how they make these vendor decisions. Who is involved in the purchase decision making? Who influences the customer's preferences and biases? Household (B2C) and organizational (B2B) consumption activities can involve several different individuals in a purchase decision.

Individuals play roles of users, buyers, influencers, decision makers, and so on, in what are called "buying centres." What are the various perspectives of each of these individuals and units engaged in the process? What are their respective roles in the decision? How is the purchase decision made, and what process do the customers follow? When and how often is the decision made? What are the preferences on the method of payment? How do these customers evaluate you and your products before purchase? Who is involved in that evaluation? This kind of detail in the purchasing activities of the customer, if gathered and utilized, can improve the effectiveness of the firm's customer acquisition efforts.

When the firm can interact directly with the customer, as in the case of services, there is the opportunity to obtain answers to these questions and respond immediately. Where there is an intermediary involved, the firm has to rely on the intermediary to represent the firm during this stage because the customer interactions are with the intermediary, not the firm. In the hand-held ("pocket PC" or "PDA") market, the competition is so fierce that companies are constantly monitoring the retailer to ensure that their products and promotions are well displayed and that the salespeople are well informed about them. The personal digital assistant maker Palm sends its agents as mystery shoppers to retailers carrying their products. Microsoft, for example, gave a free Casio EM500 Pocket PC device to salespeople who completed a Pocket PC training.

In first-time experiences with a service provider, customers may want to obtain information from the provider; thus that interaction is required prior to the consumption of the product. In situations where prices and terms of sale are negotiated, quite often the case in services, there is a significant amount of interaction. In most cases of intangible-dominant products, there is some customer involvement at least in the specification of the needs of the customer so that the specific solution can be configured for each customer.

Every firm should explore the opportunities it has for customer information to help in its acquisition efforts. The total solution includes the firm's contribution to the customer's preconsumption activities. Rich Hanks, Marriott's executive vice president of sales, recalls the early days of Marriott's Web presence. He says they did not even know that they had to put reservations on the first page. The way to design Web pages is to think like the customer and ask what the customer would like to do on the Web.

Whatever prepurchase decision-making process the customer will be using should be used in Web site design. For example, at what stage of the consumption activity cycle should a Web site charge a visitor for a service? Some visitors balk when they are asked to pay up front for a service they haven't used—they mightn't want to pay member fees when they only want one transaction, for example.

The Consumption Stage

Firms that are not customer focused are focused on product and sales. They typically pay a great deal of attention to the sales and purchase process—the preconsumption stage, but not the consumption process. During the consumption stage, it is important to understand how the customer uses the product or service and what kinds of customer activities are associated with the value that your firm's product provides. To truly understand customer value, the firm needs to dig deeper into the consumption activities of its customers. Who is involved in the use of the product? How do they use the product?

Does the customer have all of the information it needs on your firm's product to fully benefit from its use? Will the customer want to interact with the firm during the consumption stage? Will customers need customer service assistance, and if so, what kinds of usage assistance would they need? What kinds of issues dictate the effectiveness of the solution from the perspective of a consumption process?

Understanding when, where, and how a product is used is often a powerful piece of information if used effectively. Consider the following examples of firms using the context of the consumption activities as they relate to their products: Starbucks gives out free Frappuccino samples on a hot day at a busy square in Manhattan.

Unilever hands out free Lever 2000 handwipes at a food court in a shopping mall and body wash and deodorant to fitness class students at a Bally's Fitness Club. Schering-Plough provides blister treatment cushions to runners at a marathon. These firms are obtaining and using their knowledge of how their products are used at the point-of-use of the product. They are in a position to determine what customer education is necessary and what customer value improvement opportunities there may be. Product-focused firms remain focused on the product and its sale and on not much after that. To these firms, most likely, a complaining customer is the cost of doing business and a necessary evil, and is frequently cast to the unwilling hands of a customer service person. Consider the example of the "easy to assemble yourself" products that come in a box with some assembly required by the consumer. The unsuspecting customer is frequently confronted by a confusing set of directions written by someone who doesn't need directions to assemble the product.

Procter & Gamble has been actively collecting first-hand information on how consumers use their packaged household products, just to understand how the customer uses the product—rather than depend on the pencil-and-paper survey method or focus group discussions. Those methods are fine for demographics and psychographics information, but are fraught with misinformation since they rely on the accuracy of memory and communication by the consumer as well as the interpretation and visualization on the part of the firm's researcher.

In fact, P&G goes as far as to send ethnographer filmmakers who spend full days—from the time a family wakes up until bedtime—for several days, just to understand how the firm can create value for the lives of families—a way to look for new product opportunities.

In the case of service-dominant products, since production and consumption are simultaneous, the consumption phase involves the firm's production activities as well. There could be a significant degree of customer interaction and participation in the production of the solution. The customer is part of the production process, and the information regarding each interaction needs to be carefully documented and utilized to deliver customer-focused experiences.

Customer roles need to be scripted and customer performances in these roles need to be monitored and managed. This information about customer interactions is critical in improving the processes involved in service delivery. Consider what package delivery staff have to do at some of their destinations. "Please place boxes in barrel. If they (it) don't fit, put on top of barrel—Dogs will rip up if left on ground, " is a set of instructions given to Land's End by a catalog customer for package delivery by a courier. Customer data must be collected, and the value creation and delivery system should be designed to obtain and use that information appropriately.

The Postconsumption Stage

Here, customer evaluations and their disposition to be loyal to your firm is the main feature of the customer's experience. When the product is predominantly a service product, the customer might be in a formal membership relationship with the service provider, such as in the case of banking or financial services, or enrolled in an educational programme, or a fitness club, or a contractual obligation, as in a B2B context.

At the end of each interaction in the case of service products, customers may assess their experience and determine their inclination toward the solution provider. In such cases, it would be important to collect customer reactions and impressions after each consumption experience so that the relationship is intact. With packaged goods, on the other hand, where there is no interaction during the use of the product, customer assessment of the provider is made during and after the use of the product.

What is the level of satisfaction with the features of your product and with the interactions they have had with your firm? They may be pointing out systematic failures in how you are creating and delivering customer solutions. Are there fail points in your value-creation processes that need more attention? It is possible to get some very critical process-improvement suggestions from the customer. How can the benefits to the customer be improved and costs to the customer reduced so that the net customer value is improved? Which aspects of your product are most and least useful for the customer?

This information would be useful in conducting a cost-benefit analysis of the service enhancements to your product. What is the value of each customer to your firm, by transaction and in the long-run? Can the value of the customer to the firm be increased? Are there opportunities to increase the role you are playing in meeting customer needs by providing a more complete solution either by adding products or adding features to the product? Are there ways to reduce the costs of serving the customer?

Although strictly speaking not part of the consumption profile, customers may have valuable information on how well your frontline personnel are providing value to the customer. Customers can provide you with an assessment of how well your intermediaries and resellers are representing you. For example, travel agents who represent hotels, airlines, and other travel-related services might need more information, attention or encouragement to represent you appropriately. All things being equal, retailers have no incentive to sell a particular brand in a nonexclusive retail store.

As long as the customer purchases the item from their store, the retailer does not care which particular brand is purchased. Customers are the best judge of your suppliers and vendors as well. If there are aspects of your value-creation processes that are subcontracted out, customer feedback is critical in assessing whether these contracts are working as desired and whether there need to be any changes in how these processes are structured.

How will the customer want to convey feedback? Have you provided the avenues that customers are most likely to use to tell you what they think about the solution and your performance? Are your touchpoints able to solicit, record, and report customer information? The next develops these issues around customer information management.

Understanding customer value is a prerequisite for being able to create and deliver superior customer solutions. Firms need to study customers' consumption profiles to understand their needs and what they seek in the best solution. The background profile of the customer is a useful context in which to analyze the information on the consumption activities of the customer. The consumption activity framework attempts to frame the information on the customer in the three stages of consumption activities. The types of information that would be required to help understand customer value.

Companies focus attention on attracting and acquiring customers so that data collection is generally geared toward the preconsumption phase. Existing customers' transaction data is used to guide attempts to generate more sales from them. When data on consumption and postconsumption activities are gathered, a great deal more can be done to inform the entire range of the firm's decisions and activities in creating and delivering the product.

DELIVERING SUPERIOR VALUE REQUIRES A CUSTOMER FOCUS

Every firm provides a bundle of values as a product. The firm that provides the superior value bundle wins the customer. *Superior* is a key word here. Why? Consider this. Research by Jones and Sasser has shown that even satisfied customers defect. These Harvard researchers were studying the link between customer satisfaction and customer loyalty. Their findings suggest that customers are satisfied at different levels. Different levels of satisfaction result in different levels of loyalty, which in turn result in varying levels of behavioural disposition to patronage with a provider.

This logic implies that there is a range of customer satisfaction levels. Satisfied customers may not necessarily translate to loyal customers. Other researchers have introduced the notion of delighting the customer. A customer may defect to a competitor even if satisfied with the current provider because the competitor may be offering a value bundle with the perceived potential for a *higher degree* of satisfaction for that customer. Therefore, firms have to strive to achieve higher levels of satisfaction than their competition by providing superior customer value. This is the essence of achieving a sustainable competitive advantage. If you are unable to provide superior customer value, even your satisfied customers could leave you!

What can a firm do that its competitors cannot match? To answer this question, one must clearly understand the context of competition—the landscape or playing field, as it was. Pine and Gilmore might call such a competitive landscape the "experience economy, " where products are quickly commoditized and firms compete on other aspects of the total offering. People, processes, and technology combine to create products. Technology is easy to copy, but customer-oriented employees and corporate culture are much harder to copy. In fact, technology is eventually commonly available to any firm that has the necessary capital and resources. Commenting on the recovery prospects of information technology firms after the recent recession, Marc Andreassen of Netscape says that a lot of innovation is going on now. However, most innovations are quickly becoming commoditized. One reason may be that processes and systems can be designed appropriately to deliver customer satisfaction, but they can be relatively easily replicated. Employee attitudes, however, are less easily replicable.

Customers look for convenience, cost, and quality of the total experience. The service-oriented firm concentrates on the capabilities of employees and not just on the technology or the tangible features of the product. The realization that the "clicks" store is not going to replace the "bricks" store has demonstrated that technology is not the solution. Rather, it is a means to enhance the solution. In this case, technology has simply provided a different solution.

Almost all bricks-and-mortar firms now have an Internet presence; it is an inexpensive service enhancement for them compared to what the dot-com firms have to do to establish a brick-and-mortar presence. Those dot-coms that have conducted the appropriate analysis of what customer value they were creating and delivering and how they were going to be superior to existing alternatives have had a good start. Subsequently, those that figured out how to sustain it while realizing the profit potential are still around.

It is not a stretch to say that many of the dot-com failures may have occurred because they were focused on the technology and not on the customer. Meanwhile, specialty retailers who are experienced at serving the customer have combined technology with their reputed customer service to make a winning combination. With the established catalog retailers, shoppers get an audio connection in real time over the Internet with customer service personnel who help customers with any questions they may have.

Experience the L.L. Bean or Land's End service at their Web sites to understand how well these specialty catalog retailers have adopted the technology of the Internet. Customer experience with these firms with or without the technology sets them apart from the rest of the players. Technology alone will not provide a competitive advantage. The combination of superior technology and superior employees with a service orientation will contribute to achieving sustainable competitive advantage.

You need a customer-focused and service-oriented culture within the firm. It also quickly becomes evident that you need suppliers as well as distributors and agents who have a similar and compatible culture. Thus, there are two strong themes in any discussion of "creating superior customer value at a sustainable profit": a customer-focus imperative and a service orientation. If all aspects of the firm and how the firm creates and delivers value to the customer are focused on the customer, the firm can provide a superior level of customer value. Such a firm is well positioned for a sustainable competitive advantage. Now, what does it take to be a customer-focused firm? What does customer focus really mean? And, what exactly is a service orientation?

Customer Focus and Service Orientation

A customer focus necessitates a deep understanding of customers and their activities, interests, and opinions around the particular value or solution that the firm is providing. It should be an attitude that is pervasive and that permeates throughout the firm such that it becomes ingrained as a culture. Once this focus becomes a given, then the firm will find itself in the mode of serving the customer while ensuring a reasonable profit. The realization is that you cannot achieve a sustainable competitive advantage to command sustainable profits unless you are customer focused.

Serving the customer contrasts with the notion of marketing a product. It is more than providing a solution for the customer. It is about *serving* the customer. The firm looks at the customer's need in the broadest possible context, going beyond the scope of the core product that satisfies the core need in a particular consumption activity. The product is redefined to include all value-added components in a total solution. By definition, the product is extended to include several dimensions that would include as part of the total product the value added in any and all customer interactions. The service-oriented firm is one that focuses on serving the customer, regardless of whether its core product is a physical good or an intangible.

Such firms are better positioned to deliver that customer value in its products. When all competing firms provide the same core product, the competitiveness of a firm or its superiority has to come from enhancements to the core product. The key to competitiveness is in these enhancements, which are invariably provided by service dimensions. These service dimensions contribute to providing superior customer value. To successfully provide these service dimensions firms have to be service oriented. When you look around, you will find that successful firms exhibit a frame of mind that is service oriented and focused on the customer.

The service-oriented firm owns responsibilities over and above just providing a product. Such a firm is proactive in anticipating customer needs and situations in customer interactions. For example, customer education is seen as a significant responsibility of the firm. The customer-focused firm views the customer's role in consumption activities as an integral part of its solution. A customer-focused firm truly cares for the customer. Such a firm's behaviour demonstrates that it feels privileged to have the customer. When its product fails the customer, the service-oriented firm will evoke built-in customer recovery procedures implemented by customer-focused employees.

The total customer experience at such firms goes beyond the core product and is superior to other firms. The quality of the total experience includes a whole host of components or experiences other than that of the core product. The value that the customer seeks includes all of these components and not just the core product. When Lexus, Toyota's luxury division, found that its customers in the United States were having to drive hundreds of miles to buy a Lexus, the carmaker converted trucks into mobile service stations so that customers didn't have to drive that far to have the car serviced. Singapore Airlines provides its fliers a wide range of choices from what and when they eat to how and when they are entertained. The costs are worth the value the flexibility adds to the customer experience. Customers choose firms that provide this customer value in a total solution. Such firms are service oriented.

Firms add a number of dimensions typically encompassed in "services" to augment the product. Customer service is a common term used to denote these dimensions. But it is important to understand that customer service is a specific type of customer interaction and as such, it performs a narrow but necessary function. While customer service is typically involved with nonroutine customer situations such as recovering from a service failure, being "service oriented" can include, for example, anticipating that service failure and proactively initiating a service recovery. EMC, the storage devices provider, builds its products with redundant systems.

When the primary system fails and the redundant system takes over, the design and service team assigned to the client looks into the causes and alerts the client if necessary. EMC's diagnostics cover competitor products that are part of the storage and retrieval system. In service-oriented firms such as EMC, service recovery processes are built into the design of the total product offering. EMC's service orientation is reflected in the design of its products and in its concern for the customer's experience with the product performance. EMC claims a 99 percent customer retention rate. The total product offering includes serving the customer during all stages of consumption of a solution.

In service-oriented firms, services complete the product as a total solution. These services are also the primary key to a sustainable competitive advantage within that total value bundle. Providing these services requires a completely different mind-set with an understanding of the complex characteristics of services. This is true even in products where the core benefit is delivered by a physical good that the customer takes title to. The services that go along with the physical good are a significant component of the total product. As illustrated in the EMC example, this perspective is readily apparent in the business-to-business (B2B) situation, where firms are naturally inclined to focus on service to the customer. Their perspective includes service elements to augment the product and to establish and maintain customer relationships.

For manufacturing firms, the physical good is only part of the total solution toward customer needs. Indeed, the physical components of any product are easily matched by competitors, thus reducing what might have been a competitive advantage to a commodity. Firms really compete on the noncommoditized part of the total product. When these aspects of the product are meaningful to the customer and the firm can provide customer value better than the competition, the firm has a sustainable competitive advantage. Firms compete with each other on the total solution comprised of commodities and noncommodities—a complex set of benefits or value bundle.

For a number of firms, especially in the information technology industry, the product has become the service more than the physical technology itself. By the year 2000, for example, 40 percent of sales and 40 percent of profits at IBM came from its Global Services division. At Unisys, 69 percent of sales came from services. Sun's $3.3 billion services business was closely tied to its server (the black box) business. Compaq purchased DEC in 1998 for its service business. Hewlett-Packard later purchased Compaq for the same reason.

A number of articles in the popular press have lamented the sorry state of service in the United States. When packaged-goods firms are included in the list of examples, it is in the service component of the total product that the failures are apparent. Why it that firms are unable to provide the desired levels of service to satisfy customers?

Beginning in the late 1980s, there has been a great deal of research on what exactly customer orientation or "customer focuses" means and on what exactly a firm should be doing to implement such an orientation. Peppers and Rogers, known for their one-on-one marketing concept, consider customer-focused management as synonymous with relationship marketing or customer-relationship management. Information technology offered firms a way to obtain, process, and use individual customer information so that firms would be able to personalize customer experiences. Some scholars have called it "market orientation."

One set of researchers suggested that customer orientation is a subset of market orientation. Their definition for *market orientation* is "the set of cross-functional processes and activities directed at creating and satisfying customers through continuous needs-assessment." Following their lead, market orientation has been treated as being composed of three components: customer orientation, competitor orientation, and interfunctional coordination.

Can the terms *customer orientation* and *market orientation* be used interchangeably? If we accept the definition of a "market" as being a set of potential customers and treat the terms *market* and *customer* as synonymous except for the level of aggregation in numbers, then we can use the terms interchangeably. Such an argument does not necessarily negate the three-component structure of the concept of customer focus. To be truly customer focused, the firm has to be driven by the goal of providing the customer with the highest level of satisfaction. This implies that the firm concentrates on how the customer is better served (by the firm) compared to the competitive offerings and that all processes and activities in the entire firm are integrated and coordinated to accomplish this goal. The customer-focused firm has all aspects of the firm directed at providing the superior product to the customer. Thus, we can define *customer focus* as: A form of culture in a firm that directs all processes and activities of the firm toward providing superior value to the customer so as to sustain long-term profits.

It is now generally accepted that market orientation or a customer focus is a type of culture and is exhibited by a firm that is committed to providing superior customer value. When compared with different types of business cultures, the customer-focused culture has been found to be superior in delivering the best business performance. Such a customer focus was strongly correlated with the use of customer information in a study involving about 5,000 salespeople and sales managers. This study also found a strong correlation between market orientation, job satisfaction, and trust in management.

Another study of 278 salespeople and sales managers found that market orientation significantly influenced job attitudes and the customer orientation of the salespeople. A firm was seen as clearly supporting the salespeople when the salespeople perceived that the firm was being attentive to customer needs and satisfaction, aware of competitor strategies to deliver superior value, and coordinated through the entire firm. There are proven bottom-line benefits from a customer orientation. In another study using a sample of 127 strategic business units in firms listed in the Fortune 500, customer-focused firms achieved higher profitability, sales growth, and new product success.

With such evidence of strong correlations between customer-focused cultures and successful business performance, it behooves us to learn what these firms are doing to be customer focused and what it takes to be a customer-focused firm. It is clear that there are firms that have been successful in developing and implementing the customer-focused culture. Scandinavian Air Systems, Walt Disney, and British Airways are firms that pay attention to establishing the appropriate culture and climate that fosters customer orientation. The list of issues that have to be addressed runs the gamut from organizational structure and behaviour, operations, and value delivery mechanisms to internal and external metrics such as in balanced scorecards and customer loyalty measurement. This book will cover many of these issues in a comprehensive yet concise manner.

Based on the critical links in the logic espousing the merits of a customer-focused management, we first look at the elaboration of the fundamental premise of customer value and service orientation. Following this we begin to examine the specific issues in developing a customer-focused and service-oriented firm—managing customer information, creating and delivering customer value, managing customer relationships, and ensuring a customer-oriented culture.

In the middle of the continuum are products such as fast food restaurants and custom-made clothing that have an almost equal proportion, with no real predominance of tangibles or intangibles. In products that are predominantly intangible, where the customers don't take title to anything physical, such as in banking services, the service provider might use tangibles such as documentation, statements, and billing. The value for the customer is in the information contained in them.

As a proportion of what the customer is getting in the total product, the predominant source of customer value is from the intangibles in the total product. For physical goods, services enhance the core product and provide opportunities for competitive advantage. Thus, any product has some proportion of services attached to it, and this part of the product has a special nature that needs to be handled differently. If all firms provide some proportion of service components as part of the total product, it behooves them to have an understanding of the nature of services.

Only with such an understanding can we truly get into the service-orientation frame of mind. Take for example, the table salt manufacturer, Morton's. For this firm to look at itself as a packaged goods firm and therefore not concerned with services is a mistake. The fact that Morton's makes the product available at the retail store through the appropriate distribution channels is a service to the customer.

Morton's has essentially outsourced its distribution and retailing to channel intermediaries. To be truly customer focused, Morton's needs to view all the value-added it provides the customer, over and above the product of the production process—the salt—as services it provides to the customer. Morton's cannot manage its service components in the same way that it manages the production of its table salt. Most B2B manufacturing firms intuitively recognize the importance of the service component in enhancing its product. Caterpillar, the earth-moving equipment manufacturer, recognizes that prompt and reliable service is critical to its success and organizes the whole firm around customer locations. You need a service orientation to see such product enhancements as service dimensions that add value to the core product. Service orientation is

- A philosophy or frame of mind reflected in the firm's culture
- An attitude to serve the customer reflected in the firm's treatment of its customers, and
- A view of services as necessary enhancements to any core product to make a complete solution.

To provide complete and competitive solutions to the customer, one needs to understand and adopt the service orientation. The service-oriented frame of mind requires a grasp of the fundamental nature of services (whether as the product or a component of a product). Once the inherent characteristics of services are clear, it becomes apparent that their implications for the customer and the provider offer a number of opportunities and pose a variety of challenges.

As a preface to a discussion of these issues, it would be useful to note the evolution of interest in the concept of service. Prompted by the frustrations of practitioners in the service sector who were finding that marketing practices from the packaged goods world did not make sense for services, scholars began to get interested in the problem. In the late 1970s and early 1980s, for a number of reasons, the academic research community in business disciplines, particularly in marketing, operations, and human resources, began a serious intellectual debate as to whether products that were services, compared to products that were packaged goods, needed to be studied differently.

For example, could you study the marketing of hospitality services the same way as you would the marketing of toothpaste? Some scholars maintained that marketing is marketing regardless of *what* you are marketing. Either way, they argued, one had to go through the tasks of segmenting the market, positioning a product, and making product, pricing, distribution, or promotion decisions. Others argued that although that might be true, one would need to approach these tasks very differently; and they proceeded to offer the rationale for this argument. There was a great deal of interest in this effort, especially among those who recognized the tremendous growth of the services sector.

Around the same time there were environmental changes in the economy and in the competitive landscape. Services sectors such as airlines, telecommunications, and, later, banking and insurance were going through deregulation in the United States. Manufacturing was moving to cheaper labour markets in the Far East and in Latin America. Meanwhile, by the late 1980s in the United States, even professional services such as health care and legal services began to recognize the need to employ marketing practices.

Not surprisingly, even manufacturing firms were being forced to add service components to their product offerings. As these changes occurred and services were being established as an integral aspect of doing business, the United States had become a service economy. Ultimately, the debate over whether services were really different from physical products produced the rationale that the skeptics demanded. The evidence and essence of this argument epitomizes the service orientation.

Characteristics of all Services

There are certain fundamental characteristics that are inherent in all service products and in the service components of any product. Let us begin by defining service as *a deed, performance, or action.* Thus, by definition, services are intangible. The product that is a service or that component of the product that is a service cannot be seen, touched, or felt. As a deed, performance or action, a service is consumed as it is produced, such that the acts of production and consumption are inseparable. Thus, services are also perishable, in that they cannot be inventoried or produced and stored for later use. Nor can they be produced without some level of customer interaction.

Since services are produced and consumed in real time, they are inherently variable—from customer to customer, from provider to provider, and from time to time for the same customer and/or the same provider. These statements describe features that are fundamental and are inherent in products or components of products that are deeds, performances, or actions, and may sound very simplistic until you delve into the meanings and consequences of these inherent characteristics to the customer and to the provider.

It is generally accepted that services are different from physical goods along four fundamental characteristics labeled as intangibility, simultaneity or inseparability, perishability, and variability. These characteristics are conceptually inherent in all services or in the service component of any product. Although this framework is more useful as a pedagogical vehicle rather than a framework for research or practice, it is powerful in fully capturing the concept of service orientation and accomplishes the objective of placing the reader in the necessary frame of mind.

This mindset is grounded in the appreciation of the fundamental nature of services necessitating appropriate managerial decisions and actions. The fundamental character of services and the associated consequences may play out for the manager. A service orientation requires a thorough understanding of how these inherent characteristics of services are manifested for the customer and the manager.

Intangibility—Services

Services are performances. Services cannot be seen but they can be experienced. The product is a process. As a service provider, you cannot show your product as you could if you were the marketer of a packaged good. Yes, services are the result of value-creating activities, just as physical products are, and may employ tangibles or physical products in producing the service. However, the product being purchased is an experience and not a physical good. Customers cannot take ownership or title to a service. For example, hotels provide the service of overnight stay as their core product. The customer does not take title to the room that is being rented. The hotel provides the use of the room for the duration of the time that the customer has paid for. Similarly, customers don't take title to anything in air travel or in entertainment. When office copiers come with service, there is no ownership involved with the service component unlike with the copier itself. When your automobile comes with free service under warranty, unlike the automobile itself there is no real ownership of the service component.

Now, as a manager, you might say: "All this is well and good, but if it doesn't change the way I manage the product, its production, or its marketing, whether it is a packaged good or service, why should I care? Services are intangible and service components in products are intangible—yes! But so what?" Let us examine this question from the customer's point of view. For customers, one immediate consequence of the intangibility is increased perceived risk. When you cannot see the product or what you are going to get before the purchase, customers have to acknowledge a certain amount of risk they are taking. While there is perceived risk in the purchase of a packaged or physical good, you cannot return a vacation as you can a defective lawn mower.

Thus, you accept a certain amount of risk as unavoidable in the case of a service. When you book your vacation, do you really see the product? If you have previously been to the locations, you may have seen the facility, but your product was the experience. Complicating the perceived risk is the fact that the evaluation of services or the service component of the product is inherently subjective. Compared to packaged goods, customers find it harder to evaluate services before the purchase. In some cases, services are harder to evaluate even during and after their performances.

In the case of health care, for instance, you use several proxy elements, such as the cleanliness of the facility, the medical professional's "bedside manner, " and the process you had to go through. What you are evaluating is a lot more than the core product, the medical treatment itself. Being intangible, services cannot be produced until you have purchased (whether you pay before, during, or after) the service.

Simultaneity—Services

The acts of production and consumption occur simultaneously in services. This is primarily because services are produced and consumed in real time. There is a great deal of interaction before, during, and/or after the service between provider and customer. Some sort of customer interaction is necessary even if customer physical presence is not. At the very least, customers have to specify their needs and their need situations. In most if not all cases, it can be argued that production and consumption cannot be temporally separated. (Thus, this characteristic is also termed "inseparability.") A related complication for services is that in services, the provider is part of the product.

As a customer, the frontline personnel you interact with are a part of the product. In professional services, for instance, the lawyer is part of the (legal service) product, the doctor is part of the (medical care) product, the professor is part of the (education) product.

Comparing this to packaged goods: Do you have to interact with Procter & Gamble and the shop floor employee who made your particular tube of Crest toothpaste? You do interact with the retailer of the toothpaste, but remember that the retail store that makes the toothpaste available to you is a service. What you are consuming from the retailer as it is produced by the retailer is a service. In fact, you interact with the provider of the service component of the packaged good. If you interacted with P&G, it was with customer service.

Once again, let us confront the question: "So what?" To understand what difference it makes for the manager, the customer-focused firm must examine the consequences to the customer from the customer's perspective. The customer has to interact with the provider at some stage or at all stages of the production process. The customer is in the service factory in the case of an amusement park. Sometimes the service factory comes to the customer, as in the case of the landscape contractor. Sometimes the interaction is at arm's length, such as in the case of an online travel agent like Expedia.com. In each case, there is some interaction that the customer usually initiates. Thus, there is some effort on the part of the customer for the product to be produced.

The customer takes on a role in the production process. To perform the expected role, customers have to be educated and sometimes socialized into the process. For example, at a fast food restaurant, the customer needs to get familiar with the process of ordering and picking up the food. When you call your long distance phone company for a question on your bill, you need to have some information ready for the service to be performed. These days you have to be familiar with complex automated voice menus before you can get anything done over the telephone. Since consumption and production are simultaneous, the customer is consuming as the product is being produced. The product cannot be produced ahead of time and then consumed. This means that the product cannot be inventoried.

Perishability—Services

Since services cannot be produced and stored for later use, as physical products can, services are said to be perishable products. What actually perishes? In fact, what perishes is the productive capacity of the service, or more precisely, the opportunity to produce a product. A hairdresser's time is wasted or unproductive when he or she is not serving a customer. The customer service personnel ready to handle customer enquiries is not producing a service unless there is a customer to serve. An empty airline seat perishes without a passenger in it on takeoff. The factors of production such as labour, facilities, equipment, and billable time are the value-creating assets for the service provider.

The opportunity to produce the product from these assets perishes without the adequate number of customers for which the capacity is designed. And the service provider needs to maintain a certain level of capacity that is not easily adjustable. Some services are more capacity-constrained than others. A hotel cannot reduce the number of rooms in its facility when there are not enough guests. A management consulting firm with fulltime employees would be hard pressed to release its staff when there are not enough clients to fill the capacity.

For the customer, service products need to be available and accessible when and where they are needed. When the productive capacity is sometimes not able to meet the demand, customers are likely to have to wait in queues or find another provider. Whether it is on the phone for customer service, at the doctor's office, or in line for a ride in an amusement park, customers will have to get used to waiting. In some services, customers need to plan ahead of time and place reservations. That is how managers instinctively manage the utilization of capacity in the operation.

Conversely, when there is more productive capacity than there are customers to be served, service providers have to look for other customer segment opportunities for their value-creating assets. Service providers have to manage that balance between capacity and demand. They employ methods to anticipate and manage the pattern of demand and to manage the capacity accordingly.

Variability—Services

Service products as experiences vary from one experience to the next, from customer to customer, as well as for the same customer from one occasion to the next. In fact, this variability is compounded with differences among frontline personnel. When there are several steps in the service process where the customer interacts with several different personnel of the service provider, there could be variation from one interaction to another. In some cases, customers will prefer specific frontline personnel with whom they have become familiar and comfortable. Since services are produced and consumed in real time, it is clear that customers will likely see a great degree of variation in product quality.

Customers can receive a different experience each time, even at a standardized operation like McDonald's. Service managers attempt to deliver consistently high quality with frontline training and technology and to customize where possible and standardize where necessary. Customers expect customization even when it is not feasible. Managers have to balance the economics of standardization with the quality issues around customization.

Thus, the fundamental characteristics of services force their implications on the customer. The manager of services and products that involve a significant degree of tangibles are forced to orient themselves to these implications. The complexity of managerial situations as a consequence of these characteristics is manifested as opportunities and challenges. Consequently, the services manager must analyze these consequences, and be prepared to take some actions to address them.

CUSTOMER INTEGRATION MANAGEMENT (CIM)

Customer Interaction Management helps organisations execute effective and efficient interactions with their customers and prospects. These interactions must be consistent and tailored to the customer needs, based on the segment of the customer, the service required and the used channel.

Important

Today's competitive environment requires companies to ensure that the customer has a consistent experience across interactions and channels, giving him a clear sense of brand value and differentiation.

Customer Interaction specialists at Deloitte focus on the following offerings:

- *Customer Experience*: We support the organisation in describing and assessing the experience of its customer or prospect across their lifecycle, providing actionable recommendations for enriching the customer experience.

- *Multi-channel interaction management*: We provide advice regarding the ways the organisation can best reach its customers. By implementing right-channelling, we help companies maximize interaction value in a cost-efficient way.
- *Service Organisational design*: Our organisational design methods consider people and processes in order to put in place the right service models, contact flows and escalation rules.
- *Service request and SLA management*: We provide methods and tools to improve service request management and implement the appropriate service level agreements.
- *Contact Centre Implementation and Transformation*: Deloitte has a proven track-record in implementing multi-channel interaction centres, including integration with CRM processes and tools.

Predictive Customer Interaction Management

Every business needs to efficiently manage outbound and inbound interactions with customers. These interactions can occur through many channels including the web, call centres branch offices, ATMs, and e-mail. With inbound interactions, customers offer their attention. They visit a web site, make a call, or access an ATM because they want something at that moment – information about a product or help with a problem.

These interactions usually present an opportunity to communicate with a customer who is engaged by choice and ready to share information regarding his or her wants and needs.

Outbound interactions are typically used to target products to particular customer segments based on analysis of customer data.

The success of these interactions – whether through e-mail, direct mail, or other channels – depends to a great extent on the organization's understanding of the customer's wants and needs at the time of the offer. This document describes an architecture that manages inbound and outbound interactions in a consistent manner to present a unified, real-time view of each customer.

Requirements for Effective Customer Interaction Management

The following list summarizes requirements for such an architecture:

- Provides consistent customer interaction management of outbound and inbound communications.
- Addresses the uniqueness and complexities of various inbound and outbound channels. For example, in an inbound call, the business

logic might dictate that the CSR should not make an offer if the call time is greater than a given threshold.

- Allows businesses that are aligned along product lines to use both customer knowledge and data mining to publish product propensities.
- Allows customer data to be distributed across multiple systems.
- Combines rules, policies, inferencing, and analytics – both statistical and probabilistic – to produce complex models of reasoning via events, customer data, time, and analytics.
- Leverages existing investment in data mining tools such as SAS, SPSS, and others.
- Handles the low latency requirements of real-time customer interactions with sophisticated caching techniques.
- Provides flexibility, scalability, and high availability.

Key Aspects of Customer Interaction Management

How a business treats customers and manages customer relationships is a key differentiator and is critical to succeeding in highly competitive and dynamic environments.

The solution proposed in this document addresses three important aspects of customer interaction management:

1. Maintaining customer relationships using relationship events over time.
2. Driving up-sell and cross-sell opportunities using both inbound and outbound events.
3. Incorporating a feedback model to calculate the effectiveness of models over macro and micro dimensions.

4

Customer Service Management

Customer service is the provision of service to customers before, during and after a purchase. According to Jamier L. Scott. (2002), "Customer service is a series of activities designed to enhance the level of customer satisfaction – that is, the feeling that a product or service has met the customer expectation."

Its importance varies by product, industry and customer; defective or broken merchandise can be exchanged, often only with a receipt and within a specified time frame. Retail stores will often have a desk or counter devoted to dealing with returns, exchanges and complaints, or will perform related functions at the point of sale.

Customer service may be provided by a person (e.g., sales and service representative), or by automated means called self-service. Examples of self service are Internet sites. However, In the Internet era, a challenge has been to maintain and/or enhance the personal experience while making use of the efficiencies of online commerce. Writing in Fast Company, entrepreneur and customer systems innovator Micah Solomon has made the point that "Online customers are literally invisible to you (and you to them), so it's easy to short-change them emotionally. But this lack of visual and tactile presence makes it even more crucial to create a sense of personal, human-to-human connection in the online arena."

Customer service is normally an integral part of a company's customer value proposition. In their book *Rules to Break and Laws to Follow*, Don Peppers and Martha Rogers, Ph.D. write that "customers have memories. They will remember you, whether you remember them or not." Further, "customer trust can be destroyed at once by a major service problem, or it can be undermined one day at a time, with a thousand small demonstrations of incompetence."

From the point of view of an overall sales process engineering effort, customer service plays an important role in an organization's ability to generate income and revenue. From that perspective, customer service should be included as part of an overall approach to systematic improvement.

Some have argued that the quality and level of customer service has decreased in recent years, and that this can be attributed to a lack of support or understanding at the executive and middle management levels of a corporation and/or a customer service policy.

Instant Feedback

Recently, many organizations have implemented feedback loops that allow them to capture feedback at the point of experience. For example, National Express, one of the UK's leading travel companies invites passengers to send text messages whilst riding the bus. This has been shown to be useful as it allows companies to improve their customer service before the customer defects, thus making it far more likely that the customer will return next time.

Setting the Right KPIs

A challenge working with Customer Service is to ensure that you have focused your attention on the right key areas, measured by the right Key Performance Indicator. There is no challenge to come up with a lot of meaningful KPIs, but the challenge is to select a few which reflects your overall strategy. In addition to reflecting your strategy it should also enable staff to limit their focus to the areas that really matter. The focus must be of those KPIs, which will deliver the most value to the overall objective, e.g. cost saving, service improving etc. It must also be done in such a way that staff sincerly believe that they can make a difference with the effort.

One of the most important aspects of a customer service KPI is that of what is often referred to as the "Feel Good Factor". Basically the goal is to not only help the customer have a good experience, but to offer them an experience that exceeds their expectations. Several key points are listed as follows:

1. Know your product-Know what products/service you are offering back to front. In other words be an information expert. It is okay to say "I don't know", but it should always be followed up by... "but let me find out" or possibly " but my friend knows!" Whatever the situation may be, make sure that you don't leave your customer with an unanswered question.
2. Body Language/Communication-Most of the communication that we relay to others is done through body language. If we have a

negative body language when we interact with others it can show our lack of care. Two of the most important parts of positive body language are smiling, and eye contact. Make sure to look your customers in the eye. It shows that we are listening to them, not at them. And then of course smiling is just more inviting than someone who has a blank look on their face.

3. Anticipate Guest Needs-Nothing surprises your customer more than an employee going the extra mile to help them. Always look for ways to serve your customer more than they expect. In doing so it helps them to know that you care and it will leave them with the "Feel Good Factor" that we are searching for.

Standardization

There are few standards on this topic. ISO and The International Customer Service Institute (TICSI) have published the following ones:

- ISO 9004:2000, on performance improvement
- ISO 10001:2007, on customer service conduct
- ISO 10002:2004, on quality management in handling customer complaints
- ISO 10003:2007, on dispute resolution
- The International Customer Service Standard (TICSS).

There is also an Information Technology service management standard: ISO/IEC 20000:2005. Its first part concerns specifications and its second part the code of practice.

STUDY OF CUSTOMER SERVICE MANAGEMENT

The customer service study revealed that no specific tactic, technology, or mission statement is the key to effective customer service delivery. In fact, what is clear is that effective customer service delivery is organization specific, since services are designed around the targeted customers' desires and the frontline employees delivering the services.

The components of the process for producing effective customer service delivery include appropriately identifying and targeting the ideal customer, establishing a customer-focused vision that is consistent with the prioritized desires of the target customers, establishing the operational procedures and internal infrastructure that support customer service, continuously measuring customer and employee satisfaction, embracing change, and striving persistently to improve. The customer service literature clearly demonstrates that both profit-seeking and public agencies that implement effective customer service strategies realise financial benefits, either through increased profits or through reduced costs associated with long-term, informed customers; customer referrals; employee retention; improved information exchange; and streamlined service delivery.

Child support enforcement, in this case, is like any other business. In order to implement effective customer service strategies and reap the benefits of good customer service, the Office of Child Support Enforcement (OCSE) agencies will need to implement the process of developing effective customer service.

In an effort to become "more results-oriented and responsive to customers," the Office of Child Support Enforcement (OCSE) contracted with Circle Solutions, Inc. to undertake a study of public and private sector practices and outcomes in customer service. The study included a review of customer service literature, a review of the annual reports and Web sites of 40 companies mentioned in the literature, telephone interviews with companies sited as leaders in customer service in the literature, and site visits to three agencies—two private and one child support agency.

Throughout the study, an advisory group of four State child support enforcement directors provided input and feedback. As a final product of the study, this report summarizes the literature on effective approaches to customer service delivery, highlights four promising practice case studies, conjectures about the transferability of these concepts to child support, and offers future research recommendations. Child support enforcement agencies can refer to this report as a guide for improving customer service, as a resource to learn the costs and benefits of effective customer service delivery, and to inspire future inquiries into effective customer service delivery.

In the 1990s, IBM conducted global research on the question, "What will keep CEOs and senior management awake at night as we begin the twenty-first century?" The study found that, regardless of the industry or geographic location, the most common response was a desire to generate a more customer-oriented culture or business vision.

Customer service is not merely customer relations or how nice frontline workers are to customers. Rather, satisfying or even delighting customers is the goal of excellent customer service. Because customers for different types of services have different needs, customer service strategies will differ and must be tailored to the target customer.

It improves trust and information exchange: In the public sector, including child support offices, good customer service generates satisfied or delighted customers. Satisfied customers lead to increased compliance, improved information exchange, improved relationships, increased trust, and, potentially, decreased workloads or costs. For instance, police departments across the Nation have embraced the concept of community policing. Through community policing, police departments incorporate a customer focus as well as an attitude of partnership with customers, to increase satisfaction and trust and even reduce fear of crime in the community. Customers actually participate in addressing crime and disorder problems, thus reducing the workload on patrol officers.

It saves money and increases profit: In the private sector, good customer service leads to satisfied or delighted customers, which generates customer loyalty, which produces increased revenues and reduced costs. For example, during the early 1990s, IBM transformed itself into a customer-driven organization. From 1994–1999, customer satisfaction increased by 5.5 per cent, revenue increased from $63 billion to over $80 billion, cost and expense savings equaled $7 billion, and stock prices improved over 1,000 per cent.

Upon becoming CEO of Greater Southeast Hospital, a private, nonprofit community hospital, Tom Chapman refocused customer service strategy to save the faltering hospital. Instead of trying to attract more clientele outside the community or turning away the uninsured in the community it served, under Chapman's leadership, Greater Southeast sought to provide better customer service—improving the quality of life and creating community-specific services. The emphasis shifted to treating people when it was cheapest—not in the emergency room but rather when their problems were minor—and to instituting preventative care.

He opened a clinic in the high school to address minor health issues and provide health education resources to teach students about prevention. Additionally, Mr. Chapman improved coordination with the local health clinic and obtained the specific technology from which patients served by the hospital would benefit. Before his arrival, Greater Southeast spent only $20,000–$30,000 a year on a blood pressure programme, although a single stroke victim could cost $30,000 to treat.

The public and private sector customer service literature concurs on the process for delivering great customer service, even if outcomes differ. The current literature supports an outside-in strategy of customer service, rather than the traditional inside-out model for providing services. In the private sector, profit and growth are the *outcomes,* not goals.

Profit and growth are generated by customer loyalty. Loyalty is generated by customer satisfaction. Customer satisfaction is the *goal* that companies should seek and focus on, because high customer satisfaction, as a matter of course, produces customer loyalty and subsequently profit and growth. At this point, the public and private sectors converge—customer satisfaction is the *goal.*

Customer satisfaction is achieved by providing valued services and products, where value is the positive difference between customers' actual experiences and their service delivery expectations. Productive employees also create value.

Employee productivity stems from employee loyalty, and loyalty is a product of employee satisfaction. Satisfaction is generated by high-quality support services (people, information, and technology) and by being empowered to provide value and resolve customer complaints.

This customer service culture must be supported by leadership that emphasizes the importance of each customer and employee. These leaders must be creative and energetic (not lofty or conservative), participatory and caring (not removed or elitist), that is, one who can be a coach, teacher, or listener (not just a supervisor or manager).

Such a leader demonstrates company values (rather than simply institutionalizing policies) and motivates by mission (rather than by fear).

Some components of this model are cyclical. A 1991 study of property and casualty insurance companies found that employees who felt that they were meeting customer needs had twice the job satisfaction level of employees who did not believe they were meeting customer needs. In that study, when a frontline service worker left the company, customer satisfaction levels dropped from 75 to 55 per cent.

In the customer service literature, five guiding principles are adopted by public as well as private agencies delivering excellent customer service:

- Embrace change and persistently strive to improve (be a learning organization).
- Continually ask the target customers what they want and then give it to them.
- Empower, support, and reward frontline personnel.
- Harness the power of information.
- Establish an enabling infrastructure.
- Identify the Target Customer.
  - Begin by identifying the target customers and by considering the point of purchase, point of service delivery or receipt, and point of consumption.

  - Cluster or segment target customers based on their common behaviours, knowing that targeting the wrong customers can have adverse effects on the organization.
  - Determine the priorities of various clusters of customers, knowing that the capabilities of the organization are crucial in addressing these priorities.
  - When possible, focus on customers with high current or future value. (Perhaps in child support this is a custodial parent with many children in the system.) This does not mean that other customers will not receive service, but it may mean that they will receive a different level of service. Consider the frequent flier programmes that airlines and hotels offer to their customers with high current and future value. This does not mean that other passengers will not receive services, but services may not be at the same level.
  - Discourage non-target customers, those who are not likely to be satisfied by the services, and those to whom it is expensive to provide services, which is a necessary part of a customer focus. A simple example is offered as an illustration. A fire department could discourage residents from contacting the department to remove cats from trees by charging a $20 fee for performing the service and by advertising their busy emergency call load. The equipment and time investment of sending a ladder truck and several firefighters may reduce the effectiveness of the department at responding to an emergency and may not be the most prompt means of accomplishing the task for the customer.
- Determine What Customers Want..
  - Determine what target customers want (not just what they need right now) by asking them in person or as part of a mail or telephone survey or by using other mechanisms (e.g., electronic tracking and researching marketing trends) to determine what they want. Be aware that advertising, word of mouth, and public relations influence customers'expectations. Meeting customers'basic needs or expectations does not always bring high levels of satisfaction. Exceeding expectations produces high satisfaction-therefore, determine customers'ideal desires.
  - Determine how the target customers prioritize their"wants."Generally, customers want convenience, quality products and services, variety or selection, low prices, and

protection or security. However, each organization must identify what is most important to its customers.
 - Weigh how important the customer-identified"wants"are to the organization. Are the services something that the organization does, is capable of doing, or wants to pursue?
 - Determine how well the organization can meet the customers'"wants"in comparison with competitors. The success of other companies at meeting and exceeding customer expectations changes a customer's frame of reference and increases a customer's expectations.
 - Determine which"wants,"if performance delivery were to be improved, would most impact the organization's bottom line (profit, cost, loyalty, trust, or compliance).
- Establish an Organizational Culture Supportive of Customer Service.
 - Utilizing the information gathered, establish the company's customer-focused vision. The vision statement should be simple and may also identify what the company does not want to be. Some examples of simple vision statements include"Absolutely, Positively Overnight"by Federal Express and L.L. Bean's promise "Guaranteed. Period."
 - Live up to what is promised by concurrently developing and applying externally and internally oriented strategic service concepts that reflect the vision. If the organization does not implement both internally and externally oriented service strategies consistent with the vision, the organization will have good intentions but poor customer service (Thompson).
 - Continually reflect on the vision and goals and the way services are delivered to customers. Be creative about the mechanisms used to create and deliver new services. Be willing to change existing practices to integrate improvements.
- Implement an Externally Oriented Strategic Service Concept. The externally oriented strategic service concept establishes how the organization's service is designed, marketed, and delivered to target customers.
 - Take into account the costs of providing services and ways to minimize those costs while implementing quality control. The service concept must be developed with the frontline worker at its centre. Determine the necessary financial, human, and technological resources necessary, as well as how the

organizational structure and flow can enable the frontline worker to delight the customer and deliver the promised vision.

- Use advertising/educational strategies to set appropriate customer expectations.
- When planning, realise that control of information can take the place of assets. For instance, the Rural/Metro Fire Department in Scottsdale (AZ) has reduced the size of its crew and trucks because of technology that allows crews to view microfiche floor plans on the way to a fire. The added knowledge of the building layout allows fewer fire fighters to accomplish the same task that requires more firefighters when they do not have this advance knowledge.
- Provide a feedback loop for incorporating customer comments and complaints into the planning processes. Customer complaints are an invaluable resource and source of information without which organizations cannot be successful. Complaints brought to the organization are one of the most efficient and least expensive ways to obtain information about customer expectations of products and services. Complaints are a more direct means of obtaining information than conducting research studies of customer expectations, conducting transaction studies, or reviewing customer expectations in parallel industries. Another means of soliciting customer feedback that has been implemented by a number of service leaders is to interview lost customers-those who have switched service providers. (Perhaps in child support these customers were custodial parents who had been making timely payments but who stopped doing so.) Still other options are holding customer meetings, hosting social events, and attending seminars or conferences where customers are present.

Ensure that the complaint resolution strategy supports the customer-focused vision. Most research shows, "...if customers believe their complaints are welcomed and responded to, they will more likely repurchase." British Airways found that 67 per cent of its complaining passengers fly again if their complaints are handled well. British Airways even implemented a creative and convenient way to allow customers to complain by installing video booths at Heathrow Airport so that customers could immediately go into a booth and state a complaint, even during non-business hours. The videotapes are reviewed and addressed during business hours.

   - One final element of an externally oriented service strategy is to regularly measure customer satisfaction or delight in the products and services.
- Implement an Internally Oriented Strategic Service Concept.

The internally oriented strategic service concept establishes how the organization's internal processes will support the customer-focused vision. The premise behind the internally oriented strategic service concept is "...capable workers who are well trained and fairly compensated provide better service, need less supervision, and are much more likely to stay on the job. As a result, their customers are likely to be more satisfied...". A study by Sears in 1989 found that "employee turnover and customer satisfaction are directly correlated."

Stores with high customer service ratings had a 54 per cent sales force turnover versus 83 per cent in stores with low customer service ratings. This is supported by examples throughout the literature. Taco Bell found that the 20 per cent of stores with the lowest employee turnover rates have 55 per cent higher profits (an outcome of customer satisfaction) than the 20 per cent of stores with the highest turnover rates.

A number of other studies provide convincing evidence as to why companies should avoid employee turnover. Merck and Co. found in 1990 that turnover costs were 1.5 times an employee's annual salary. Clearly this varies based on a number of cost factors (e.g., workers compensation claims, hiring process costs, training costs, and lost business), but it is commonly noted that employee turnover is an expensive problem. Abt Associates studied an automobile dealer's sales and determined that it cost $36,000 to replace a salesperson with 5–8 years of experience with a salesperson with less than 1 year of experience. The economic costs of excessive employee turnover in one trucking company were analysed, and it was determined that the company could increase profits by 50 per cent by cutting driver turnover in half.

- Ensure that leaders of the learning organization exhibit the company values. Leaders must foster the creation and testing of new ideas and be unabashedly willing to change existing practices to integrate improvements.
- Identify employee groups important to implementing the externally oriented service concept. Frontline workers are of central importance.
   - Identify the characteristics and needs of the employee group(s) and how well those needs are met. This may include resources needed to successfully perform the job or needs can refer to compensation, work environmental factors, or personal needs.

Understanding employee needs helps an organization to develop successful processes as well as employee retention policies. Learn how targeted employees perceive the proposed customer services. An organization cannot change without the participation of its employees.

- Focus on recruiting employees who support the customer service vision. The costs of employing people who do not support the customer service vision are considerable. Forum Corporation research in the service industry showed, "...only 14% [per cent] of customers who stop patronizing service businesses do so because they are dissatisfied with what they bought. More than two-thirds defect because they find service people indifferent or unhelpful." Oftentimes, the right employees are those that fit in with the corporate culture's customer service vision, not necessarily those with the most experience in the industry. Additionally, develop career paths that allow successful customer-oriented employees to remain on the frontline.
- Focus on training and employee development throughout employment. A study by Ryder Truck from 1988 through 1989 found that increased training meant lower employee turnover.
- Empower frontline employees to do what it takes to satisfy the customer. Management must support employee empowerment by clearly defining the parametres of the empowerment, while remaining flexible within the parametres. This will encourage creativity. Rules should be simple and few—Continental Airlines actually had an employee handbook burning party to signify the change from a procedural environment to one of empowered customer service. Also, in support of internal customers, the Department of Defence reduced its 230 pages of travel regulations to 17 pages.
- Ensure that management supports employee decisions and judgment calls, even if this means that the cost of satisfying customers initially increases. In positions of high customer contact, quality control is not met by increased supervision, but by the use of incentives to emphasize quality, making service providers highly visible to customers, and by building a peer group to instill a sense of pride and teamwork.
- In addition to skills and empowerment, equip frontline personnel with the technology, information, and internal resources to do what it takes to satisfy the customer. The literature is replete with examples of how incorporating the latest information technology can improve employee productivity. For example, Charles Schwab

developed IWIN, a system that allows an agent to identify and view electronically Charles Schwab literature to respond to customer questions received by telephone. Before this system was implemented, agents who were unfamiliar with the literature in question could not provide immediate and succinct answers to customer questions.

- Ensure that divisions and individuals within the organization communicate. Frontline employees and other employees need information and a support network. A customer should never have to tell one employee what another employee already knows.
- Develop cross-functional teams for operations and improvement tasks. First ask those who are doing the work for suggestions to improve productivity. The Social Security Administration nearly doubled its telephone-answering capacity by implementing automated features, utilizing additional technology to change the way employers' reports of wages are recorded, and cross training its employees to work outside their normal areas of responsibility during peak periods.
- Link all employees' compensation to (and offer rewards for) good customer service performance. Rewards can be money, status, praise, acknowledgement, or perks such as trips or special events. While Charles Schwab does provide monetary incentives based on the amount of money a broker team brings into the company, if the customer service survey for the quarter does not show strong customer service by the team, the reward is reduced or even eliminated for the quarter. This policy in a profit-seeking environment leaves no doubt that customer satisfaction is the primary goal.
- Finally, measure employee satisfaction regularly. Leaders in the service industry have employed such methods as toll-free numbers, periodic roundtable meetings, and surveys to collect employee satisfaction information.

UNDERSTANDING AND MANAGING CUSTOMER PERCEPTION

In today's globalising economy competition is getting more and more fierce. That means it becomes more difficult for products and services to differentiate themselves from other offerings than ever before. Not only is the number of competitive offerings rising due to globalisation of production, sourcing, logistics and access to information. Many products and services face new competition from substitutes and from completely new offerings or bundles from industry outsiders. Since product differences are closed at an increasing speed and many companies try to win the battle for customers by price reductions, products and services tend to become commodities.

On the other hand, customer behaviour becomes more hybrid. On one hand, customers are increasingly price sensitive – searching for bargains at marketplaces like ebay or buying their groceries at discount markets. On the other hand they enjoy branded and luxury goods. One and the same person may plan a weekend trip with a no-frills airline and a stay at a five-star-hotel.

In the result, customers have a wider choice of often less distinguishable products and they are much better informed. For many offerings the balance of power shifts towards the customer. Customers are widely aware of their greater power, which raises their expectations on how companies should care for them.

Bringing it all together, it becomes ever more difficult to differentiate a product or service by traditional categories like price, quality, functionality etc.

In this situation the development of a strong relationship between customers and a company could likely prove to be a significant opportunity for competitive advantage. This relationship is not longer based on features like price and quality alone. Today it is more the perceived experience a customer makes in his various interactions with a company (e.g. how fast, easy, efficient and reliable the process is) that can make or break the relationship. Problems during a single transaction can damage a so far favourable customer attitude. The consequence for companies is that they have to adapt their ways of competing for customers. Traditionally, companies have focused their efforts of customer relationship management on issues like customer satisfaction and targeted marketing activities like event marketing, direct marketing or advertising. Although doubtless necessary and beneficial, these activities are not longer enough. They narrow the relationship between company and customer down to a particular set of contacts in which the company invests its efforts. Most likely this will produce not more than a satisfied customer who is well aware of the companies offerings and has a positive attitude towards them. However, a satisfied customer is not necessarily a loyal one.

If a customer is satisfied that means that a product of service has met his expectations and that he was not dissatisfied by it. Customer satisfaction is doubtlessly very important. It is the precondition for repeat purchases and it prevents the customer from telling others about his disappointing experiences. A loyal customer, however, is more than a customer who frequently purchases from a company.

The difference is the emotional bond which links the customer so closely to the company that he develops a clear preference for these products or brands and is even willing to recommend them to others. Loyal customers truly prefer a product, brand or company over competitive offerings. Thus loyalty goes beyond a rational decision for known quality or superior price-performance-ratio. It is about the customers' feelings and perceptions about the brand or product.

When the customer makes his buying decision, he evaluates the benefits he perceives from a particular product and compares them with the costs. The value a customer perceives when buying and using a product or service go beyond usability. There is a set of emotional values as well, such as social status, exclusivity, friendliness and responsiveness or the degree to which personal expectations and preferences are met.

Similarly, the costs perceived by the customer, normally comprise more than the actual price. They also include costs of usage, the lost opportunity to use an other offering, potential switching costs etc. Hence, the customer establishes an equation between perceived benefits and perceived costs of one product and compares this to similar equations of other products.

Based on this, customer loyalty can be understood as to how customers feel about a product, service or brand and whether their perceived total investments with a it live up to their expectations.

The important point here is the involvement of feelings, emotions and perceptions. In today's competitive marketplace, these perceptions are becoming much more important for gaining sustainable competitive advantage. Customer perceptions are influenced by a variety of factors. Besides the actual outcome – i.e. did the product or service deliver the expected function and did it fulfil the customers need – the whole process of consumption and all interactions involved are of crucial importance. In today's globalised information driven economy this can also comprise issues like

- How other customers or influencing groups perceive the product or brand.
- The degree to which the customer feels the actual marketing campaign addresses the most important issues.
- Responsiveness and service quality of any affiliates, e.g. distribution partners.

Customer perceptions are dynamic. First of all, with the developing relationship between customer and company, his perceptions of the company and its products or services will change.

The more experience the customer accumulates, the more his perceptions will shift from fact-based judgements to a more general meaning the whole relationship gains for him. Over time, he puts a stronger focus on the consequence of the product or service consumption.

Moreover, if the customers' circumstances change, their needs and preferences often change too.

In the external environment, the offerings of competitors, with which a customer compares a product or service will change, thus altering his perception of the best offer around. Another point is that the public opinion towards certain issues can change. This effect can reach from fashion trends to the public expectation of good corporate citizenship. Shells intention to dump its Brent Spar platform into the ocean significantly altered many customers perception of which company was worth buying fuel from.

Research has been don on the impact of market share on the perceived quality of a product. Depending on the nature of the product and the customers' preferences, increasing market share can have positive or negative effects on how the customer perceives the product.

BENEFITS OF IMPLEMENTING CRM

Customer relationship management is meant to shore up less than adequate efforts in the past at understanding who your most profitable customers are. This means creating a profile of desirable customers, developing marketing and sales campaigns to reach those prospects, and maintaining your best customers to increase the lifetime value of the relationship.

In short, CRM should provide the benefits of:

- Selling to your best prospects, and
- Retaining your best customers for
- Improving the profitability of your institution.

However, Ernst & Young reports that 63% of respondents to their e-commerce/CRM survey did not know how much their profitability increased as a result of their CRM projects. Unfortunately, the CRM process is so new that bankers we talked with have not had any time to obtain measurable results. Most CRM projects are being implemented on the faith that obtaining and analyzing customer data will enable the bank to be more profitable. As a side benefit, CRM systems help the bank present a consistent view of the customer relationship across all delivery channels, CRM is costly. It generally requires new database management systems, integration with legacy system, analysis and decision support systems, campaign management systems, new messaging and routing systems, and sales tracking systems. When done right, CRM is an enterprise-wide endeavor. It requires the melding of employee behaviors with information technologies, for the benefit of the customer.

Warnings and Pitfalls

In today's CRM environment, there is a danger we see with multiple vendors offering systems built on relational database technology and touting theirs as the one customer relationship management tool you need. Because most new banking applications are being developed with a database that aggregates customer data, a "data mart," these vendors are jumping on the CRM bandwagon. The problem will come when you have implemented multiple CRM data marts to handle various applications, and then find you cannot reconcile the data in each database. It will be better to implement a single CRM system first and then hang multiple applications off the core database.

You should think of CRM technologies as basically handling two major operations:

- Back office customer data aggregation and analysis
- Front office end-user data presentation and manipulation

All CRM solutions are built on a relational database, often called "middleware" because it suits between the legacy systems that handle the transaction processing and the front end systems that deliver the data across end points. Between the back office and the front office are many technologies that facilitate analysis and presentation.

The end-user may be a banker or the customer. End-user touch points may be in the bank, at the credit officer's workstation, in the call center, at the teller line or on the platform, or on remote, at an ATM machine, a kiosk, on the telephone, via internet, or soon, through wireless devices.

The question is where should you begin your CRM implementation? In the rush to provide new, or enhance old delivery channels-from call centers, to ATMs, to the Internet-with consistent customer relationship record at each touch point, you run the internet banking solutions, and total delivery channel solutions, is the inherent customer relationship management technology on which they are based.

Principles Of Service In Banking

1. By satisfying the clients' business objectives a bank can satisfy their own professional and personal objectives.
2. Every bank wants their client to regard the organization as their partner of choice time after time.
3. Satisfied customers/clients become engaged clients when they trust the bank the are linked with and feel a sense of pride through an association with it.
4. Engaged clients form a significant source of continued and improved growth.
5. An engaged client will actively sell the bank's product and services to others.
6. Engaged client forms a sound commercial foundation for the existing bank.
7. Don't keep good news to yourself-inform the client of every success.
8. Give every customer a reason to trust the bank.
9. Do what you said; you could do it, when you said you would do it.
10. Take personal ownership& responsibility for keeping the client informed of progress in any matter they have raised.

Findings & Conclusion

The main objective of the report has been to assess the current state of the CRM development within Indian credit institutions and to evaluate its organizational impacts.

The study has identified issues that need to be assessed if CRM is to be used more productively to take advantage of new opportunities.

STEPS THAT BANKERS' CAN FOLLOW TO BULID UP LONG TERM RELATIONSHIP WITH THEIR CUSTOMERS:

- WELCOME CALL
- PROFILE SHEET
- BANK CUSTOMER INTERACTION DETAIL FILE
- APPOINTMENT DIARY
- IMPORTANT DATES TRACK ALARM

CRM should be viewed neither as a new competitive tool nor as a cluster of technologies, but rather as a set of business processes that help manage client credit institutions relationships and improve internal credit institutions workflow. CRM in fact, is a process that helps to maximize medium to long term profits as a result of a better customer knowledge, customized treatment of customers or a perception of it, and improved fulfillment of customer needs. These goals can be better reached by adoption of enabling ICTs. Ideally, an effective CRM project needs to be very well integrated in the credit institution organization.

Implementing a CRM process means gathering flows of information concerning actual and potential customers. Information flows coming from delivery channels should ideally be consolidated into a customer database in order to develop customer profiles that enable banks to improve customer services CRM based on ICT can strengthen the marketing strategy of the financial organization by making more effective the management of all the information concerning customers.

The exploitation of CRM appears to have a positive impact on the quality and quantity of information conveyed to customers. This is particularly relevant for the most sophisticated customers, i.e. those who are used to dealing with new technological tools and are not afraid of interacting with the bank through the telematics channels. Nevertheless, distant interaction is not as effective as personal interaction between customers and their bank. Therefore, according to almost all of the bank representatives, e-business supports low value information needs, while more sophisticated requests for information can be addressed only through personal interaction between the bank and the customer that usually takes place at the branch.

Almost all the credit institutions have adopted the strategy of launching their e-business services as an additional service rather than as an alternative to offline services. The impact of e-business in banks is being limited by their strategic decision not to cannibalize their branches. This research highlights how some of the credit institutions which had originally invested only in the development of a virtual channel had to drastically re-define their customers or by opening a call centre. The credit institutions representatives argued that their customers want a choice of channels and they are adopting a multi-channel strategy. Most of the banks consider that since Internet and telephone are most useful for managing operational and low value added tasks, the traditional delivery structure still has a fundamental role and can be developed to specialize in high added value tasks and consultancy services.

Most financial suppliers believe that customer support services are a core business in the financial industry. Most of the financial organizations choose to internalize the customer support contact center, whereas others choose to outsource front-office customer care tasks to contact centre companies. But the final elaboration of data on customers and their exploitation for CRM strategy is maintained in house and involves the bank management personnel.

The customer retention is the result of an increasing degree of product personalization and differentiation. Credit institutions apparently prefer to compete on quality (product information, broader range of product and services) rather than on price (meant as product acquisition cost to the customer: price, mode of payment, delivery). Therefore product innovation (cross-selling, product differentiation and personalization) seems to be the crucial issue of the CRM strategy.

Financial institutions have to realize the importance of the technology scalability as well as the reengineering of the business processes.

A medium to long term CRM strategy requires significant innovation in the organization of the banks' flow of information.

Ideally, CRM technologies and processes could make the slogan "the right customer with the right product at right place and in the right moment" possible.

But many banks face the problem of having multiple database with customer information, so that multiple entries refer to the same customer if he/she holds more than one product with the company. This makes it difficult for sales people or relationship managers to have a full view of their customers. A number of CRM deployments have failed because of inconsistent customer data. This problem results in companies sending, for example, the same offer twice to the same customer.

Hence CRM is a vital tool for financial institution to prosper.......

What Is Banking?

Banking in a traditional sense is the business of accepting deposits of money from public for the purpose of lending and investments. These deposits can have a distinct feature of being withdrawal by cheques, which no other financial institution can offer.

In addition, banks also offer various other financial services, which includes: –

- Issuing Demand Draft and Travelers Cheques
- Credit Card
- Collection of Cheques, Bills of Exchange
- Safe Deposit Lockers
- Issuing Letters of Credit and Letters of Guarantee
- Sale and Purchases of Foreign Exchange

- Custodial Services
- Investment and Insurance services

The business of banking is highly regulated since banks deal with money offered to them by the public and ensuring the safety of this public money is one of the prime responsibilities of any bank. That is why banks are expected to be prudent in their lending and investment activities. Every bank has Compliance department, which is responsible to ensure that all the services offered by the banks and the processes followed are in compliance with the local regulation and the bank's corporate policies:

- Banking Regulation Act, 1949
- Foreign Exchange Management Act, 1999
- Indian Contract Act, 1872
- Negotiable Instrument Act, 1881

Banks lend money either for productive purposes to individuals, firm corporate etc. or for buying house property, cars and other durable and for investment purposes to individuals and others. However banks do not finance any speculative activity. Lending is risk taking; having prudent norms for lending should cover the risk. The depositors of banks are also assured of their money by deploying some percentage of deposits in statutory reserve like SLR and CRR.

BANKING INDUSTRY IN INDIA

Banking in India has its origin as early as the Vedic period. It is believed that the transition from money lending to banking must have occurred even before Manu. The great Hindu Jurist, who has devoted a section of his work to deposits and advances and lay down rules relating to rate of interest. During the Mogul period, the indigenous banker played a very important role in lending money and financing foreign trade and commerce. During the days of the East India Company it was the turn of the agency houses to carry on the banking business.

The General Bank of India was the first joint Stock Bank to be established in the year 1786. The others, which followed, were the Bank of Hindustan and Bengal Bank. The bank of Hindustan is reported to have continued till 1906 while the other two failed in the meantime.

In the first half of the 19th century of East India Company establish three banks; The Bank of Bengal in 1809, the Bank of Bombay in 1840 and the bank of madras in 1843. These three banks also known as presidency Bank were independent units and functioned well. These three banks were amalgamated on 27th January 1921. With the passing of the State Bank of India Act in 1955 the Reserve Bank of India Act 1934. In the wake of the Swadeshi Movement, a number of bank with Indian management were establish in the country namely, Punjab National Bank Ltd., Bank of India Ltd., the Central Bank of India Ltd., Indian Bank Ltd., the Bank of Baroda Ltd., and the Central Bank of India Ltd. On July 19, 1969 fourteen major banks of the Country were nationalized & in 15th April 1980 six more commercial private sector banks were also taken over by the Government.

Today the commercial banking system in India may be distinguished into:

Public Sector Banks:

State Bank of India & its associate bank called the State Bank Group, 20 nationalized banks, Regional Rural Banks mainly sponsored by public sector banks Old generation private bank, New generation private bank, foreign banks in India, Scheduled co-operative bank, non-scheduled banks.

Co-operative Sector Banks:

The co-operative sector has been developed in the country to the supplement the

Village moneylender. The co-operative banking sector in India is divided into four components State Co-operative Banks, Central Co-operative Banks, Primary Agriculture Credit Societies, Land Development Banks, Urban Co-operative banks, Primary Agriculture Development Banks, Primary Land Development Banks, and State Land Development Banks.

Development Banks:

Industrial Finance Corporation of India (IFCI)

Industrial Development Bank of India (IDBI)

Industrial Credit and Investment Corporation of India (ICICI)

Industrial Investment Bank of India (IIBI)

Small Industrial Development Bank of India (SIDBI)

National Bank for Agriculture and Rural Development (NABARD)

Export Import Bank of India (EXIM)

National Housing Bank:

The Indian banking can be broadly categorized into Nationalized, Private Banks & Specialized Banking Institution. The RBI Acts as a centralized body, monitoring and discrepancies and short coming in the system. Since the Nationalization of Banks in 1969, the public sector banks have accrued a place of prominence and have since then seen tremendous progress. Conservative banking practices allowed India Banks to be insulated partially form the Asia currency crises, India banks are now quoting all higher valuation when compared to Bank to other Asian countries that have major problems linked to huge NPA's and payment defaults. Co-operative banks are nimble footed in approach and armed with efficient branch network focus primarily on the high revenue niche retail segments. The India banking was finally worked up to the competitive dynamic of the new India market and is addressing the relevant issues to take on the multifarious challenges of globalization.

Private Banks has been fast on the uptake and is reorienting their strategies using the interest as a medium. The Internet has emerged as the new and challenging frontier of marketing.

The large dose of liberalization have largely brought this transformation and economic reforms that allowed banks to explore new business opportunities rather generating revenues from conventional streams i.e. borrowing and lending.

The banking in India is highly fragmented with banking unit contributing to almost 55 of deposits and 60% of advances. Indian nationalized banks continue to be the major lender in the economy due to their sheer size and penetrative networks which assures them high deposit mobilization. The India banking can be broadly categorized into nationalized, private banks and specialized banking institutions. The RBI acts as a centralized body monitoring any discrepancies and shortcoming in the system. It is foremost monitoring body in the Indian financial sector. The nationalized banks continue that out of commercial banks operating in India, banks are in the public sector and 5 are in the private sector.

CUSTOMER RELATIONSHIP SERVICE

One person's excellent service may represent barely adequate service to someone else. What impresses one customer may make absolutely no impression on another. To complicate matters, what a customer believes to be good service in one context may be unacceptable in another situation or at another time. Service is perceptual; it is individualized; and it is situational. So how can you figure out what customers want from you in terms of service? The kind and level of service that you must deliver depends on who the customer is, what her expectations are, what experience she has had with you and other firms, what your strategy is and what role customer service plays in its delivery—along with a host of other things.

Many managers and executives are uncomfortable with this notion of variable service delivery; they would much prefer to be able to pin down service and to be able to standardize it so that it can be consistently delivered. But I don't believe service should be the same for everyone. In fact, the value of service as a relationship-building tool is its customizability. Simply out, some customers require and deserve better service than others. Several studies have examined the importance for a business of retaining its customers in great depth, with evidence suggesting that retention leads to increase market share and eventually greater profits. Marketing tools that businesses can employ for retaining customers may, therefore, provide for a competitive advantage. For example, tools may contribute to product and service differentiation, as well as to create barriers for customers switching to other products and services.

Today's businesses are facing fierce and aggressive competition while operating in both domestic and global markets. Most managers and marketers would of course agree that establishing long-term business relationships is about development and survival. According to Lewis (1991), the world has never been so interdependent. All trends point to cooperation as a fundamental, growing force in business. Marketing is also about how to integrate the customer into the design of the products/services and how to design a systematic process for the interaction that will create substance in relationships. In a competitive world, companies have to work hard to gain any added value. They have to work with their customers to discover the new ways for running the business more efficiently for themselves and more effectively for the customers.

Four Levels of Service

Another element that gets in the way of impressive service delivery is management's very simplistic view of customer service. I can think of at least four levels of customer service, each of which involves the creation of progressively more emotional value for customers. To the customer, service involves more than just the functional delivery of service (the first level, which, in a world where companies like FedEx have practically perfected technical service provision, customers take as a given). Customers care how easy you make it for them to communicate with you. This opens the door to a discussion of your phone system, your web site and your customer service center—not to mention whether customers can find someone to serve them in your store. Increasingly, when you keep them on hold for 20 minutes, don't respond to their email inquiries and ask them to deal with unknowledgeable and unhelpful staff, they will walk away.

At the third level, companies need to understand how customer service is linked to the people they employ. My experience suggests that customers are most likely to equate the notion of service with the way they are treated by employees. Finally, the level of service that customers experience is a powerful influence on how customers feel emotionally toward a company. Poor service can make a customer feel neglected, unimportant, frustrated, angry or even humiliated. Surprisingly good service leads to emotions such as comfort, relief, delight or excitement.

Holistic View

Yet, many companies have a less-than-holistic view of their value proposition. Customer service must be seen to be an integral part of what we offer the customer. I recently encountered a major company that has separate marketing, sales and customer service departments, each of which prepares its own annual plan and sets its own budgets, without consulting with the others. In that firm, customer service is defined mainly as the operation of the call center. To the customer, service means much more.

Customer service is not optional. It's not trivial. And it's not easily standardized. Don't make the mistake that one Canadian bank made of treating customer service as a promotion. That bank offered customers $5 if they had to wait in line more than five minutes in its branches. Customers were generally not impressed. To them, a wait time of five minutes was not the issue. Of course, wait time is important—but not nearly as important as being served politely and efficiently once you reach the counter. Customer service is extremely complex, much like value, satisfaction and the increasingly popular customer experience. To apply such concepts effectively, management must appreciate their complexity. To utilize customer service to increase customer loyalty, to reinforce the positioning of the brand and to gain a competitive advantage, companies much have a strategy to guide its development and implementation.

Customer Relationship Management

Before we begin to examine the conceptual foundations of CRM, it will be useful to define what CRM is. A narrow perspective of customer relationship management is database marketing emphasizing the promotional aspects of marketing linked to database efforts. Shani and Chalasani1 define relationship marketing as "an integrated effort to identify, maintain, and build up a network with individual's consumers and to continuously strengthen the network for mutual benefit of both sides, through interactive, individualized and value-added contacts over a period of time". In today's hyper competitive scenario, more than three quarters of the money and time spent by companies go towards acquiring and retaining customers. Customer-centricity has become the buzzword and the ones with clear and relentless focus on customers, enjoy a better competitive position. This is proved time and again. Reading the customer demographics and understanding their needs (both explicit and implicit) is what customer insight is all about. Customer insight is the basic point or the foundation for building a customer centric organization. Everything in the value chain revolves around this. This is the raw material. This is more a conversion process rather, since the end product is Customer Loyalty! Over decades, many organizations had successfully completed the conversion process and tasted higher returns, most organizations miserably failed in their efforts.

CRM evolved from business concepts and processes such as relationship marketing and the increased emphasis on improved customer retention through the effective management of customer relationships. CRM emphasize that customer retention affects company profitability in that it is more efficient to maintain an existing relationship with a customer than create a new one.

CRM is defined as:

"Customer relationship management (CRM) is a business strategy to acquire and manage the most valuable customer relationships. CRM requires a customer-centric business philosophy and culture to support effective marketing, sales and service processes. CRM applications can enable effective customer relationship management, provided that an enterprise has the right leadership, strategy and culture (Brayn)."

Crm Objectives In Banking Sector

The idea of CRM is that it helps businesses use technology and human resources gain insight into the behavior of customers and the value of those customers. If it works as hoped, a business can: provide better customer service, make call centers more efficient, cross sell products more effectively, help sales staff close deals faster, simplify marketing and sales processes, discover new customers, and increase customer revenues. It doesn't happen by simply buying software and installing it.

For CRM to be truly effective an organization must first decide what kind of customer information it is looking for and it must decide what it intends to do with that information. For example, many financial institutions keep track of customers' life stages in order to market appropriate banking products like mortgages or IRAs to them at the right time to fit their needs.

Next, the organization must look into all of the different ways information about customers comes into a business, where and how this data is stored and how it is currently used. One company, for instance, may interact with customers in a myriad of different ways including mail campaigns, Web sites, brick-and-mortar stores, call centers, mobile sales force staff and marketing and advertising efforts.

Company analysts can then comb through the data to obtain a holistic view of each customer and pinpoint areas where better services are needed. In CRM projects, following data should be collected to run process engine: 1) Responses to campaigns, 2) Shipping and fulfillment dates, 3)Sales and purchase data, 4) Account information, 5) Web registration data, 6) Service and support records, 7) Demographic data, 8) Web sales data.

Banking And Loyalty

During the past decade, the financial service sector has undergone drastic changes, resulting in a market place which is characterized by intense competition, little growth in primary demand and increased deregulation. In the new market place, the occurrence of committed and often inherited relationships between a customer and his or her bank is becoming increasingly scarce.

Several strategies have been attempted to retain customers. In order to increase customer loyalty, many banks have introduced innovative products and services (Meidan, 1996). However, as such innovations are frequently followed by similar charges; it has been argued that a more viable approach for banks is to focus on less tangible and less easy-to-imitate determinants of customer loyalty such as customer evaluative judgments like service quality and satisfaction (Worcester, 1997; Yavas and Shemwell, 1996). Banking has traditionally operated in a relatively stable environment for decades. However, today the industry is facing a dramatically aggressive competition in a new deregulated environment. The net result of the recent competition and legislation is that traditional banks have lost a substantial proportion of their domestic business to essentially non-bank competition.

Competition will undoubtedly continue to be a more significant factor. Finding a place in this heating sun becomes vital to the long-range profitability and ultimate survival of the bank. Banks begin to realize that no bank can offer all products and be the best/leading bank for.

A bank has to create the customer relationship that delivers value beyond the provided by the core product. This involves added tangible and intangible elements to the core products, thus creating and enhancing the "product surrounding". Positioning is an attempt to distinguish the bank from its competitors along real dimensions in order to be the most preferred bank for a certain market segment or in other words, if a bank can position itself favorably within a particular marketplace, relative to competitors, that bank is a competitive one.

Competitiveness means that a bank, in terms of its competitive position, its management and marketing strategies, its use of information technology, the quality of its products/services and its ability of managing long term customer relationship must be increasingly responsive to the market consideration and customer orientation. The increasing importance of relational marketing in recent years, particularly in the servicing and manufacturing industries, such as banks, has been accompanied by a bundle of works on customer loyalty. Several authors emphasize the positive relationship existing between customer loyalty and business performance (Beerli et al., 2004; Reichheld and Sasser, 1990). Loyal customers not only increase the value of the business, but also enable it to maintain the costs lower than those associated with attracting new customers (Beerli et al., 2004).

Problem Statement

Service quality offers a sustainable competitive advantage to a bank because it creates value and also customer satisfaction. However, service quality is reduced drastically by service breakdowns. The results of service breakdowns are customer dissatisfaction and possibly customer defection depending on the customer's trust, knowledge and the availability of alternative service provider. In the banking sector, to maintain and having a closer relationship with the entire or existing customers are very important. The maintenance of consumer trust in the retail banking industry is of considerable importance as it can impact on the likelihood of retaining existing customers and attaining new ones. Furthermore, trust in a bank can also be more important to a bank customer than price. So, each bank must make sure that their services fulfill their customers' needs and wants.

The focus on this research is to identify the common relationship marketing underpinnings such as trust, commitment, empathy, values and conflict handling on customer loyalty in banking sector. This research will also look whether all dimensions mentioned contribute equally or differentially towards the loyalty of the customer. My thesis is concerned on mainly issues with most customers complain in HBL because they acquire service with certain expectations, and, for any number of reasons, those expectations were not met. CR officers help in this scenario controlling delays, failures and troubles like problems to the customers of HBL. CRM can fill the gaps between the HBL and customers, so this is total concern of my thesis that how and when CR officers can impart their knowledge and role in HBL.

Objectives

HBL Customer relationship management circumferences on these objectives those are important to customer approaches.

- To elucidate the customer relation activities in the HBL.
- To gauge the impact CRM on the customer relations in the Bank.
- To evaluate the impact of motivated CRO's on the organizational effectiveness of the Bank.
- To analyze without proper CRM in bank it has negative effect on the performance of the bank.

Hypothesis

H0 =Customer relationship officer activities do not have any impact on organizational effectiveness of HBL.

H1 =Customer relationship officer activities have impact on organizational effectiveness of HBL.

Significance Of Study

The project is significant in the way that after studying through all the contents of research project, the user can effectively judge that how effectively Customer Relationship is being done in HBL along with important issues, problems and challenges faced by it. My study can be helpful for business students, HRM related issues, marketing plans and for other institutions related with customers and organizations.

Delimitation

Reliance upon secondary sources of information as the data had to be gathered more from employees' experiences and observations rather than direct focus on the customers. I have interviewed many of customers, employees but more significant and satisfactory answers related to the problems and effectiveness of Customer Relationships are provided by the employees of different HBL Branches, I visited.

SERVICE AS A PROCESS

Marketers don't usually need to know the specifics of how physical goods are manufactured— that responsibility belongs to the people who run the factory. However, the situation is different in services. Because their customers are often involved in service production and may have preferences for certain methods of service delivery, marketers do need to understand the nature of the processes through which services are created and delivered. Furthermore, they should be involved in any decisions to change the nature of a given process if that change will affect customers. A process is a particular method of operation or a series of actions, typically involving multiple steps that often need to take place in a defined sequence.

Think about the steps that Susan went through at the hair salon: phoning in advance to make an appointment, arriving at the store, waiting, having a shampoo, discussing options with the cutter, having her hair cut and styled, tipping, paying, and finally leaving the store.

Service processes range from relatively simple procedures involving only a few steps—such as filling a car's tank with fuel—to highly complex activities like transporting passengers on an international flight. The characteristics of the processes that might be used in a particular service operation necessarily reflect the nature of the business. Within certain constraints, the choice of processes may also be shaped by customer expectations and preferences. Looking at the processes *currently* used is only part of the story, since alternative processes may be available for exploration.

People Processing

From ancient times, people have sought out services directed at themselves. To receive these types of services, customers must physically enter the service system. Because they are an integral part of the process, they cannot obtain the benefits they desire by dealing at arm's length with service suppliers. They must enter the service factory, which is a physical location where people or machines create and deliver service benefits to customers. Sometimes, of course, service providers are willing to come to customers, bringing the necessary tools of their trade to create the desired benefits in the customers' choice of locations. If customers want the benefits that a people-processing service has to offer, they must be prepared to cooperate actively with the service operation. For example, Susan cooperates with her hair stylist by sitting still and turning her head as requested.

She will also have to be part of the process when she visits the optometrist for her next eye exam. The level of involvement required of customers may entail anything from boarding a city bus for a five-minute ride to undergoing a lengthy course of unpleasant treatments at a hospital. In between these extremes are such activities as ordering and eating a meal; having one's hair washed, cut, and styled; and spending some nights in a hotel room.

The output from these services is a customer who has reached her destination or satisfied his hunger or is now sporting clean and stylishly cut hair or has had a good night's sleep away from home or is now in physically better health. It's important for managers to think about process and output in terms of what happens to the customer because it helps them to identify what benefits are being created. Reflecting on the service process itself helps to identify some of the non-financial costs—such as time, mental and physical effort, and even fear and pain—that customers incur in obtaining these benefits.

Possession Processing

Often, customers ask a service organisation to provide treatment for some physical possession— which could be anything from a house to a hedge, a car to a computer, or a dress to a dog. Many such activities are quasi-manufacturing operations and do not always involve simultaneous production and consumption. Examples include cleaning, maintaining, storing, improving, or repairing physical objects—both live and inanimate—that belong to the customer in order to extend their usefulness. Additional possession-processing services include transport and storage of goods; wholesale and retail distribution; and installation, removal, and disposal of equipment—in short, the entire value-adding chain of activities that may take place during the lifetime of the object in question.

Customers are less physically involved with this type of service than with peopleprocessing services. Consider the difference between passenger and parcel transportation. In the former you have to go along for the ride to obtain the benefit of getting from one location to another. But with package service, you drop the package off at a mailbox or post office counter and wait for it to be delivered to the recipient. In most possession-processing services, the customer's involvement is usually limited to dropping off the item that needs treatment, requesting the service, explaining the problem, and later returning to pick up the item and pay the bill.

If the object to be processed is something that is difficult or impossible to move, like landscaping, installed software, heavy equipment, or part of a building, the service factory must come to the customer, with service personnel bringing the tools and materials necessary to complete the job on-site. The service process could involve applying insecticide in a house to get rid of ants, trimming a hedge at an office park, repairing a car, installing software in a computer, cleaning a jacket, or giving an injection to the family dog. The output in each instance should be a satisfactory solution to the customer's problem or some tangible enhancement of the item in question. In Susan's case, the cleaners disappointed her because her suit wasn't ready when promised.

Mental Stimulus Processing

Services that interact with people's minds include education, news and information, professional advice, psychotherapy, entertainment, and certain religious activities. Anything touching people's minds has the power to shape attitudes and influence behaviour. So, when customers are in a position of dependency or there is potential for manipulation, strong ethical standards and careful oversight are required.

Receiving these services requires an investment of time on the customer's part. However, recipients don't necessarily have to be physically present in a service factory— just mentally in communication with the information being presented.There's an interesting contrast here with people-processing services.

Passengers can sleep through a flight and still arrive at their desired destination. But if Susan falls asleep in class or during an educational TV broadcast, she will not be any wiser at the end than at the beginning! Services like entertainment and education are often created in one place and transmitted by television, radio, or the Internet to individual customers in distant locations.

However, they can also be delivered to groups of customers at the originating location in a facility such as a theater or lecture hall. We need to recognise that watching a live concert on television in one's home is not the same experience as watching it in a concert hall in the company of hundreds or even thousands of other people. Managers of concert halls face many of the same challenges as their colleagues in people-processing services.

Similarly, the experience of participating in a discussion-based class through interactive cable television lacks the intimacy of people debating one another in the same room. Because the core content of all services in this category is information based, it can easily be converted to digital bits or analog signals; recorded for posterity; and transformed into a manufactured product, such as a compact disc, videotape, or audiocassette, which may then be packaged and marketed much like any other physical good. These services can thus be "inventoried" because they can be consumed at a later date than when they were produced. For instance, Susans

Spanish videotape can be used over and over again by students visiting the language lab.

Information Processing

Information processing, one of the buzzwords of our age, has been revolutionised by computers. But not all information is processed by machines. Professionals in a wide variety of fields also use their brains to perform information processing and packaging.

Information is the most intangible form of service output, but it may be transformed into more enduring, tangible forms as letters, reports, books, tapes, or CDs. Among the services that are highly dependent on the effective collection and processing of information are financial services and professional services like accounting, law, marketing research, management consulting, and medical diagnosis.

The extent of customer involvement in both information and mental stimulus processing is often determined more by tradition and a personal desire to meet the supplier face to face than by the needs of the operational process.

Strictly speaking, personal contact is quite unnecessary in industries like banking or insurance. Why subject your firm to all the complexities of managing a people-processing service when you could deliver the same core product at arm's length? As a customer, why go to the service factory when there's no compelling need to do so?

Susan appears comfortable dealing at arm's length with both her bank and her insurance company, using a self-service ATM for her banking transactions and receiving mail communications from her insurance company. Habit and tradition often lie at the root of existing service delivery systems and service usage patterns. Professionals and their clients may say they prefer to meet face to face because they feel that in this way they learn more about each other's needs, capabilities, and personalities. However, experience shows that successful personal relationships, built on trust, can be created and maintained purely through telephone or e-mail contact.

5

Consumer Behaviour

The study of consumers helps firms and organizations improve their marketing strategies by understanding issues such as how:

- The psychology of how consumers think, feel, reason, and select between different alternatives;
- The psychology of how the consumer is influenced by his or her environment;
- The behaviour of consumers while shopping or making other marketing decisions;
- Limitations in consumer knowledge or information processing abilities influence decisions and marketing outcome;
- How consumer motivation and decision strategies differ between products that differ in their level of importance or interest that they entail for the consumer; and
- How marketers can adapt and improve their marketing campaigns and marketing strategies to more effectively reach the consumer.

One "official" definition of consumer behaviour is "The study of individuals, groups, or organizations and the processes they use to select, secure, use, and dispose of products, services, experiences, or ideas to satisfy needs and the impacts that these processes have on the consumer and society." Although it is not necessary to memorize this definition.

It brings up some useful points:

- Behaviour occurs either for the individual, or in the context of a group or an organization.
- Consumer behaviour involves the use and disposal of products as well as the study of how they are purchased. Product use is often of great interest to the marketer, because this may influence how a product is best positioned or how we can encourage increased consumption. Since many environmental problems result from product disposal this is also an area of interest.

- Consumer behaviour involves services and ideas well as tangible products.
- The impact of consumer behaviour on society is also of relevance. For example, aggressive marketing of high fat foods, or aggressive marketing of easy credit, may have serious repercussions for the national health and economy.

There are four main applications of consumer behaviour:

1. The most obvious is for *marketing strategy—i.e.*, for making better marketing campaigns. For example, by understanding that consumers are more receptive to food advertising when they are hungry, we learn to schedule snack advertisements late in the afternoon. By understanding that new products are usually initially adopted by a few consumers and only spread later, and then only gradually, to the rest of the population, we learn that,
   - Companies that introduce new products must be well financed so that they can stay afloat until their products become a commercial success and
   - It is important to please initial customers, since they will in turn influence many subsequent customers' brand choices.
2. A second application is *public policy*. In the 1980s, Accutane, a near miracle cure for acne, was introduced. Unfortunately, Accutane resulted in severe birth defects if taken by pregnant women. Although physicians were instructed to warn their female patients of this, a number still became pregnant while taking the drug. To get consumers' attention, the Federal Drug Administration took the step of requiring that very graphic pictures of deformed babies be shown on the medicine containers.
3. *Social marketing* involves getting ideas across to consumers rather than selling something. Marty Fishbein went on sabbatical to work for the Centres for Disease Control trying to reduce the incidence of transmission of diseases through illegal drug use. The best solution, obviously, would be if we could get illegal drug users to stop. This, however, was deemed to be infeasible. It was also determined that the practice of sharing needles was too ingrained in the drug culture to be stopped. As a result, using knowledge of consumer attitudes, Dr. Fishbein created a campaign that encouraged the cleaning of needles in bleach before sharing them, a goal that was believed to be more realistic.
4. As a final benefit, studying consumer behaviour should make us better consumers. Common sense suggests, for example, that if you

buy a 64 liquid ounce bottle of laundry detergent, you should pay less per ounce than if you bought two 32 ounce bottles. In practice, however, you often pay a size *premium* by buying the larger quantity. In other words, in this case, knowing this fact will sensitize you to the need to check the unit cost labels to determine if you are *really* getting a bargain.

There are several units in the market that can be analysed. Our main thrust in this course is the *consumer*. However, as suggested, also need to analyse our own firm's strengths and weaknesses and those of *competing firms*. Suppose, for example, that we make a product aimed at older consumers, a growing segment. A competing firm that targets babies, a shrinking market, is likely to consider repositioning towards our market. To assess a competing firm's potential threat, we need to examine its assets against pressures it faces from the market. Finally, we need to assess conditions. For example, although we may have developed a product that offers great appeal for consumers, a recession may cut demand dramatically.

CONSUMER RESEARCH METHODS

Market research is often needed to ensure that we produce what customers really want and not what we *think* they want. Primary vs. secondary research methods. There are two main approaches to marketing. *Secondary* research involves using information that others have already put together.

For example, if you are thinking about starting a business making clothes for tall people, you dont need to question people about how tall they are to find out how many tall people existthat information has already been published by the U.S. Government. *Primary* research, in contrast, is research that you design and conduct yourself. For example, you may need to find out whether consumers would prefer that your soft drinks be sweater or tarter.

Research will often help us *reduce risks* associated with a new product, but it *cannot take the risk away entirely*. It is also important to ascertain whether the research has been complete. For example, Coca Cola did a great deal of research prior to releasing the New Coke, and consumers seemed to prefer the taste. However, consumers were *not* prepared to have this drink replace traditional Coke.

Often, we take *cultural* influences for granted, but they are significant. An American will usually not bargain with a store owner. This, however, is a common practice in much of the World. *Physical* factors also influence our behaviour. We are more likely to buy a soft drink when we are thirsty, for example, and food manufacturers have found that it is more effective to advertise their products on the radio in the late afternoon when people are getting hungry. A person's *self-image* will also tend to influence what he or she will buy—an upwardly mobile manager may buy a flashy car to project an image of success. *Social* factors also influence what the consumers buy—often, consumers seek to imitate others whom they admire, and may buy the same brands. The social environment can include both the mainstream culture and a subculture. Thus, sneaker manufacturers are eager to have their products worn by admired athletes. Finally, consumer behaviour is influenced by *learning*—you try a hamburger and learn that it satisfies your hunger and tastes good, and the next time you are hungry, you may consider another hamburger.

BEHAVIOURAL INTENTION

The behavioural intention is what the consumer plans to do with respect to the object. As with affect, this is sometimes a logical consequence of beliefs but may sometimes reflect other circumstances—*e.g.*, although a consumer does not really like a restaurant, he or she will go there because it is a hangout for his or her friends. Changing attitudes is generally *very difficult*, particularly when consumers suspect that the marketer has a self-serving "agenda" in bringing about this change.

Here are some possible methods:

- *Changing affect*: One approach is to try to change affect, which may or may not involve getting consumers to change their beliefs. One strategy uses the approach of *classical conditioning* try to "pair" the product with a liked stimulus. For example, we "pair" a car with a beautiful woman. Alternatively, we can try to get people to like the advertisement and hope that this liking will "spill over" into the purchase of a product. For example, the Pillsbury Doughboy does not really emphasize the conveyance of much information to the consumer; instead, it attempts to create a warm, "fuzzy" image. Although Energizer Bunny ads try to get people to believe that their batteries last longer, the main emphasis is on the likeable bunny. Finally, products which are better known, through the *mere exposure* effect, tend to be better liked—that is, the more a product is advertised and seen in stores, the more it will generally be liked, even if consumers to do not develop any specific beliefs about the product.

- *Changing behaviour*: People like to believe that their behaviour is rational; thus, once they use our products, chances are that they will continue unless someone is able to get them to switch. One way to get people to switch to our brand is to use temporary price discounts and coupons; however, when consumers buy a product on deal, they may justify the purchase based on that deal and may then switch to other brands on deal later. A better way to get people to switch to our brand is to at least temporarily obtain better shelf space so that the product is more convenient. Consumers are less likely to use this availability as a rationale for their purchase and may continue to buy the product even when the product is less conveniently located.
- *Changing beliefs*: Although attempting to change beliefs is the obvious way to attempt attitude change, particularly when consumers hold unfavourable or inaccurate ones, this is often difficult to achieve because consumers tend to resist. Several approaches to belief change exist:
- *Change currently held beliefs*: It is generally very difficult to attempt to change beliefs that people hold, particularly those that are strongly held, *even if they are inaccurate*. For example, the petroleum industry advertised for a long time that its profits were lower than were commonly believed, and provided extensive factual evidence in its advertising to support this reality. Consumers were suspicious and rejected this information, however.
- *Change the importance of beliefs*: Although the sugar manufacturers would undoubtedly like to decrease the importance of healthy teeth, it is usually not feasible to make beliefs less important—consumers are likely to reason, why, then, would you bother bringing them up in the first place? However, it may be possible to strengthen beliefs that favour us—*e.g.*, a vitamin supplement manufacturer may advertise that it is extremely important for women to replace iron lost through menstruation. Most consumers already agree with this, but the belief can be made stronger.
- *Add beliefs*: Consumers are less likely to resist the addition of beliefs *so long as they do not conflict with existing beliefs*. Thus, the beef industry has added beliefs that beef
  - Is convenient and
  - Can be used to make a number of creative dishes.

  Vitamin manufacturers attempt to add the belief that stress causes vitamin depletion, which sounds quite plausible to most people.

- *Change ideal*: It usually difficult, and very risky, to attempt to change ideals, and only few firms succeed. For example, Hard Candy may have attempted to change the ideal away from traditional beauty towards more unique self expression.

CUSTOMER BEHAVIOUR & CUSTOMER RELATIONSHIP

In my opinion the very best athletes shift the momentum of the game at critical moments, and as spectators this pivot can take our breath away. Nearly any sports fan can recall a game-changing play that enabled the team to take the upper hand and demoralize the competition. Businesses today need to be equally agile when managing their customer relationships. They must be able "to turn on a dime" to capture new markets and break away from the competition. To attract and retain customers, high-performance organizations are moving from a transactional view of their customer to one that measures the value of their relationship as the sum of each and every experience. Those experiences are defined by an increasingly complex set of interactions. And the interactions that make up today's experiences cut across the enterprise and have varying degrees of significance. But making the pivot and successfully connecting with your customers can be intimidating.

Banks typically offer numerous products and services via many channels and with multiple partners, thereby making the prospect of planning, designing and executing effective customer experiences daunting. While Banks must acknowledge the importance of the experience when managing the customer relationships, strategic and operational changes are also required to complete the pivot. The fact is that Banks are at different stages of maturity when it comes to designing and deploying satisfying customer experiences. But regardless of where they are in the process, the bar representing customer expectations has been raised, and the pace of change often exceeds a company's ability to respond. Moreover, an organization must look across industries to understand the types of services their customers are accustomed to, which they will also be expected to deliver.

Perhaps the most important hurdle to clear, however, is the one a company sets for itself – its brand promise. Failing to live up to a brand expectation can damage a company's shareholder value as it creates a gap between what customers expect and what they deliver.As the gap widens, customer frustration takes over and results in disloyalty and churn. Curing this ailment requires a customer-centric approach, including developing market focus and positioning, defining distinctive capabilities and enabling a performance anatomy. High-performance businesses have remarkable clarity when it comes to setting strategic direction, especially regarding big decisions. They always seem to be in the right place at the right time. This occurs as a result of a company's market focus and positioning. They know where and how to compete when they set their business strategy. They also invest in distinctive capabilities which inherently provide direct value to the customer. They design product functions, features and services with the customer experience in mind. Often this means working across the enterprise in addition to multiple channels and business partners.

In this context, a sound performance anatomy within the organization and flawless execution are key factors for success. A corporation's "culture" must breed a mind-set that creating positive customer experiences is the responsibility of all employees, especially those on the front line. Equally important is having the commitment to follow through when times get tough. This means outperforming the competition, which always requires having an effective coach to call the right plays. Naming the right coach in today's environment is an emerging dilemma requiring attention. Banks have wrestled with similar questions before. Some Banks will conclude that they need a customer advocate and change agent in the boardroom – especially if the transformation to customer-centricity is a long-term one. In some cases this responsibility can be filled by a traditional line of business player; in other instances a "chief customer officer" may be the answer. Whatever decision Banks make regarding who should lead the charge, the fact is that making the pivot to this new CRM mind-set is critical and urgent. Delivering the customer interactions that produce optimal experiences to produce long-term relationships is the new mission of CRM executives. Achieving high performance in any industry will depend on the ability to bring all the dimensions of a company together to deliver satisfying outcomes. Now some brief introduction of some CRM and related definitions

Customer

The word derives from "custom," meaning "habit"; a customer was someone who frequented a particular shop, who made it a habit to purchase goods of the sort the shop sold there rather than elsewhere, and with whom the shopkeeper had to maintain a relationship to keep his or her "custom," meaning expected purchases in the future (Hougas).

Customer Relations

The approach of an organization to winning and retaining customers. The most critical activity of any organization wishing to stay in business is its approach to dealing with its customers. Putting customers at the center of all activities is seen by many as an integral part of quality, pricing, and product differentiation (Harry)

History Of CRM

Customer Relationship Management (CRM) is one of those magnificent concepts that swept the business world in the 1990's with the promise of forever changing the way businesses small and large interacted with their customer bases. In the short term, however, it proved to be an unwieldy process that was better in theory than in practice for a variety of reasons. First among these was that it was simply so difficult and expensive to track and keep the high volume of records needed accurately and constantly update them.

In the last several years, however, newer software systems and advanced tracking features have vastly improved CRM capabilities and the real promise of CRM is becoming a reality. As the price of newer, more customizable Internet solutions have hit the marketplace; competition has driven the prices down so that even relatively small businesses are reaping the benefits of some custom CRM programs.

In the beginning...

The 1980's saw the emergence of database marketing, which was simply a catch phrase to define the practice of setting up customer service groups to speak individually to all of a company's customers. In the case of larger, key clients it was a valuable tool for keeping the lines of communication open and tailoring service to the clients needs. In the case of smaller clients, however, it tended to provide repetitive, survey-like information that cluttered databases and didn't provide much insight. As companies began tracking database information, they realized that the bare bones were all that was needed in most cases: what they buy regularly, what they spend, what they do.

Advances in the 1990's

In the 1990's companies began to improve on Customer Relationship Management by making it more of a two-way street. Instead of simply gathering data for their own use, they began giving back to their customers not only in terms of the obvious goal of improved customer service, but in incentives, gifts and other perks for customer loyalty. This was the beginning of the now familiar frequent flyer programs, bonus points on credit cards and a host of other resources that are based on CRM tracking of customer activity and spending patterns.

True CRM comes of age

Real Customer Relationship Management as it's thought of today really began in earnest in the early years of this century. As software companies began releasing newer, more advanced solutions that were customizable across industries, it became feasible to really use the information in a dynamic way. Instead of feeding information into a static database for future reference, CRM became a way to continuously update understanding of customer needs and behavior.

Branching of information, sub-folders, and custom tailored features enabled companies to break down information into smaller subsets so that they could evaluate not only concrete statistics, but information on the motivation and reactions of customers. The Internet provided a huge boon to the development of these huge databases by enabling offsite information storage, where before companies had difficulty supporting the enormous amounts of information. The Internet provided new possibilities and CRM took off as providers began moving toward Internet solutions. With the increased fluidity of these programs came a less rigid relationship between sales, customer service and marketing.

CRM enabled the development of new strategies for more cooperative work between these different divisions through shared information and understanding, leading to increased customer satisfaction from order to end product. Today, CRM is still utilized most frequently by companies that rely heavily on two distinct features: customer service or technology. The three sectors of business that rely most heavily on CRM — and use it to great advantage — are financial services, a variety of high tech corporations and the telecommunications industry. The financial services industry in particular tracks the level of client satisfaction and what customers are looking for in terms of changes and personalized features. They also track changes in investment habits and spending patterns as the economy shifts. Software specific to the industry can give financial service providers truly impressive feedback in these areas.

In recent years however, several factors have contributed to the rapid development and evolution of CRM. These include:-

1. *The growing de-intermediation process* in many industries due to the advent of sophisticated computer and telecommunication technologies that allow producers to directly interact with end-customers. For example, in many industries such as airlines, banks insurance, software or household appliances and even consumables, the de-intermediation process is fast changing the nature of marketing and consequently making relationship marketing more

popular. Databases and direct marketing tools give them the means to individualize their marketing efforts.

2. *Advances in information technology,* networking and manufacturing technology have helped companies to quickly match competition. As a result product quality and cost are no longer significant competitive advantages.
3. *The growth in service economy.* Since services are typically produced and delivered at the same institution, it minimizes the role of the middlemen.
4. *The total quality movement.* Another force driving the adoption of CRM has been the total quality movement. When companies embraced TQM it became necessary to involve customers and suppliers in implementing the program at all levels of the value chain. This needed close working relationships with the customers. Thus several companies such as Motorola, IBM, General Motors, Xerox, Ford, Toyota, etc formed partnering relations with suppliers and customers to practice TQM. Other programs such as JIT and MRP also made use of interdependent relationships between suppliers and customers.
5. *Customer expectations* are changing almost on a daily basis. Newly Empowered customers who choose how to communicate with the companies across various available channels. Also nowadays consumers expect a high degree of personalization.
6. *Emerging real time,* interactive channels including e-mail, ATMs and call centre that must be synchronized with customer's non-electronic activities. The speed of business change, requiring flexibility and rapid adoption to technologies.
7. *Hyper competition.* In the current era of hyper competition, marketers are forced to be more concerned with customer retention and customer loyalty.
8. *Retaining customers is less expensive.* As several researches have found out retaining customers is less expensive and more sustainable competitive advantage than acquiring new ones.
9. *Few suppliers.* On the supply side it pays more to develop closer relationships with a few suppliers than to develop more vendors.

CRM Programs

Today, many businesses such as banks, insurance companies, and other service providers realize the importance of Customer Relationship Management (CRM) and its potential to help them acquire new customers retain existing ones and maximize their lifetime value. At this point, close relationship with customers will require a strong coordination between IT and marketing departments to provide a long-term retention of selected customers. This paper deals with the role of Customer Relationship Management in banking sector and the need for Customer Relationship Management to increase customer value by using some analytical methods in CRM applications.

CRM is a sound business strategy to identify the bank's most profitable customers and prospects, and devotes time and attention to expanding account relationships with those customers through individualized marketing, reprising, discretionary decision making, and customized service-all delivered through the various sales channels that the bank uses. Under this case study, a campaign management in a bank is conducted using data mining tasks such as dependency analysis, cluster profile analysis, concept description, deviation detection, and data visualization. Crucial business decisions with this campaign are made by extracting valid, previously unknown and ultimately comprehensible and actionable knowledge from large databases.

The model developed here answers what the different customer segments are, who more likely to respond to a given offer is, which customers are the bank likely to lose, who most likely to default on credit cards is, what the risk associated with this loan applicant is. Finally, a cluster profile analysis is used for revealing the distinct characteristics of each cluster, and for modeling product propensity, which should be implemented in order to increase the sales.

Customer Relationship Management

In literature, many definitions were given to describe CRM. The main difference among these definitions is technological and relationship aspects of CRM. Some authors from marketing background emphasize technological side of CRM while the others considers IT perspective of CRM. From marketing aspect, CRM is defined by [Couldwell 1998] as ".. a combination of business process and technology that seeks to understand a company's customers from the perspective of who they are, what they do, and what they are like". Technological definition of CRM was given as ".. the market place of the future is undergoing a technology-driven metamorphosis" [Peppers and Rogers 1995]. Consequently, IT and marketing departments must work closely to implement CRM efficiently. Meanwhile, implementation of CRM in banking sector was considered by [Mihelis et al. 2001]. They focused on the evaluation of the critical satisfaction dimensions and the determination of customer groups with distinctive preferences and expectations in the private bank sector.

The methodological approach is based on the principles of multi-criteria modeling and preference disaggregation modeling used for data analysis and interpretation. [Yli-Renko et al. 2001] have focused on the management of the exchange relationships and the implications of such management for the performance and development of technology-based firms and their customers. Spesifically the customer relationships of new technology-based firms has been studied. [Cook and Hababou, 2001] was interested in total sales activities, both volume-related and non-volume related. They also developed a modification of the standard data envelope analysis (DEA) structure using goal programming concepts that yields both a sales and service measures. [Beckett-Camarata et al. 1998] have noted that managing relationships with their customers (especially with employees, channel partners and strategic alliance partners) was critical to the firm's long-term success.

It was also emphasized that customer relationship management based on social exchange and equity significantly assists the firm in developing collaborative, cooperative and profitable long-term relationships. [Yuan and Chang 2001] have presented a mixed-initiative synthesized learning approach for better understanding of customers and the provision of clues for improving customer relationships based on different sources of web customer data. They have also hierarchically segmented data sources into clusters, automatically labeled the features of the clusters, discovered the characteristics of normal, defected and possibly defected clusters of customers, and provided clues for gaining customer retention. [Peppers 2000] has also presented a framework, which is based on incorporating e-business activities, channel management, relationship management and back-office/front-office integration within a customer centric strategy. He has developed four concepts, namely Enterprise, Channel management, Relationships and Management of the total enterprise, in the context of a CRM initiative. [Ryals and Knox 2001] have identified the three main issues that can enable the development of Customer Relationship Management in the service sector; the organizational issues of culture and communication, management metrics and cross-functional integration-especially between marketing and information technology.

CRM Objectives in Banking Sector

The idea of CRM is that it helps businesses use technology and human resources gain insight into the behavior of customers and the value of those customers. If it works as hoped, a business can: provide better customer service, make call centers more efficient, cross sell products more effectively, help sales staff close deals faster, simplify marketing and sales processes, discover new customers, and increase customer revenues. It doesn't happen by simply buying software and installing it. For CRM to be truly effective, an organization must first decide what kind of customer information it is looking for and it must decide what it intends to do with that information. For example, many financial institutions keep track of customers' life stages in order to market appropriate banking products like mortgages or IRAs to them at the right time to fit their needs.

Next, the organization must look into all of the different ways information about customers comes into a business, where and how this data is stored and how it is currently used. One company, for instance, may interact with customers in a myriad of different ways including mail campaigns, Web sites, brick-and-mortar stores, call centers, mobile sales force staff and marketing and advertising efforts. Solid CRM systems link up each of these points. This collected data flows between operational systems (like sales and inventory systems) and analytical systems that can help sort through these records for patterns. Company analysts can then comb through the data to obtain a holistic view of each customer and pinpoint areas where better services are needed. In CRM projects, following data should be collected to run process engine: 1) Responses to campaigns, 2) Shipping and fulfillment dates, 3)Sales and purchase data, 4) Account information, 5) Web registration data, 6) Service and support records, 7) Demographic data, 8) Web sales data.

CONSUMER BEHAVIOUR

Consumers go through a decision-making process that can include up to five steps.

We will use an adapted version of these steps to organize the information in this chapter:

- Need recognition the customer has a need to fulfill or a problem to solve.
- Information search the customer seeks out infor-mation to help satisfy the need.
- Evaluation of alternatives The customer selects a subset of the alternatives and "evaluates them.
- Purchase The customer chooses a particular brand and then buys it.

- Purchase outcomes The customer evaluates the choice made and "decides whether it lives up to expecta-tions.

Using an adaptation of the basic consumer decision-making process shown in we have organized this chapter into four main categories:

- Information search,
- Evaluation- of alternatives,
- Purchase and—consumption, and
- Post purchase evaluation . In purchase of services, these categories do not occur in a lin-ear sequence the way they most often do in the purchase of goods.

As you will see in this chapter, once of the major differences between goods and services is that a greater portion of the evaluation of services succeeds purchase and consumption than is the case with oods. Therefore, while our categorization here follows the sequence consumer's use with goods, we will show how these stages in services depart from evalu-ation of goods.

Analyzing Consumer's Buying Behaviour

The core function of the marketing department is to understand and satisfy consumer need, wants and desire. Consumer behaviour captures all the aspect of purchase, utility and disposal of products and services. In groups and organization are considered within the framework of consumer. Failing to understand consumer behaviour is the recipe for disaster as some companies have found it the hard way. For example, Wal-Mart launched operations in Latin-America with store design replicating that of US markets. However, Latin America consumer differs to US consumer in every aspect. Wal-Mart suffered consequences and failed to create impact.

Social, cultural, individual and emotional forces play a big part in defining consumer buying behaviour. Cultural, sub-culture and social class play an important is finalizing consumer behaviour. For example, consumer growing up in US is exposed to individualism, freedom, achievement, choice, etc. On sub-culture level influence of religion, race, geographic location and ethnicity define consumer behaviour. Social class consists of consumer with the same level of income, education, taste, feeling of superiority and inferiority. Over time consumer can move from one social level to another.

Culture alone cannot define consumer behaviour; social forces also play an important role. Social forces consist of family, friends, peer groups, status and role in society. Groups which have direct or indirect influence on consumer are referred to as reference groups. Primary groups consist of friends, family and peers with whom consumer has direct contact for considerable time. Secondary groups are association where interaction is at formal level and time devoted is less.

Consumer buying behaviour is influenced by individual's own personality traits. These personality traits do not remain the same but change with the life cycle. The choice of occupation and corresponding income level also play part in determining consumer behaviour. A doctor and software engineer both would have different buying pattern in apparel, food automobile etc. Consumers from similar background, occupation and income levels may show a different lifestyle pattern.

An individual buying behaviour is influenced by motivation, perception, learning, beliefs and attitude. These factors affect consumer at a psychological level and determine her overall buying behaviour. Maslow's hierarchy, Herzberg Theory and Freud Theory try and explain people different motivational level in undertaking a buying decision. Perception is what consumer understands about a product through their senses. Marketers have to pay attention to consumer's perception about a brand rather than true offering of the product. Learning comes from experience; consumer may respond to stimuli and purchase a product. A favorable purchase will generate positive experience resulting in pleasant learning. Belief is the pre-conceived notion a consumer has towards a brand. It is kind of influence a brand exerts on consumer. For example, there is a strong belief product coming through German engineering are quality products. Companies may take advantage of this belief and route their production through Germany.

Companies need to think beyond buying behaviour and analyze the actual buying process. Complex buying behaviour requires high involvement of buyers, as it is infrequent in nature, expensive, and they are significant differences among the available choice e.g. automobile. Grocery buying is referred to as habitual buying, which requires less involvement as few differences among brands, frequent and inexpensive. Buying process involves purchase need, decision makers, information search, alternatives evaluation, purchase decision and post purchase behaviour. Companies try hard to understand consumer experience and expectation at every stage of buying process.

Marketers need to figure the right combinations which will initiate purchase need e.g. marketing programs. Companies should ensure consumer have readily available information to take the decision e.g. internet, friends.

Consumers evaluate alternatives based on their brand perception and belief. Companies need to work hard to develop products, which match this perception and belief every time. Final purchase decision is taken looking other's perception of the brand. Post purchase if expectations meet actual performance consumer is satisfied and more likely to repurchase or recommend the brand to others.

Consumer markets are defined by various geographical, social and cultural factors. Furthermore, consumer behaviour is influenced by psychological, personality, reference groups and demographic reasons. Finally actual buying process involves complex process and cycle. Companies have to keep a tab on all three factors in formulating strategy.

Process of Consumer Behavior

Consumer behavior involves the psychological processes that consumers go through in recognizing needs, finding ways to solve these needs, making purchase decisions (e.g., whether or not to purchase a product and, if so, which brand and where), interpret information, make plans, and implement these plans (e.g., by engaging in comparison shopping or actually purchasing a product).

Sources of Influence on the Consumer

The consumer faces numerous sources of influence. Often, we take *cultural* influences for granted, but they are significant. An American will usually not bargain with a store owner. This, however, is a common practice in much of the World. *Physical* factors also influence our behavior. We are more likely to buy a soft drink when we are thirsty, for example, and food manufacturers have found that it is more effective to advertise their products on the radio in the late afternoon when people are getting hungry. A person's *self-image* will also tend to influence what he or she will buy—an upwardly mobile manager may buy a flashy car to project an image of success. *Social* factors also influence what the consumers buy—often, consumers seek to imitate others whom they admire, and may buy the same brands. The social environment can include both the mainstream culture (e.g., Americans are more likely to have corn flakes or ham and eggs for breakfast than to have rice, which is preferred in many Asian countries) and a subculture (e.g., rap music often appeals to a segment within the population that seeks to distinguish itself from the mainstream population). Thus, sneaker manufacturers are eager to have their products worn by admired athletes. Finally, consumer behavior is influenced by *learning*—you try a hamburger and learn that it satisfies your hunger and tastes good, and the next time you are hungry, you may consider another hamburger.

Consumer Choice and Decision Making: Problem Recognition

One model of consumer decision making involves several steps. The first one is *problem recognition*—you realize that something is not as it should be. Perhaps, for example, your car is getting more difficult to start and is not accelerating well. The second step *is information search*—what are some alternative ways of solving the problem? You might buy a new car, buy a used car, take your car in for repair, ride the bus, ride a taxi, or ride a skateboard to work. The third step involves *evaluation of alternatives.* A skateboard is inexpensive, but may be ill-suited for long distances and for rainy days. Finally, we have the *purchase* stage, and sometimes a post-purchase stage (e.g., you return a product to the store because you did not find it satisfactory). In reality, people may go back and forth between the stages. For example, a person may resume alternative identification during while evaluating already known alternatives.

Consumer *involvement* will tend to vary dramatically depending on the type of product. In general, consumer involvement will be higher for products that are very expensive (e.g., a home, a car) or are highly significant in the consumer's life in some other way (e.g., a word processing program or acne medication).

It is important to consider the consumer's motivation for buying products. To achieve this goal, we can use the Means-End chain, wherein we consider a logical progression of consequences of product use that eventually lead to desired end benefit. Thus, for example, a consumer may see that a car has a large engine, leading to fast acceleration, leading to a feeling of performance, leading to a feeling of power, which ultimately improves the consumer's self-esteem.

A handgun may aim bullets with precision, which enables the user to kill an intruder, which means that the intruder will not be able to harm the consumer's family, which achieves the desired end-state of security. In advertising, it is important to portray the desired end-states. Focusing on the large motor will do less good than portraying a successful person driving the car.

Information Search and Decision Making

Consumers engage in both *internal* and *external* information search. *Internal* search involves the consumer identifying alternatives from his or her memory. For certain low involvement products, it is very important that marketing programs achieve "top of mind" awareness. For example, few people will search the *Yellow Pages* for fast food restaurants; thus, the consumer must be able to retrieve one's restaurant from memory before it will be considered. For high involvement products, consumers are more likely to use an *external* search. Before buying a car, for example, the consumer may ask friends' opinions, read reviews in *Consumer Reports*, consult several web sites, and visit several dealerships. Thus, firms that make products that are selected predominantly through external search must invest in having information available to the consumer in need—e.g., through brochures, web sites, or news coverage.

A *compensatory* decision involves the consumer "trading off" good and bad attributes of a product. For example, a car may have a low price and good gas mileage but slow acceleration. If the price is sufficiently inexpensive and gas efficient, the consumer may then select it over a car with better acceleration that costs more and uses more gas. Occasionally, a decision will involve a *non-compensatory* strategy. For example, a parent may reject all soft drinks that contain artificial sweeteners. Here, other good features such as taste and low calories *cannot* overcome this one "non-negotiable" attribute.

The amount of effort a consumer puts into searching depends on a number of factors such as the *market* (how many competitors are there, and how great are differences between brands expected to be?), *product characteristics* (how important is this product? How complex is the product? How obvious are indications of quality?), *consumer characteristics* (how interested is a consumer, generally, in analysing product characteristics and making the best possible deal?), and *situational* characteristics.

Two interesting issues in decisions are:

- *Variety seeking* (where consumers seek to try new brands not because these brands are expected to be "better" in any way, but rather because the consumer wants a "change of pace," and
- *"Impulse" purchases*—unplanned buys. This represents a somewhat "fuzzy" group. For example, a shopper may plan to buy vegetables but only decide in the store to actually buy broccoli and corn. Alternatively, a person may buy an item which is currently on sale, or one that he or she remembers that is needed only once inside the store.

A number of factors involve consumer choices. In some cases, consumers will be more *motivated*. For example, one may be more careful choosing a gift for an in-law than when buying the same thing for one self. Some consumers are also more motivated to *comparison shop* for the best prices, while others are more *convenience* oriented. *Personality* impacts decisions. Some like variety more than others, and some are more receptive to stimulation and excitement in trying new stores. *Perception* influences decisions. Some people, for example, can taste the difference between generic and name brand foods while many cannot.

Selective perception occurs when a person is paying attention only to information of interest. For example, when looking for a new car, the consumer may pay more attention to car ads than when this is not in the horizon. Some consumers are put off by perceived *risk*.

Thus, many marketers offer a money back guarantee. Consumers will tend to change their behavior through *learning*—e.g., they will avoid restaurants they have found to be crowded and will settle on brands that best meet their tastes. Consumers differ in the *values* they hold (e.g., some people are more committed to recycling than others who will not want to go through the hassle). We will consider the issue of lifestyle under segmentation.

The Family Life Cycle

For purposes of this discussion, a "couple" may either be married or merely involve living together. The breakup of a non-marital relationship involving cohabitation is similarly considered equivalent to a divorce. In real life, this situation is, of course, a bit more complicated. For example, many couples undergo divorce. Then we have one of the scenarios:

Single parenthood can result either from divorce or from the death of one parent. Divorce usually entails a significant change in the relative wealth of spouses. In some cases, the non-custodial parent (usually the father) will not pay the required child support, and even if he or she does, that still may not leave the custodial parent and children as well off as they were during the marriage. On the other hand, in some cases, some non-custodial parents will be called on to pay a large part of their income in child support. This is particularly a problem when the non-custodial parent remarries and has additional children in the second (or subsequent marriages).

As a person gets older, he or she tends to advance in his or her career and tends to get greater income (exceptions: maternity leave, divorce, retirement). Unfortunately, obligations also tend to increase with time (at least until one's mortgage has been paid off). Children and paying for one's house are two of the greatest expenses.

Note that although a single person may have a lower income than a married couple, the single may be able to buy more discretionary items.

Note that although a single person may have a lower income than a married couple, the single may be able to buy more discretionary items.

Family Decision Making

Individual members of families often serve different roles in decisions that ultimately draw on shared family resources. Some individuals are *information gatherers/holders*, who seek out information about products of relevance. These individuals often have a great deal of power because they may selectively pass on information that favours their chosen alternatives. *Influencers* do not ultimately have the power decide between alternatives, but they may make their wishes known by asking for specific products or causing embarrassing situations if their demands are not met. The *decision maker(s)* have the power to determine issues such as:

- Whether to buy;
- Which product to buy (pick-up or passenger car?);
- Which brand to buy;
- Where to buy it; and
- When to buy.

Note, however, that the role of the decision maker is separate from that of the *purchaser*. From the point of view of the marketer, this introduces some problems since the purchaser can be targeted by point-of-purchase (POP) marketing efforts that cannot be aimed at the decision maker. Also note that the distinction between the purchaser and decision maker may be somewhat blurred:

- The decision maker may specify what kind of product to buy, but not which brand;
- The purchaser may have to make a substitution if the desired brand is not in stock;
- The purchaser may disregard instructions (by error or deliberately).

It should be noted that family decisions are often subject to a great deal of conflict. The reality is that few families are wealthy enough to avoid a strong tension between demands on the family's resources. Conflicting pressures are especially likely in families with children and/or when only one spouse works outside the home. Note that many decisions inherently come down to values, and that there is frequently no "objective" way to arbitrate differences. One spouse may believe that it is important to save for the children's future; the other may value spending now (on private schools and computer equipment) to help prepare the children for the future. Who is right? There is no clear answer here. The situation becomes even more complex when more parties—such as children or other relatives—are involved. Some family members may resort to various strategies to get their way. One is *bargaining*—one member will give up something in return for someone else. For example, the wife says that her husband can take an expensive course in gourmet cooking if she can buy a new pickup truck. Alternatively, a child may promise to walk it every day if he or she can have a hippopotamus. Another strategy is *reasoning*—trying to get the other person(s) to accept one's view through logical argumentation. Note that even when this is done with a sincere intent, its potential is limited by legitimate differences. Also note that individuals may simply try to "wear down" the other party by endless talking in the guise of reasoning.

Various manipulative strategies may also be used. One is *impression management*, where one tries to make one's side look good (e.g., argue that a new TV will help the children see educational TV when it is really mostly wanted to see sports programming, or argue that all "decent families make a contribution to the church"). *Authority* involves asserting one's "right" to make a decision (as the "man of the house," the mother of the children, or the one who makes the most money). *Emotion* involves making an emotional display to get one's way (e.g., a man cries if his wife will not let him buy a new rap album).

The Means-End Chain

Consumers often buy products not because of their attributes *per se* but rather because of the ultimate benefits that these attributes provide, in turn leading to the satisfaction of ultimate values. For example, a consumer may not be particularly interested in the chemistry of plastic roses, but might reason as follows:

The important thing in a means-end chain is to start with an *attribute*, a concrete characteristic of the product, and then logically progress to a series of consequences (which tend to become progressively more abstract) that end with a *value* being satisfied. Thus, each chain *must start with an attribute and end with a value.* An important implication of means-end chains is that it is usually most effective in advertising to *focus on higher level items*. For example, in the flower example above, an individual giving the flowers to the significant other might better be portrayed than the flowers alone.

Attitudes

Consumer attitudes are a composite of a consumer's (1) beliefs about, (2) feelings about, (3) and behavioural intentions toward some "object"—

within the context of marketing, usually a brand, product category, or retail store. These components are viewed together since they are highly interdependent and together represent forces that influence how the consumer will react to the object.

Beliefs: The first component is *beliefs.* A consumer may hold both positive beliefs toward an object (e.g., coffee tastes good) as well as negative beliefs (e.g., coffee is easily spilled and stains papers). In addition, some beliefs may be neutral (coffee is black), and some may be differ in valance depending on the person or the situation (e.g., coffee is hot and stimulates—good on a cold morning, but not good on a hot summer evening when one wants to sleep). Note also that the beliefs that consumers hold need not be accurate (e.g., that pork contains little fat), and some beliefs may, upon closer examination, be contradictory.

Affect: Consumers also hold certain feelings toward brands or other objects. Sometimes these feelings are based on the beliefs (e.g., a person feels nauseated when thinking about a hamburger because of the tremendous amount of fat it contains), but there may also be feelings which are relatively independent of beliefs. For example, an extreme environmentalist may believe that cutting down trees is morally wrong, but may have positive affect toward Christmas trees because he or she unconsciously associates these trees with the experience that he or she had at Christmas as a child.

Behavioural intention: The behavioural intention is what the consumer plans to do with respect to the object (e.g., buy or not buy the brand). As with affect, this is sometimes a logical consequence of beliefs (or affect), but may sometimes reflect other circumstances—e.g., although a consumer does not really like a restaurant, he or she will go there because it is a hangout for his or her friends.

Changing attitudes is generally *very difficult*, particularly when consumers suspect that the marketer has a self-serving "agenda" in bringing about this change (e.g., to get the consumer to buy more or to switch brands). Here are some possible methods:

- *Changing affect.* One approach is to try to change affect, which may or may not involve getting consumers to change their beliefs. One strategy uses the approach of *classical conditioning* try to "pair" the product with a liked stimulus. For example, we "pair" a car with a beautiful woman. Alternatively, we can try to get people to like the advertisement and hope that this liking will "spill over" into the purchase of a product. For example, the Pillsbury Doughboy does not really emphasize the conveyance of much information to the consumer; instead, it attempts to create a warm, "fuzzy" image. Although Energizer Bunny ads try to get people to believe that their batteries last longer, the main emphasis is on the likeable bunny. Finally, products which are better known, through the *mere exposure* effect, tend to be better liked—that is, the more a product is advertised and seen in stores, the more it will generally be liked, *even if consumers to do not develop any specific beliefs about the product*.

- *Changing behavior*. People like to believe that their behavior is rational; thus, once they use our products, chances are that they will continue unless someone is able to get them to switch. One way to get people to switch to our brand is to use temporary price discounts and coupons; however, when consumers buy a product on deal, they may justify the purchase based on that deal (i.e., the low price) and may then switch to other brands on deal later. A better way to get people to switch to our brand is to at least temporarily obtain better shelf space so that the product is more convenient. Consumers are less likely to use this availability as a rationale for their purchase and may continue to buy the product even when the product is less conveniently located.
- *Changing beliefs*. Although attempting to change beliefs is the obvious way to attempt attitude change, particularly when consumers hold unfavorable or inaccurate ones, this is often difficult to achieve because consumers tend to resist. Several approaches to belief change exist:
- *Change currently held beliefs*. It is generally very difficult to attempt to change beliefs that people hold, particularly those that are strongly held, *even if they are inaccurate*. For example, the petroleum industry advertised for a long time that its profits were lower than were commonly believed, and provided extensive factual evidence in its advertising to support this reality. Consumers were suspicious and rejected this information, however.
- *Change the importance of beliefs*. Although the sugar manufacturers would undoubtedly like to decrease the importance of healthy teeth, it is usually not feasible to make beliefs less important—consumers are likely to reason, why, then, would you bother bringing them up in the first place? However, it may be possible to strengthen beliefs that favour us—e.g., a vitamin supplement manufacturer may advertise that it is extremely important for women to replace iron lost through menstruation. Most consumers already agree with this, but the belief can be made stronger.

- *Add beliefs.* Consumers are less likely to resist the addition of beliefs *so long as they do not conflict with existing beliefs*. Thus, the beef industry has added beliefs that beef (1) is convenient and (2) can be used to make a number of creative dishes. Vitamin manufacturers attempt to add the belief that stress causes vitamin depletion, which sounds quite plausible to most people.
- *Change ideal.* It usually difficult, and very risky, to attempt to change ideals, and only few firms succeed. For example, Hard Candy may have attempted to change the ideal away from traditional beauty toward more unique self expression.
- *One-sided vs. two-sided appeals.* Attitude research has shown that consumers often tend to react more favourably to advertisements which either (1) admit something negative about the sponsoring brand (e.g., the Volvo is a clumsy car, but very safe) or (2) admits something positive about a competing brand (e.g., a competing supermarket has slightly lower prices, but offers less service and selection). Two-sided appeals must, contain overriding arguments why the sponsoring brand is ultimately superior—that is, in the above examples, the "but" part must be emphasized.

BEHAVIOURAL SEGMENTATION

By segmenting the consumer markets according to their behavioural patterns, a company can target the acquisition and retention of highly profitable and potentially lucrative customers. The benefits of performing customer behavioural analysis can thus be listed as:

- Gaining meaningful insight and actionable business intelligence at reasonable costs
- It is now practical to develop extremely cost-effective and highly targeted marketing campaigns
- Businesses now focus on knowing their customers as real people with real needs and preferences, leading to better customer satisfaction and hence attraction
- Behaviour is a stable element on which to base a website as it evolves slowly over time
- Businesses stop throwing away money spent on marketing to the wrong customers as they can now known who their customers are and what they desire
- Best point of contact for credible dialogue can be identified
- Loyal customers cost less than acquiring new ones and are a great source of information to create new and innovative services

By knowing their customers, a business can be assured of the fact that they will always be kept ahead of their competition. The information obtained after customer behaviour analysis is performed allows businesses to gain insight into how their potential customers interact with their websites, what is working on their sites, and what is not. Customer-focused marketing is therefore essential as part of the activities performed to ensure the success.

Customer-Focused Marketing

All marketing is done with the customer in mind. Marketing can in fact be referred to as an on-going conversation occuring between business and customer. It is therefore necessary for businesses to gain in-depth knowledge of their relative customers so that the best marketing strategies can be employed in order to attract these potential buyers. This can effectively be done by performing activities such as customer behaviour analysis to ensure customer retention. Listed below are a number of tips to aid businesses striving towards customer retention through marketing efforts:

Marketing as a Conversation

Direct interaction with customers is necessary to essentially find out what it is that they are wanting. This marketing conversation involves a process running from action - reaction - feedback - repeat. Businesses need to be willing to take the time to listen to their customers as this can ensure a business of putting something up for offer which is of great worth amongst their targeted consumers, and is relative to their particular needs and desires.

It is required for businesses to constantly perform marketing promotion so that these customers will come back for more. Giving satisfaction to first-time buyers can prove effective for a business in the long-run for the reason that by giving customers what they desire the first time round, customer retention is encouraged through this form of customer loyalty.

Active Customers

Making customers feel as though they are in control is an effective strategy in customer-focused marketing. This is done by transforming consumers into active customers who are given the ability to make choices for themselves by actively engaging in promotions and, hereby, deciding on the best possible products and services their money can buy. Customer retention is encouraged through this interaction with customers which aids in customer loyalty. Businesses need to make each and every one of their customers feel good about themselves by giving them something to do. Therefore, retaining customers means keeping them happy by keeping them active.

Determining Future Customer Behaviour

This is most effectively done through an analysis of the actual behaviour of past and present customers. Actual behaviour needs to be differentiated from demographic behaviours (which are implied consumer characteristics). Actual behaviour is, as such, better at predicting the future which is done by keeping a watch over the actions customers perform with regard to online purchases and the products they purchase over the Internet.

Allocating Resources for Marketing

B usinesses need to take their budget into consideration when allocating resources for promotions. It is well-known amongst businesses that some marketing activities will generate higher profits than others and data therefore needs to be created by interacting with customers in order to consequentially identify the most profitable promotions, which will be delivered to the right customer at the right time, without wasting time or money.

Hereby, effective marketing means avoiding unprofitable promotion which will as such mean not reaching the right customers and wasting money.

What Can Intoweb Do For You?

Customer behaviour analysis forms a major part in the process of overall website analysis. Customer behaviour can be tracked on the Internet with the right Internet business solutions in place and therefore the variety of website analysis applications and software which is available enables Intoweb to detect important changes in potential customer value; which can then be applied to a new or existing website to help increase website success.

Intoweb can with regard to customer behavioural analysis offer our clients the following:

- Place emphasis on the ads, media and products creating long-term high potential value customers, while downplaying the ones that do not
- Create high ROI marketing programs

- Make more money selling to customers by driving higher sales while all the more reducing costs
- Predict when your best customers are about to leave you and react with customer retention and save-a-customer programs
- Quantify the effects of marketing and operational initiatives by linking them to a change in potential customer value
- Plan and implement the most effective marketing campaigns for our clients with a top-down strategic focus
- Target campaign activities to increase campaign velocity, flexibility, and return-on-investment
- Optimise plans made to increase campaign velocity, flexibility and ROI
- Learn by measuring campaign results and integrating new knowledge into refined strategies and future campaigns so that our services only get better over time
- By performing web analytics, we are indeed known for our reliability and our capability to get the best desired results possible for each and everyon of our clients

CONSUMERISM, CONSUMER BEHAVIOUR AND IDENTITY: THE EXTENT IN POLICY DECISION-MARKETING

Today's market is characterized by highly competitive organizations which are all vying for consumer's loyalty. Profit-oriented firms are faced with the challenge to maintain their own competitive edge in order to survive and be successful. Strategies are carefully planned and executed to gain the ultimate goal of all: company growth. However, internal factors are not the only elements which influence growth. There are also external factors and components working within the organization which shape the direction of the organization. Among this is the consumer - the fuel of the organization.

The dynamics of contemporary living define most of the aspects of human life today. From traditional ways to technologically driven mechanisms, life indeed is no longer the same decades and centuries ago. The recent developments and revolutionary processes resulting to increased convenience of people in various applications contributed to the topical standards of living. Along with the changing business world, customers change as well, becoming more demanding, knowledgeable and highly sophisticated.

Before, it is enough if they have purchased a product or service the best way and condition possible. Now, the process of commercial interaction does not end that way. There are more complex steps to be completed to be able to achieve satisfactory results. In turn, company management had shifted their focus on their clients or customers so as to stay successfully in business. This transition meant that organizations have to completely reformulate their conventional business aims and purposes from being process-focused to customer-centred.

In the business, the consumers eventually developed as a result of the radical emergence and amalgamation of innovative and manipulative processes in the global marketplace. Established characteristics in terms of their behaviour and identity are important aspects to consider in studying the significant role they play in any economic endeavor. Furthermore, the subject of consumerism in given societies is becoming popular and a sought-after area of research. In connection, the presence of consumer policies and laws in the global market serve as controlling mechanisms to regulate the diversity of the international economic battlefield. This makes the buying experience even more multifaceted and interactive.

Advertising is the common playground where consumers ensnare themselves with products/services available in the market. The adverse effects of advertising are perceived to be reinforcing elements in the development of consumerist behaviour and culture. This is where the aspect of policy decision making is applicable. The creation of regulating policies in connection to advertising and its effects to consumerism and consumer behaviour is quantified.

This document aims to critically analyse the extent of the relationship of consumerism, consumer behaviour and identity with respect to policy decision-making of the state and business organizations predominantly in terms of the advertising medium. Specifically, it opts to qualify the extent of consumerism in relation to consumer behaviour and culture. Guidelines in advertising are the parametres to be used in policy decision-making. Additionally, it will provide several conceptual backgrounds about the said areas of the general consumer. To fully substantiate the arguments and findings in this research, information taken from vast sources of literature is used as supporting documents. There are also specific examples to be used to show the claims.

Initially, the understanding buyer behaviour is one of the more perplexing tasks confronting every manager. The difficulty arises from the heterogeneity of buyers, from their being groups of individuals who differ from one another. But differences notwithstanding, consumers do share attitudes, opinions, reactions, and desires at various times. Business experience, marketing research, theoretical constructs and models, and trial-and-error methods help to find some of the common denominators.

Believing on the idea that the consumers are the fuel of every profit and/or non-profit organization, studying their behaviour and identity remains parallel and important in every decision-making activity. Consumers have always been regarded as vital factors in relation to different organizational operations and functioning. They live and act in a constantly changing cultural, social, technological, legal, and economic environment. Shaped by the environment, marketing institutions, and activities in return have a major/minor impact on it. Their behaviour and identity, on the other hand, significantly determine the business future in a particular part of country and given culture. As we all know, as region varies on its own, so does the consumer behaviour and identity of such group of people in a region. Through observations of the consumer behaviour, the category in competition, organization, and the marketing strategies of businesses are well evaluated. Consumer behaviour is influenced by different aspects in its environment. It can be viewed with different factors such as the cultural, personal, psychological and social factors of the consumers.

The study of consumer behaviour is one of the most interesting and challenging as well as important aspects in marketing management. Practically, essential decisions that are taken in developing an effective marketing mix for specific product/service are based in the systematic knowledge of the consumers that make up its permanent target market. Believes that understanding the behaviour of the consumer is the most basic step in helping marketing authorities to visualize and predict future trends, reactions, and changes in the marketing mix. It may also serve as a reference in determining the potentials of new products and its adoption. Consumer behaviour is said to be closely associated to marketing research – another important field that deserves further comprehensive investigation.

Each organization provides some products/services that are used by consumers, even though they may not always recognize as products/services by the consumers as such. For example, it seems fairly obvious that the college students who drink a cola produced by a specific beverage company are the consumers of that beverage product.

In a general sense, we can all think of public high school students as the consumers of a state's educational product; voters can be thought of as consumers of a political candidate's leadership and administration product; and, the members of a religious group might be viewed as consumers of a church's spiritual product. Thus, the study of the behaviour of consumers involves an examination of a wide range record of everyday human buying behaviour.

Consumer behaviour as defined by is "the activities that people engage in when selecting, purchasing, and using products and services so as to satisfy needs and desires". continued: "...such activities involve mental and emotional processes, in addition to physical actions". In general perspective, consumer behaviour studies individuals, groups or organizations with regards to obtaining, using and disposing of products and services. It also accounts the decision processes that lead and follow these behaviours. Consumer behaviour investigates consumers' actions, as well as the reasons for those behaviours. In order to fully understand the broad spectrum of consumer behaviour, identified its macroscopic and microscopic perspectives.

Consumer behaviour in a macro level categorizes marketers to look for demographic shifts as well as the general public's values, beliefs and practices which affect their interaction with the economic marketplace. Meanwhile, the micro level indicates consumer behaviour focused on human behaviour and the motivations underlying these behaviours. These concepts are drawn out from sociological and psychological perspectives as proven results of studies in the said aspect.

There are many factors that determine these activities, and the product/ service is just one of them. There are some frameworks that helps explain customer behaviours. Among these are brand orientation model and integrated framework for cross-cultural consumer behaviour. Others, on the other hand, are expressed through demographic research, such as the relationship of culture on consumer behaviour. These models and studies are applicable to consumer behaviour in general products/services. But delving into such topic discussion will make this report technical and might astray away from its real objectives.

In the recent years, the study of consumer behaviour and consumer decision-making has become a sought-after research field. Topics in the various fields of consumer science are considered hot stuffs in scholastic as well as marketing management sectors. Theoretically, consumer science includes the former discipline of home economics – the foundation of basic consumption. The consumer science discipline also evolves around consumer behaviour and decision making concerning the necessities of live and survival. Among these are foods and nutrition, clothing and textiles, housing and interior merchandise in everyday living. Believe that the providence of the aforementioned goods will result to physical, psychological, socio-psychological and financial satisfaction in a complex micro and macro environment. Of specific importance, observed that buying and consumer decision-making are complicated as based on the result of external influences that have to be handled within an internal frame of reference that has come about through consumer socialization.

The complex phenomenon of consumer behaviour is dependent to some considerable factors in the working environment of people. It is somewhat innate or even cultural in its foundation, external or internal in nature, or just a by-product of the common circumstances in the purchasing experience.

Advertising is among the external factors that plays a great role in the buying experience of people. For the record, an average American household exposure to television advertising is about an estimated 7 hours per day times 9 to 16 minutes of nonprogram material per hour. Additionally, advertising traditions hold that the average consumer is exposed to over 1,500 radio, television, newspaper, magazine, and/or billboard advertisements per day. As a result, it could be said that advertising and its component influence the behaviour of consumers. The promises of advertised products/services are subject to trial and materialization by the consumer. Thus, purchasing the said product/service is the sole way to prove its claims.

The daily exposure of people to all the different kinds of media makes it accessible and convenient for them to recognize the presence of the latest product/service in the market. With the assistance of ads, consumers are engaged in buying experience. As a part of their consumer behaviour stimulation, there are internal assessments that are occurring within the limits of the human nature. In Taiwan, and colleagues studied the behaviour of consumers in relation to the medium. They indicated that the elements of advertising, the manner of presentation, or a certain ad for instance, greatly affect the culture, concept and emotions, and other human attributes of a certain setting. More often than not, advertising contributes to the development of changes in connection to the existing behaviour and identity of the consumer. It may also lead to the practice of consumerism.

According to, most advertising agencies keep on striking into insights on how to gain a deeper understanding on the reason why consumers behave the way they do. Further, advertising practitioners found assessment in probing the thoughts of every individual by using focus groups as variables in eliciting ideas for new products and promotional campaigns to be established. In advertising, I believe that people who are only exposed to recurring ads focus and elaborate on tangential cues such as the credibility of the source. For instance, a controversial political figure endorsing a product/service will simply be viewed as trash among its critics. Thus, the purchase of the product/service is almost impossible. This certain example is related in the process of forming brand attitude among the ordinary consumer that falls under the capacity of the advertising medium.

Largely, researchers linked consumer decision making in the study of perception. The study of perception is largely bounded on what humans consciously or subconsciously add to or subtract from their raw sensory inputs to produce a private and selective picture of the world. In general term, it is the process that involves the individual's decision in selecting, interpreting, and organizing stimuli into a meaningful and coherent picture of the world. A stimulus is any unit of input to the senses – may it be products, packages, brand names, advertisements, and commercials. In studies of consumerism, it has become almost a cliché to claim that the purchase, use and display of goods in some way expresses social identities and is rooted to the persuasive effects of advertising. The relationship of consumerism and customer behaviour plus advertising has been long overdue. Its interconnection opened up various horizons for academic marketing and management probing.

Consumerism is already deep-rooted part of every given culture. It has become so disturbing on a global scale. Defining consumerism is always equated into a negative image. However, with this report, consumerism will be tackled in connection to the rights of consumers as well as its association to consumer behaviour and identity towards policy decision-making. Traditionally, consumerism is known as the purchasing of products beyond the basic requirement of consumption.

Indicates: "In a Buddhist view of mutual co-arising and radical interrelatedness the cause of consumerism is boundlessly plural—a virtual infinity of conditions affecting and being affected by countless other conditions. The desires of individuals have been conditioned by the way parents raised them, by the historical conditions... by the use of media, and so on."

Furthermore, consumerism is related to environmental conditions that are persuasive. These conditions are contributory factors along with politics, economics, social institutions, industrial technology, and ideological tendency. Take for example, the consumerist behaviour of Filipino people during the holiday season perfectly show the factors affecting the practice.

With the various criticisms in consumerism, it has been connected with media applications such as advertising. In advertising, consumerism is a powerful mechanism that is driven by considerable sums spent on advertising. These are designed to generate both a desire to follow trends and the consequential personal self-reward scheme based on personal procurement. The basic idea of materialism and consumerism is one of the by-products of overt advertising.

The presence of consumerism in various cultures is studied in relation to policy decision making. The regulations made by the state are directed to the welfare and being of every buying individual. Laws on consumer rights are created to protect people against abuses in the economic marketplace. There are given considerations that are taken at hand when passing and eventually implementing such laws. The extent of consumer behaviour and identity as well as the relationship of culture are fully considered in realizing its intended purpose. For instance, the advertising medium proliferate consumerism. Every advertisement is produced with the aims to procure interest among the buyer and persuade him/her to have the product/service. The aesthetics of advertising easily provoke a culture of consumerism. Paradoxically, quaintness in advertising shows consumerism correcting itself, disassociating itself from its own conceited techniques, hiding consumerism from the consumer and ostensibly rejecting the commercialism on which it is based. Thus, animated or unrealistic presentation of some advertisements could easily attain its goal - persuasion.

In reference to my personal experiences, advertising materials that are too-good-to-be-true are appealing to me. The tendency is that I am persuaded to try on the product/service being advertise. My buying behaviour was stimulated by the ad. Therefore, it creates an identity that can lead to addiction and constant purchase beyond my normal consumption. As a result, I am practicing a culture of consumerism.

As of the moment, there are government policies that control media like advertising standards. Countries like UK, Canada, and some developing nations maintain protocol in using the said medium. It is always subject to regulation and continuous assessment. The measurement of its extent of applicability in connection to the personal characteristics of consumers is strictly implemented. Its degree of interdependency to consumer behaviour and the present existing culture is not fully taken into considerable contemplation. This is the reason why the extent of policies must be measured in connection to consumer behaviour as well as identity.

The emphasis on consumerism and an increasing awareness of environmental and ethical issues all have their implications for marketing strategists. Many firms are blending communications activities with public purpose policy decision making. Of course, innovation and the production of the new are intrinsic to consumerism and tend to structure the conceptual field of the study of consumerism. The connection of creating advertising policies to the release of new products/services is undeniable. Thus, advertising is among the medium where policies must be evaluated.

New connections between the cultural and the political, the visual and the material, advertising and personal belonging, consumerism and the rights of citizenship has been premeditated issues tackled by each government worldwide. Within European nation-states, individuals' access to citizenship rights has increasingly been framed through discourses of consumerism. The presence of communal and societal awareness and battle against consumerism is another turning point for legislative undertakings of the state's authorities. People in various countries individually contribute to the cessation of consumerist behaviours or practices. The sense of national belonging and citizenship to consumerism and focus on choice as a prime mechanism in the production of consumer-citizenship identities linked the idea of individual behaviour and culture. Thus, the fight against consumerist attitudes is unyielding.

With the present realities, the intervention of state policies in the subject of consumerism is appropriate. State policies must deal with the basics of consumer behaviour. Considering the various factors affecting the decision making of consumers, the government is expected to regulate advertising processes in all sorts of medium – print or broadcast. While advertising is a recognizable media to proliferate economic activity, policies created must deal with the common protection of consumers. However, the degree of effect to consumerism is boundless due to the fact that consumers possess the freedom to choose.

This is aside from the truth that every consumer differs in behaviour and identity. In advertising standards created, implemented, and promoted by authority, it is highly needed that every advertisement must present only what is real and substantial to consumers. The ethics of advertising is necessary for every media regulating system. Advertising policies and standards posed by authorities must be in accordance to the general moral discretion of the society and organizations. Thus, advertisements of organizations must maintain its commitment to corporate social responsibility. Prior to its public release, every advertisement must be taken into legal scrutiny in order to identify its effect in establishing the culture of consumerism. The protection of consumers' rights and welfare is the main concern of the state as well as the business organization.

Furthermore, the measurement of the extent of consumerism, consumer behaviour and identity in policy decision making of government is rooted on the natural laws of what is acceptable and not. As previously stated, ethics in advertising is the name of the game.

For instance,: "... The Federal Trade Commission should become concerned with regulating... type of potentially unfair advertising.... the FTC prohibits a company from stating that its product will cure an illness when such is not the case, the FTC might begin prohibiting a company from stating that its product will encourage sexual satisfaction, make one more masculine/feminine, or promote a happier homelife when such is not the case".

There are more concerns that the government and lawmakers need to qualify in relation to advertising regulation. But then again, the dynamic state in every given situation of human life is a significant factor in determining the extent in policy decision making and taking.

Materialism in modern life is rooted in the innate freedom and quest for satisfaction of people. In the U.S., personal freedoms and life satisfaction or the need to optimize on life's happenings are both integral elements in lifestyles. By this fact, the tendency to acquire a consumerist behaviour is ubiquitous.

It is indeed true. There are internal processes that occur during a buying experience. This is simply apparent due to the personal characteristics of certain consumers especially to the environment. and colleagues stated that "the standards and values that stem from the environment greatly influence consumer behaviour, affecting purchasing and consumption activities, and the business organizations concerned."

The cultural context of consumer behaviour can be defined as "the totality of the customs, arts, sciences, religions, politics, and economics that distinguishes one society from another, and that influences the individual consumer's behaviour". The presence of subculture among the main culture makes the difference. Subculture is usually defined as a category of people who share a sense of identification that is distinguishable from that of the culture as a whole. This shared sense of identification may result from a shared set of values, from a common history, or from similarity in socio-demographic attributes. Social class is perhaps the type of subculture that is most often used by consumer psychologists. The attribute that distinguishes between levels of social class is the relative level of social benefits. In connection to principles of consumerism, it could be assumed that this process is now a subculture.

All in all, the premise on economic interpretation of consumerism as the belief in the freedom to choose among consumers should indicate the economic structure of a society. This must be the basis of evaluating the extent of policy decision making of the states as well as business organizations. The relationship of consumerism, consumer behaviour and identity in connection to activities, policies, and actions taken by the state and business organization must be based and dependent on the consumer's behaviour and identity.

The practice of consumerism, consumer behaviour and identity will always be pertinent to the buying experience of consumers. Thus, proper regulation of such laws implemented must be strictly determined and observed. This will eventually serve the welfare of the ultimate beneficiaries – the consumers.

6

Customer Knowledge Management

Among other reasons firms have a low return on their information technology investments is that they only poorly understand what the technology makes possible. The objectives and role of information in customer-focused management must be understood. Customer-intelligent firms use their customer knowledge to drive all of the firm's activities and decisions.

When firms have so much opportunity to interact with their customers, why is it that they treat their customers like strangers? The reason is not lack of information on their customers, but a lack in a firm's managing of that information. Firms may have the ability to capture that information, but may not process and utilize the knowledge to manage relationships with their customers. Information technology has only placed this realization in sharp focus.

On the other hand, the power of information technology has also raised the ugly specter of abuse of privacy when firms have access to a vast amount of customer information. Network Solutions, the first company that registered addresses on the .com, .org, and .net domains for the Internet, now a unit of VeriSign, raised eyebrows when it planned to sell names, street addresses, and other information gathered from businesses and individuals who signed up for an Internet address. There are several examples of Internet companies that have been reined in for their use of customer information. DoubleClick Inc., decided against combining Web-tracking data with offline databases. Toysmart was not allowed to sell its customer database when it shut down.

Hagel and Rayport suggest that customers will become savvy about their personal information and be reluctant to divulge it unless they receive some value for it. They predict that customers will win the battle over their information and firms they call "infomediaries" will "become custodians, agents and brokers of customer information, marketing it to businesses on consumers' behalf while protecting their privacy at the same time."

Nevertheless, customer information is crucial for a customer focus because of the need to make and execute customer-focused decisions in all aspects of the business. Firms will continue to require customer information to do business. Information technology will continue to challenge a firm's judgment in obtaining and using customer information.

Traditionally, research on the customer has been at the aggregate level, most utilized during the new product development process, to test new product ideas, in test marketing, and to test new campaign concepts in the realm of advertising. Marketing research has been standard practice preceding the launch of new products or advertising campaigns. Most firms conduct regular market research activities to direct segmentation decisions such as targeting and to determine how to reach segments.

Scholars have implored managers to "spend a day in the life of your customer" and to "get inside the lives of your customers, " so as to obtain a deeper understanding of customers. The quality of the knowledge on the customer is much greater because of direct observation. Obtaining that knowledge is only the first step. The basic skill of listening involves competence in sensing, evaluating *and* responding. A study of 500 new car buyers found customer perceptions of these three dimensions of listening to be strongly linked to trust in the salesperson.

There are also benefits within the firm when the practice of listening to customers is emphasized by senior managers. Senior managers at First Chicago discovered that in emphasizing listening to the customer they found a cultural change within the organization. Customer knowledge gained from firsthand customer contact is very persuasive. Smart CEOs at firms like IBM, Cisco, and EMC intuitively realize this, and their senior managers contact their major customers on a regular basis. These firms also act on that information to improve relationships with those important customers.

The benefits of customer knowledge management have concentrated at the individual level. For example, Dreyfus, like other mutual fund firms, keeps track of client activity, claiming that they can predict when a client is going to shift money out of their mutual funds. Clients receive a call from a Dreyfus representative, who wants to know how the client feels about the investment and if his or her goals are being met. If Dreyfus is able to track clients at all stages of the consumption process, then the firm has a better chance of retaining the customer. A number of CRM- and ERP-type software programmes allow companies to track processes in the life of a specific sales order from order entry all the way to delivery to customer. Of course, FedEx introducing package tracking is a well-known example from years ago. There are a number of benefits of information technology for firms of any size.

Siebel software allows Honeywell to spot problems and opportunities by tracking and analyzing all customer interactions; and at Marriott, Siebel empowers sales reps to respond more quickly to customer needs by integrating customer information from different departments. Lexmark International used Microstrategy software to help build what they call a data warehousing solution that accomplished a reduction in product delivery time by 70 percent, a threefold improvement in being able to deliver a customer's order on the desired date, and a 60 percent reduction in the information costs.

Package delivery firm UPS's selfservice tracking system, built by IBM, saved the company $450,000 a day in customer service expenses; and, the Clarify call centre software helped payroll-processing firm ADP improve customer retention rate by 5 percent and increase revenues by $100 million in 1999 simply by providing its customer service reps with customer information on its 8000 clients. There are numerous such examples of technology-based customer information management systems having a profound impact on a firm's productivity and in customer retention. Both outcomes are the basis for achieving and sustaining profits.

The marketing research practice has undergone a major transformation in recent years. A primary function of marketing research activities is to collect and analyze customer information. Technology has enabled all phases of the marketing research process ranging from sampling and data collection to analysis and reporting. With newer technologies and faster cycle times, firms conduct research at all stages of the product life cycle and not just at the product development stage or the test marketing stage.

This is at the aggregate level, whereas there is another change in research on the customer at the individual level, where technology is enabling customers to interact with the firm in a multitude of different ways not previously possible. These interactions can now occur during all stages of consumption. At every interaction with the customer, a firm has the opportunity to acquire valuable customer information, as well as to process and utilize the information for creating and delivering superior customer value. Once the data is available, the challenge is to provide the user of the information and decision maker with targeted information.

Enter rulesbased approaches, which are simply programmes that make sense of data using preconceived models. Sadly, the majority of CRM and ERP packages fail the firm not for lack of data, but simply because the firm does not have the appropriate understanding and appreciation of the fundamentals of customer-focused management. The rules for decision-making should be founded on customer-focused management principles.

The better the understanding of the customer and the utilization of that knowledge, the more customer focused the rules are. The best technology is only as good as what you tell it to do. CRM and ERP packages are really knowledge management software, tools to manage knowledge of the customer and enable the processes within the firm that are working to meet specific customer needs. To be more effective with these tools, firms need to gather the information, analyze and process it to obtain a good understanding of the customer, and utilize it at every opportunity in the value-creation and delivery process. Therefore, for a thorough understanding on how to manage customer information, it is important to understand the principles of knowledge management, in general.

Organizational Learning

What is knowledge management? To answer this question, we have first to deal with a more fundamental question: what is the difference between data, information, and knowledge? Are these terms just synonyms that are interchangeable? No, they are not! The simplest way to understand the differences among these terms is to picture a continuum. As we add value to data, it becomes information; and as we add value to information, information becomes knowledge. When we interpret data in a context, we convert that data into information that has some meaning. When we categorize and elaborate on that information with explanations, then we have added more value and the information can now be considered knowledge.

Thus, *knowledge management* is the management of data and information so that a firm can optimally capture, process, and utilize its knowledge for effective decision-making and operation. *Customer knowledge management* is the management of the acquisition, processing, and utilization of customer information for effective customer-focused decision making. Knowledge management practice has been studied in the context of how organizations learn. Before we discuss the methods of managing customer knowledge, it would be useful to understand knowledge management and, specifically, information processing from the perspective of organizational learning. Organizational learning can be broadly depicted as a three-stage process:

- Information acquisition or generation
- Information transmission or dissemination
- Information analysis or interpretation

Studies have demonstrated that a customer-focused firm has a formal and systematic method for gathering, interpreting and using customer information. To be customer-focused, therefore, firms need to be committed to the importance and value of customer information and to the use of customer information in guiding the creation and delivery of customer value. Thus, recognizing information's value to the firm and realizing when and where it is accessible is a prerequisite for knowledge management.

Richard Schulze, CEO of Bestbuy, the runaway success in electronics retailing, says: The best way to find out whether a store is running smoothly is by asking the cashier. "The cashier really understands where the problems lie. They're the last people to see the customer." To consider all of the sources of customer information we also need to first identify the natural state of the information. Customer information is available as tacit and as explicit knowledge.

The explicit knowledge is present in the databases of the firm or as documented information. Customer information files in databases are usually quantitative data. More and more firms are also using qualitative data when the technology is used to accommodate that type of data. Otherwise, most of this rich information remains as hidden knowledge. This information that is not recorded is the tacit knowledge that is usually resident with the employees and managers of the firm. For example, records of customer service interactions capture the actual transaction, complaint, or feedback from the customer. At the same time, employees, based on their prior experience, will unconsciously record and bring to bear their judgments of the situation, which are not necessarily documented. The knowledge that employees have that is not recorded anywhere is deemed the tacit knowledge of the firm.

While at the individual level information is available from customer information files in the firm's databases, other types of information at the aggregate level may be gathered during the course of product development activities and other specific projects and reside in research reports. There is information on the customer at several locations within the firm, from sales to customer service, to name the most obvious areas.

Besides this explicit knowledge, there is a wealth of information at both the aggregate and the individual levels. Wherever the firm has interfaced with the customer, the "touch-points, " there is information on the customer. It immediately becomes apparent that several product and service delivery contact points within the firm have access to customer information, but not all are part of the customer information management system.

CRM software packages enable the firm to capture all of the information gathered at each touch-point into a central database and make it available at any touch point. To determine all of the opportunities for gathering information on the customer, firms can develop a blueprint of the order delivery or customer service processes depicting all of the touch-points from the consumption cycle when the customer interacts with the firm.

Knowledge gained on the customer from each and every customer interaction when recorded and made available can be valuable in improving the customer focus of any of the firm's decisions or actions. The major sources for customer knowledge are discussed below.

Customer Information Files are typically transaction-related and purchase-related individual-level customer data found in sales records, customer interaction records, and customer service incident records. What is perhaps not in these files, which needs to be considered as a necessary component of individual customer profiles where available, is information related to the activities of preconsumption, consumption, and postconsumption.

Research Reports have segment-level aggregate data that are found in product development reports, advertising research reports, sales and marketing reports, and customer service reports. What needs to be seen is whether research on market segments is an ongoing pursuit of the firm—to indicate that the firm is proactively assessing customer value being delivered by the firm.

Knowledge held by employees and managers—Tacit knowledge of the customers—is by definition not completely identified and its utility not realized. If there is no formal process to regularly capture and utilize this information, a wealth of knowledge resident in the firm is being ignored.

Upstream and downstream sources: When suppliers and intermediaries are regularly included in discussions of value-creation and delivery decisions, there is an opportunity to discover information on market trends, technology, ideas for product improvement, and so on that are useful at the aggregate level. At the individual level, where there are (downstream) intermediaries, if it is possible, it would be highly valuable to obtain individual customer level information.

Now let us look at opportunities that may be missed by firms that are not proactive in looking for customer information. For example, how many firms capture and utilize data on referrals? If it is appropriately captured and analyzed, firms can use this information to proactively stimulate referrals. Firms can identify customers who could be bringing in new customers. Firms can determine what incentives would be effective in stimulating referrals. From the referring and referred customers, firms can learn what messages are being conveyed about the firm and which messages are most effective in stimulating product trial from new customers.

Firms can learn what types of customers are most liable to switch from their current patronage based on word of mouth. Firms can track and follow the patronage behaviour of these new customers and nurture their loyalty and referral behaviour. Firms can also find out from these new customers valuable information on the competition as well. Similarly, what about prospective customer queries? How well is this information captured and utilized? What would such information contain?

They are a good source of what customers look for in a product, a reflection of their choice criteria. How many firms systematically record information on complaints and praises? This type of information would be very helpful in understanding how the firm is faring on creating and delivering customer value. It could highlight failpoints in the value-creating processes and provide input into frontline evaluation and motivation activities.

Many firms have loyalty programmes to reward the frequent user. What sort of frequent-user data do these firms maintain? How many firms really use the frequent-purchase data? Some firms who know their customers well recognize the importance of sorting out the most profitable customers from their customer base and treating them differently. Some customers are indeed more equal than others! Most firms use frequent-purchaser data for targeting specials and promotions. However, this data can also provide invaluable information on customer value and customer profile information to align the firm's value-creation and delivery processes.

Traditionally, firms have gathered routine customer information only at purchase and when a customer returns a product for a refund or invokes a guarantee. Firms have also attempted to obtain customer reactions through customer feedback mechanisms. Feedback forms and customer surveys are administered on a regular basis in some firms. However, most often the information gathered from these efforts is worthless because of faulty designs and worse, sometimes even result in misdirected decisions because of flawed survey methodology. More often than not, the surveys are neither reliable nor valid.

While reliability and validity as statistical measures of the psychometric stability of a scale are important for a scientific, unbiased study, management can improve the utility of customer surveys with a rather simple analysis. Examine the design, administration, and use of any survey along the dimensions of structure, content, and process. Structural features such as length and the time it would take the respondent to fill out the survey, the layout of the various questions in the survey, and the response format for the questions affect the effectiveness of the survey.

Content decisions, such as the categories of information sought from the respondent and information identifying the type of respondent filling out the survey, affect the utility of the survey, which will only be as good as the effectiveness of its administration and its usability. Thus, the process of survey delivery, customer response delivery mechanisms, and the customization of the reports to the decision maker and user of the information in their value-creating and delivery roles is critical to the success of the customer feedback exercise.

There are other sources of customer information that the firm has access to and may not fully utilize. The systematic way of determining what these sources might be is to list all the possible touch-points where customers interact with the firm and placing them in sequence in the three phases of consumption. In the preconsumption phase, customers may interact with salespeople or customer service or other frontline personnel.

Recognizing what these touch-points are and what kinds of information is shared between the firm and the customer is an important step. Firms must decide what data needs to be captured at the touch-points and how it is to be used in guiding decisions and activities.

How many firms systematically utilize frontline operations personnel for gathering customer information? Frontline operations personnel are in an ideal position to gather customer information. They can be trained on when, what, and how to observe or elicit information from customers. They need to be motivated and recognized for their ability to obtain, process, and disseminate such information.

Similarly, there are also the intermediaries or resellers of the firm's products and services that represent the firm in different ways. These intermediaries might perform functions of delivery and distribution, promotion, or customer service on behalf of the firm. Walmart recognized and wielded the power it held with such customer information in negotiating terms with powerful packaged goods manufacturers, including Procter & Gamble.

In the consumption phase, customers may call for assistance in using the product or on some aspect of how the solution works. This information needs to be captured and incorporated into customer education activities such as product directions-for-use instructions, or used in product development and improvement efforts. There is also a wealth of information within the firm available from customer complaints and suggestions.

Service failures and recovery situations provide valuable information on customers and their experiences with the firm and its solutions. If these are recorded and maintained on a systematic basis, they can be "mined" for patterns that yield insights not otherwise available. For example, recurrent complaints about customer service response time might suggest that the customer service process needs redesigning.

Often when the data is not available on which to base a decision, the firm has to collect that information. For example, say the firm has received several complaints about customer service access and wants to determine what changes need to be made to the customer service operation. In this case, the firm may want to conduct some research in order to determine the customer needs and preferences with regard to customer service.

For each decision that directly relates to a customer, the firm has first to determine what kind of information is needed to make the most effective customer-focused decision. Some of this information is available in existing databases, while some may have to be gathered. To gather information, the firm needs to set up a method of determining what information needs to be gathered, how it can be obtained, and in what form it will be available.

WORKING FOR CUSTOMERS

FMC stresses the importance of creating a holistic customer service culture by beginning with upper-level management and actualizing this goal among all staff including frontline personnel. The framework for the customer service culture at FMC includes learning what the customers want; implementing steps to provide for those wants for which a business case can be made; equipping frontline employees with training, information, empowerment, and motivation; and monitoring success through customer and employee feedback mechanisms.

When the U.S. call centres were being developed, the director researched other call centres to find a model for their design. In favour of economies of scale (related to technology, resources, and personnel), FMC implemented call centre access on a national scale at four sites. Even with this consolidated design, FMC is committed to providing personalized service.

Call centre management utilizes customer telephone and mail survey results as well as focus group findings to guide implementation. Once analysed, this information is provided to the areas within the call centre for which it applies. (For example, customer feedback about loan rates goes to employees responsible for making policy decisions about rates. Customer input about experiences and interactions with personnel are provided to staff in training and human resources.)

Call centre managers are expected to coach and mentor call takers, based on performance during quality control checks. FMC management utilizes formal feedback initiatives to ensure that communication between the frontline and management remains open. One of these programmes is the Voice of the Customer Committee.

On this committee, frontline workers meet with management during a monthly meeting at which staff relay what customers want, based on their interactions with customers that month and over time. Another mechanism, the Ideas Programme, offers an opportunity for frontline personnel to submit a proposal to management on how to improve customer service. Employees are rewarded for submitting proposals, and when ideas are implemented, a gift card is provided.

Frontline employees, especially through the Voice of the Customer Committee, have made important contributions to improving customer service at FMC. For example, frontline staff identified necessary changes in the voice menu wording, suggested options that should be added and some to omit from the phone tree menu, and identified customers' information needs. Frontline personnel are encouraged not only to report to management any processes that are not working, but to offer potential solutions.

The key to hiring someone on the front line, according to FMC management, is to hire staff with a passion for customer service. Training for FMC staff includes training on teams, as well as learning how to give and receive feedback, how to be a good team member, and how to improve telephone communication skills.

One important motivator for employees is the policy within the company that includes customer satisfaction as a determining factor in employee compensation. Quarterly, customer telephone survey results are tabulated, and employees receive bonuses that are tied directly to their scores. Also, prizes are offered for customer letters or phone calls of praise. Lunches are offered to teams who perform well in customer service.

In an effort to make the payment process as convenient as possible for customers, FMC piloted a phone pay system through Western Union.

Currently, this programme produces 350,000 transactions each month. Other pay options include direct electronic payments from a bank account or payroll deduction and Internet-based payment processing. Twenty-two per cent of FMC payments are processed electronically. At the time of this report, they are also considering whether to permit credit card payments.

During a month when the customer simply cannot pay, FMC works with customers who struggle to make full and timely payments. For example, a customer may be permitted to skip a payment and add that payment to the end of the loan. Another option is reducing the amount of the monthly payment and extending the length of the loan. Accountability is enforced through late payment charges and reports made to the credit bureau.

Customer service is key to the day-to-day operation of Cherner Automotive Group (Cherner). This sentiment is echoed from the frontline employee to the upper-level executive. The Cherner philosophy of customer service delivery is customer satisfaction through continued friendly communication and interaction, coupled with accessibility and responsiveness. Cherner's approach is very individualized, and they believe that customer service is relative to the customer being served. In no case did a Cherner employee claim to be in the business of selling vehicles; rather, employees view themselves as"in the people business."Building customer relationships is underscored. Cherner employees realise that exemplary customer service brings in new customers, as well as repeat customers. This is accomplished by reputation or referral.

Cherner operates two dealerships, both of which are located in the Northern Virginia technology corridor. Cherner has a wide customer base that includes retired persons, business professionals, members of Congress, and community residents. Many Cherner customers are repeat customers or referrals.

Cherner is a family-owned and -operated business. The corporate culture embraces change; strives to learn what customers want and gives it to them; and seeks both customer and employee loyalty. Cherner considers customers'first impressions to be important and strives to create a warm and inviting environment. Cherner employees attempt to make customers feel welcome and to provide individualized attention.

The only"formal"policies for making this occur include the"10-foot rule,"whereby employees who are in the area should acknowledge customers within this range and ask to be of assistance, and a policy that all customers who enter the dealership are acknowledged within 30 seconds. Cherner employees understand the value of smiling and being pleasant to all customers.

According to Cherner staff at all levels of the company, customers deserve responsiveness. The ability to individualize service is, in their opinion, what sets them apart in customer service delivery. There are no written guidelines, but employees have a degree of autonomy in making decisions.

For example, the service advisor has the latitude to refund money or to adjust a charge ticket. The core ideology is that each employee is encouraged to do whatever it takes within reason-based on the situation-to serve a customer immediately. Employees are discouraged from having a"this is my job or that is not my job"attitude. Rather, all employees work for the same company and every employee is responsible for serving customers and making them happy.

Integral to Cherner's customer service delivery is the need to understand customer expectations. Cherner listens to their customers and provides convenient forums for customer feedback. The most widely used method is their customer satisfaction survey. Each customer who purchases an automobile receives a questionnaire from Ford Motor Company. The results are shared with the dealer. Also, Cherner hires an outside company to phone a sample of their service customers to collect data on customer satisfaction. These findings are presented in the monthly report"Viewpoint."The service area also has a customer feedback/suggestion box, posted beside the cash register.

Staff at all levels of the organization articulated their customer service orientation as:

- Being pleasant and smiling at customers.
- Being a good listener (and being empathetic to customers'situations).
- Doing the job right the first time.
- Being accountable.
- Building trusting relationships with customers.
- Treating people fairly.
- Making customers fully happy.
- Being willing to apologize.

Cherner's owners and managers set the tone for the company. Managers are expected to"lead by example."The general manager adheres to a policy of"Management by Walking Around."In other words, he and other managers try to stay connected with employees throughout the organization by working side-by-side with them. Senior-level executives have an open-door policy and solicit employee input during staff meetings. Calls are not screened, so customers also can contact managers directly.

Managers attempt to empower employees by providing a supportive environment in which employees are encouraged to make decisions. Managers are expected to coach frontline staff. During interviews, frontline personnel indicated that if a frontline employee were experiencing difficulties, managers would speak with that individual and coach him/her. However, frontline staff felt that improvement would be expected and that the employee would be held accountable for improving, or the employee would be terminated. As an employee's experience increases, so does the amount of discretion allotted to the employee.

Cherner frontline personnel perceive that they are supported by management in that whatever they feel they cannot handle can be turned over to management, with frontline staff confident that the situation will be addressed. Management also listens and responds to the needs of the employees. This is handled in different ways. For example, when employees in service determine that they need some training or equipment to do the job better, they can write the request on a white board designed for this purpose, and a member of management will address the request (and keep the notation on the board until the request is resolved). The white board is also an information-sharing tool for frontline employees. Employee meetings are an another forum for raising and addressing issues.

Most of the dealership's employees have longevity with the company. During each discussion with Cherner employees, regardless of organizational level, the interviewee acknowledged that to deliver great customer service, a company must hire and retain the right people. Managers added that "the right person" is one who can get along with others, possesses good judgment, can work on a team, is motivated, and possesses the desire to grow and learn. Cherner wants to hire sales personnel who are motivated not by money, but rather by the desire to help people.

Cherner offers multifaceted, ongoing training for employees. In order to continually provide effective customer service, employees are trained both in-house and by the manufacturers. Ford Star Satellite training, Ford's training facility in Centreville (VA) and printed training materials from KIA and ISUZU are designed to keep employees current on various features and aspects of the products being sold and serviced. Other training offered is designed to enhance selling techniques and customer service and to update technicians on vehicle and repair technology. In the past, employees received gender sensitivity training that was offered to improve customer service for female customers. Among the most creative training strategies is Cherner's frontline mentoring system, whereby a senior salesperson mentors a new salesperson for 90 days. The senior salesperson is responsible for teaching sales basics, orienting the new employee to Cherner culture and attitude, describing Cherner products, and detailing processes. One frontline employee stated that this type of mentoring is a key component to great customer service that is transferable to other organizations.

At all levels of the organization, employees reported being very self-motivated—driven by personal pride and the desire to do a great job. This may be a result of Cherner's hiring policies as well as employees' positive perceptions of their work environment.

Most of those that were interviewed commented that separate and distinct from the actual family ownership of the dealership, the working environment feels like a family environment. Employees know and talk with one another, even across departments; employees support one another; employee picnics and gatherings allow families to get to know each other; and employees simply "get along." This family environment proves to be a strong motivator for Cherner employees at all levels.

Another motivator that was mentioned comes directly from individual customers. Employees reported receiving Christmas cards, gifts, notes, and personal appreciation and friendship from satisfied customers. Cherner, as well as the vehicle manufacturers, offers incentives to foster and sustain employee motivation. Cherner sponsors contests, and the winners are given free tickets to sporting events or dinner coupons, monetary awards, and other "per's" (e.g., use of a vehicle, recognition, etc.) Rewards are also offered based on customer survey scores, reported by Ford. At times, there are luncheons or dinners.

Rather than a point-in-time formalized evaluation process, employees are continuously recognized for good service. Similarly, management addresses negative behaviour as it is observed or identified via customer surveys or complaints and seeks to correct this behaviour through mentoring and coaching.

Technology is a resource primarily used for training and in the service area. Service employees are linked to each of the manufacturer's databases and have access to sophisticated on-line reference manuals. They are connected to nationwide databases that have background information on the history of the car, as well as customer history. This allows for a more detailed, efficient, and expedient service call and better customer service.

Ford Star is a satellite training initiative that allows employees to remain at the dealership while receiving training. Employees can even take the required tests and receive their scores via the Internet. This lends convenience for employees being trained.

The attitude of customer responsiveness holds true for complaints. Employees echoed the same sentiment: "If you receive it, handle it. If you can't handle it, find someone who can until the problem is solved." Employees explained that complaints are an information resource for them, and that they utilize the information to improve services.

Cherner boasts a low turnover rate, estimated at approximately 10 per cent. In fact, an average employee will remain with Cherner for 10 years. The General Manager has been with Cherner for 29 years. This low turnover is attributed to the family-oriented atmosphere, competitive wages, and knowledge that the jobs at Cherner are secure (as Cherner does not have a history of layoffs).

One challenge to this positive environment has been a recent decision to respond to customer and manufacturer desires to operate on Saturdays. As such, employees who used to be off each weekend now find themselves working on some Saturdays. In an effort to reduce employee burnout or turnover that such a change may produce, Cherner offers special incentives to these employees. For example, an employee who works on Saturday may choose to take the following Monday off (service advisors can take Friday) or to be paid for an extra day of work at overtime rates. Management also provides lunch for employees who work on Saturday.

Cherner focuses on outcomes rather than the process. Cherner offers its vehicle repair customers a shuttle back to work, within a reasonable distance, or to the transit station. However, Cherner recognizes that because of local traffic conditions, offering this service during evening rush hour is counterproductive. Therefore, customers are reimbursed for cab fare back to Cherner when traveling from the transit station to Cherner to pick up a vehicle during evening rush hour. While Cherner could have told customers that the shuttle does not run during rush hour and that transportation would have to be arranged on their own or during non-rush hours, Cherner went the extra mile with customers and found a mutually beneficial way of providing this service.

Cherner aims to exceed customer expectations. When customers have their vehicles at Cherner to be serviced, they are provided with complementary car washes. Cherner proclaims that the benefits of customer service delivery are happier customers, high employee morale, employee and customer loyalty, free advertising (word of mouth), and sales generation.

"If you do it right the first time, you won't have to do it again." This is the premise from which they operate. Satisfaction the first time results in not having to spend more labour hours rectifying a situation. This, in turn, makes daily business operations more fluid and service more efficient. Satisfaction the first time also enhances the dealership's community reputation as that of a professional, people-oriented business. This business stance generates a larger customer base. High employee morale is also a benefit of good customer service. Employees take pride in their work.

The costs to Cherner for delivering great customer service include employee incentive costs, salaries, and bonuses; training costs; car wash expenses; shuttle service expenses; and write-off costs for services performed but not charged to the customer. As part of its external customer service strategy, the Child Support Division in Texas has developed a programme called *Compact with Texans,* which outlines the vision, guiding principles, and goals of the division and explains how external customers can continue to provide feedback on child support.

The guiding principles are:

- Always do what is best for the child, by putting children first.
- Treat everyone with dignity, respect, honesty, and courtesy.
- Walk in the customer's shoes—have empathy.
- Be a leader in doing the right thing, not just in doing things right.
- Participate and contribute in finding solutions—work as a team.
- Maintain objectivity and be nonjudgmental.
- Respect customer' privacy.
- Bear in mind that the customers' perceptions of reality are their reality.

These principles are designed as the framework for action at the agency and individual levels when serving both internal and external customers. Everyone in the division is provided with a copy of these principles to hang on their office walls, and these principles are also posted in conference rooms and hallways throughout the office. To advance these principles, the customer service action plan addresses:

- Improving access to services and staff by implementing regional call centres; expanding and publicizing the Office of the Attorney General (OAG) Child Support Web site—including online application for services; publicizing the complaint process on posters and the Internet; considering a plan to increase office hours; and putting computers in six office lobbies, on which customers may access some case information as well as conduct job searches.

- Ensuring comprehensive, accurate, and easily accessible information that is easy to understand by recording information about billing and interest, credit bureau reporting, and license suspension laws on a toll-free line; providing telephone access to information about mail-out dates; providing call takers with screen pops; providing parents with an information packet and video (and also including it on the Web site) about customer expectations, services, procedures, and timeframes when they first enter the system; providing presentations in public forums or for selected groups regarding child support; comprehensively training new employees; and providing staff with information online.
- Ensuring prompt action on new case information and responses to customer requests and inquiries by instituting several policies, including: the service delivery process must begin within 20 days of receiving an application for services; telephone messages must be addressed within 2 business days, and action must be taken within 2 business days of information receipt; actions taken on a case or information received must immediately be documented; responses must be made to written inquiries within 10 days; follow-up efforts to telephone inquiries must be undertaken within 15 business days; automated wage withholdings must be acted upon within 2 business days of receiving information about a new employer; either customers are seen when they walk in or appointments must be scheduled to occur within 10 days of the customer's request. Additionally, prompt action is actualized by improving the automated computer system and allowing parents to make address changes on an automated toll free line.
- Improving accuracy and quality by revising forms, standardized letters, and publications as necessary to ensure that they are clear and current and that they use plain language; training all central office staff in writing techniques; training managers in leadership development; creating a compliment-tracking system; establishing an employee recognition programme (including revising performance plans and defining merit raise criteria); providing automated management reports; conducting a workload study; sharing best practices; and creating a customer service advisory team.
- Treating customers professionally, courteously, and respectfully by pilot testing privacy measures in waiting rooms, providing customer service and other professional training to all staff, creating individual staff training plans, attaching information about court procedures

to court notices (including expected wait time), and instituting a regular customer feedback process.

The Child Support Division of the Texas OAG works with mothers, fathers, and legal guardians of children to locate absent parents; establish paternity; establish, enforce, and adjust child and medical support orders; and collect and distribute the money associated with these orders. They have over 1 million active cases. In 1997, the Texas legislature mandated the Sunset Advisory Commission to review the OAG Child Support Division to determine whether the OAG should continue to administer the State's child support programme. Legislators were receiving too many complaints about the Division from constituents. The Sunset Commission conducted its review in 1998 and recommended that the OAG continue to administer the programme for a 2-year probationary period. The Commission made a number of recommendations for improving the programme. The highest priority was improving customer service and, in particular, accessibility. Too often, customers needing information about their cases could not get through to staff for information. Of the 1.5 million calls a month that child support received, only 14 per cent of those who wished to speak with staff could do so. Thousands of calls each day were abandoned. A customer service survey revealed that 48 per cent of customers were dissatisfied.

Shortly after the Commission issued its report, a new Attorney General took office. He hired a new Deputy Assistant Attorney General for child support, and they both made customer service a top priority, with answering the phones as the number one objective. A full-time staff person was hired to develop the customer service strategy and action plan. The process included focus groups with internal and external customers, a customer satisfaction survey, and an employee satisfaction survey, as well as and soliciting input from various special interest groups.

Customers said that they were most concerned with obtaining timely and accurate information, preserving their personal dignity, and being respected. Employees wanted empowerment and discretion.

To make the plan "stick," the administration realised that they needed to communicate, improve staff development, measure performance, and increase employee accountability and recognition. Quarterly, the regions report on their progress through action plans.

TECHNOLOGY-ENABLED CUSTOMER INFORMATION MANAGEMENT

Technology has revolutionized customer information management. Information technologies allow firms to gather, store, and interpret demographic and behavioural data so that each subsequent interaction with the customer is customized, based on historical data gathered from each customer interaction. Digitized purchase transactions in commerce have enabled numerous opportunities to track customer interactions. Chip technology has progressed so rapidly that soon there could be a computer chip in just about any product that would enable mindboggling links to improve customer value and the customer-firm relationship.

For example, take the Internet and e-commerce. Most Web sites will ask simple unobtrusive questions of customers when they browse the site. This information identifies the customer and tracks the customer's activities or "clickstreams" on the Web site. Subsequently, software can use this information to personalize the Web site and the experience for the customer.

A number of firms have emerged that provide customer information management software. Such software can customize Web pages for each customer depending on the customer's profile, which is created based on the customer's previous interactions with the firm and the Web site. Vignette's software allows Web sites to dynamically generate pages that are custom-made for each customer. Silknet's virtual sales assistant guides customers through a series of questions about their need situations and then makes product recommendations.

Marriott has an enterprise-wide software that integrates information on customers from different departments so that its sales reps can anticipate and respond more quickly to customer needs. Similarly, H&R Block uses software from Clarify to combine and coordinate customer records from its tax offices, discount brokerages, its customer service centre, and its Web site so that customer interaction personnel in each department have access to all of the information on the customer.

There are a variety of methods for analyzing data. Data mining techniques attempt to discern patterns in the data where one set of characteristics affects another set in a certain way. SAS Enterprise Dataminer software helps detect patterns in databases and construct models to predict customer response to the firm's actions. Software from iMarket looks at customers' most recent or most frequent purchase decisions and the monetary value of these purchases for the firm and helps decision makers select a subset of customers for targeting specific promotions or new product introductions. Epiphany and Digimine are examples of firms that use a set of their own proprietary algorithms to analyze customer data for their clients.

Early clients of Epiphany included Charles Schwab and Hewlett Packard, and for Digimine include Nordstrom. Edify has software that will link customer feedback such as survey responses to individual customer profiles for anlaysis. There is also software such as Nudist available for the analysis of qualitative data. When firms are able to sort through their customer databases and group customers by the relevant characteristics with such datamining software, the power of segmentation and targeting is fully realized with such datamining software.

In general, data is useless for decision making unless it is organized for interpretation. When organized appropriately, data can be contextualized so as to be transformed into information. Displaying and disseminating information is critical to the firm's success. Without proper reporting procedures, decision makers do not benefit from the information that the firm has.

For example, ESRI has a programme called Arcview that allows the user to spatially display numerical data. The user can view the data in his or her preferred format to match individual cognitive styles. As Peter Drucker notes, no two executives organize the same information in the same way. Therefore, software that allows the users to display information in their own preferred formats is valuable in customer information management.

The task of the customer information management system is to generate intelligence on the customer so that firm can be more customer-focused in its serving the customer. Intelligence generation capability has been shown to be positively correlated to superior customer value. In a study that involved hour-long in-depth interviews and surveys of sixty-six of the largest one thousand electronic firms by scholars interested in the characteristics of the market-oriented firm, firms are urged to treat learning about the customer as an investment.

Ultimately, customer information is useless unless it is available to the user. Scholars researching the value of information have called this the "value in use" metric. The more the information is used, the more value it has! Customer information management, therefore, involves determining how the information needs to be made available, to whom, when, and in what form. The focus here is on who needs the information.

In the spirit of customer focus, the information system serves an internal customer—the decision maker. What will the user need the information for? What specific information is needed for the firm's decisions and activities? Is the user of the information able to enhance customer value with the information?

At what level of aggregation is the information used: policy level and customer level, segment level, and individual level? Such decisions need to be made so as to prioritize the customer information according to its impact on customer value. In making judgments about committing resources to managing and leveraging customer information, the firm should consider the worth of the information in terms of how it would help the firm provide superior customer value at a reasonable profit.

Customer information must drive any business process and activity. Customer-focused management requires a customer-focused analysis of the information necessary for designing processes and making decisions regarding value creation in the firm. These run the gamut of decisions regarding creating and delivering customer solutions, product improvements, attracting and retaining customers, customer service, recovering from product failures, hiring and motivating employees, and ensuring a customer-oriented climate and culture.

Creating and Delivering Superior Customer Value

Firms create and deliver customer value as a bundle of benefits contained in a core and supplementary product. Since the core of any product is a commodity, the competitive advantage comes from the supplementary product. Designing and delivering superior customer value is all about adding value to the customer's value chain and doing it better than the competition. Paying careful attention to the details in each and every encounter with the customer ensures a customer-focused delivery of the value created by the firm.

Since the customer-focused firm competes on service, it also faces the classic challenge of any service firm—matching demand and supply. In order to maximize the profitability from its value-creating assets, firms have to determine the most profitable mix of segments for its customer portfolio.

Designing and Developing Superior Customer Value

How do you design customer-focused solutions that compete on service? Let customer information drive the decision on how best to leverage the productive assets of the firm. Market-based as well as asset-based assessments are necessary to configure value-creating assets into core and supplementary product benefits that provide a sustainable competitive advantage.

How does a small startup bank beat the big boys of the banking industry in their own backyard? Commerce Bancorp in New Jersey is not your standard bank. You will find their branches open at 8:00 AM and at 8:00 PM, and for most of the day on weekends. Vernon Hill, founding

CEO of the bank, who also owns Burger King franchises, has embraced retailing practices in successful firms such as Walmart, Home Depot, and Starbuck's. The core product at Commerce Bancorp is the business of banking, of course. But the total solution includes access and convenience benefits for the customer that most definitely distinguish it from other banks.

There are even bathrooms for patrons in each branch at Commerce Bancorp. The total solution for any product includes a core product with supplementary features that in combination present a resultant value to the customer. Product differentiation and superior customer value is not in its core product, but in that total solution. The total solution for Commerce Bancorp is not just banking delivered by human or automated tellers in physical branches, it is banking at the customer's convenience when, where, and how the customer wants it.

Indeed, the difference in a customer-oriented firm is very evident at any Commerce Bancorp branch. Commerce bank has found powerful ways of differentiating itself by being customer focused and then it has been able to execute its customer-focused value creation and delivery.

Firms create and deliver value from their assets. Firms must determine how they might be able to create customer value that is superior to the alternatives available to the customer. With a customer focus, the firm seeks to design a superior solution that will provide the firm with sustainable profits. This covers issues and decisions involved in conceiving, designing, and delivering the customer-focused product offering. What must happen to ensure that the productive assets of the firm, facilities, processes, and people, are set up to create and deliver customer-focused value?

TRANSLATING CUSTOMER NEEDS TO PRODUCT CONCEPT

The assessment must be done both at the aggregate, segment level and at the individual, customer level, where appropriate. The aggregate, segment-level assessment orients the firm's thinking about overall product strategy. When a firm directly interacts with its customer, the individual, customer-level assessment helps the firm configure the product within that strategy to the individual customer.

In keeping with the view that a product is really a bundle of benefits, the core value in any product for any firm is the primary benefit that the firm provides. The supplementary product includes as parts of the solution additional benefits that augment the core product.

Typically, a large part of the supplementary product is comprised of services. For the most part, the core product is a commodity, as in the example of Commerce Bancorp. All banks offer deposits, withdrawals, and investments and banking products such as checking and savings accounts, and fixed and variable income securities, and today most banks offer mutual funds. These products comprise the core product for banks.

How these products are different from bank to bank is represented in the supplementary components of the total product. Commerce Bancorp offers free checking and money orders and does not compete on its lower interest on its savings accounts and CDs. Thus, Commerce Bancorp differentiates itself on a number of different supplementary benefits to the customer, ranging from the quality of its customer interactions to a number of facilitating services such as bathrooms in its branches. Similarly, most if not all banks have an online presence, but customers at banks like Allfirst Financial can talk with bank personnel via their home personal computer.

The hotel industry is one that grew out of its room-and-board days to a total product offering that today includes a multitude of facilitating services. "Room and board" was the commodity. As all hotels in a certain level, competitors in the same segment, began offering the same set of supplementary services, such as room service, meeting and conference rooms, a swimming pool, a gift shop, personal grooming salon service, business services, cable, or Internet service in each room, these became commodity and part of the core product.

By March 2001, 78 precent of all Ritz-Carlton hotels offered highspeed Internet. While only two hotel chains—Omni and Westin hotels—have laptops available for guests, most hotels in that class offer two phone lines. Thus, over time, as competing firms add supplementary services, these previously differentiating value components become a commodity and lose their differentiating ability.

Consider the recent "advances" in the form of supplementary services in the hotel industry. Electronic kiosks can not only check you in with your room key and print your bill at checkout, but can also be an electronic concierge providing a guest with directions or maps to locations of interest. Human butlers are back in the hotel industry.

A growing number of hotels at the top end will provide a bath butler to prepare your luxury bath, a technology butler to solve your gadget problems, a private butler to pack your clothes or make your plans. If you are traveling with a baby or young child, you can find a hotel that offers a room for a nanny and kiddie perks such as baby-sitting, some one to read a bedtime story with live actors, or toys and activities for the child. If you are bringing a pet along, some hotels will even offer you special pet services for a fee! Over time, hotels in the premium category will all be offering some or all of these supplementary features. These features become part of the standard offering and reduce themselves into a commodity for that category of hotels. You can expect that the "technology butler" service will be adopted by hotels for the business traveller segment, briefly providing a differentiating feature only very quickly to become standard fare. In designing superior customer value, a firm must translate customer needs to the specifications of a solution in terms of core and supplementary benefits.

All hotels need not have the same core product. That statement might seem confusing. Consider the Station Inn, in Pennsylvania, between Pittsburgh, and Harrisburg. It sits 125 feet from the railroad tracks. Railroading buffs sleep at the hotel just to see the freight trains, about 60 of them in a space of 24 hours. Same industry as hotels—but a somewhat different core product. Precise definition of a product can only emerge from deep inspection of the "What business are we in?" analysis.

The Supplementary Product

If product differentiation is derived from the enhancement that the supplementary product provides the core benefit, what constitutes supplementary product? Starting with the familiar: customer service is a common supplementary product (sometimes mistaken as the only element in the supplementary product). There are elements of the supplementary product, such as billing and payment, that are also common to all firms. They are required to facilitate the core product. These must also be viewed as part of the supplementary product to the extent that they affect customer value.

A firm can add to the customer value when its billing and payment process is customer focused or can detract from customer value if it is unpleasant in the customer's experience. Thus, there are some supplementary features that are found in all products that may not necessarily be recognized as such.

Services marketing scholar Christopher Lovelock visualized this concept as a flower with petals. Think of the supplementary product as composed of elements of the total value bundle that facilitate and enhance (or detract from) the primary benefit sought in a product. Visualize these elements in three broad categories: facilitating services, quality of customer experience, and brand image.

Facilitating Services

Facilitating services are all those features of the product and activities of the firm that serve to facilitate the consumption of the core product. All firms have to provide some of these services at some level. Large retailers such as Sears, Walmart, and Lowe's will provide assembly and installation services for a fee and sometimes for no charge. The four broad categories of facilitating services—complementary services, customer education, customer access, and customer service. Customer-focused firms differentiate themselves by excelling in these facilitating services.

Complementary services are those related to the consumption of the core product. Some are almost necessary, like the waiting area in a physician's clinic or parking facilities at a hotel. Passengers on long international flights enjoy a wide range of inflight entertainment activities such as films, TV channels, and even casino-style gambling or electronic shopping and services such as being able to rent a car or book hotel rooms from the technology at their seats. Some complementary services are product differentiators.

For example, recognizing that some of its customers were coming in to the bank to conduct their business bringing little children with them, some Wells Fargo branches have a play area with television cartoons, Nintendo, and the like—and even sells toys to children. Washington Mutual offers calculators, pens, and piggy banks for a small fee.

To compete for advertising within its *Mutual Funds* magazine for instance, the publisher, Time, Inc. offers its advertising customers anything from primary research and use of its subscriber list to assistance in customizing gifts and promotions to readers or sponsorship featured on special cover-wraps. These are examples of complementary services that help differentiate value created by different providers.

Only with an intimate understanding of the customer's value chain consumption (and creation) activities can firms begin to see what opportunities there might be to facilitate the consumption of the core product. Sometimes complementary products are outsourced and provided directly to the customer by the supplier, as Wells Fargo did when it invited Starbuck's to open locations at some of its branches.

Ultimately, these complementary products ought to be consistent with the positioning strategy for the product. When a complementary feature is offered by all competitors in a particular product category, it becomes a commodity and part of the core product for that category and ceases to be a product differentiator.

Customer education is a form of facilitating service in that it provides information to the customer about the firm or the product in such a way that it facilitates the acquisition and consumption of the product. Instruction manuals and product support via telephone, fax, or the Internet are examples of customer education. Consider what some banks are doing to be more accessible for customers looking for assistance.

Tellers and managers are dressed in khakis and casual shirts to appear approachable and friendly. Bank of America has tested concierges in their lobby to help direct customer questions. Home Depot provides free classes on home improvement projects. Once again, the service feature might be a necessary component of the total product, but how it is designed and delivered may be a source of product differentiation.

Customer access has to do with everything that the firm does to make its products available to the customer and to facilitate the acquisition and consumption of the product. The hours of operation and location are a simple example of customer access for a service. The various touch points that are available to the customer to access the services of the firm or to reach someone within the firm would be a measure of the customer access. The methods of billing and payment for the product would relate to access to the product and can be a product differentiator.

For example, the convenience of payment by credit card was once a source of competitive advantage. Convenience and ease of use is a critical component of customer value for any product. Services such as financing options are also related to this idea of customer access. If these are not customer-focused, they will fail the customer and the firm.

Customer service is a key facilitating service and includes the commonly understood activity of businesses related to product complaints or failures, product returns, refunds, and such. The accommodation of special requests or adapting to unusual or irregular customer situations would be an example of customer service as well. Poor customer service reduces customer value and risks losing the customer.

Quality of Customer Experience

When the total product provided by all firms contains the same set of facilitating services, the product is not necessarily a commodity. The quality of the service offered remains a source of differentiation and therefore a supplementary feature of the product. Perceived quality enhances, and lack thereof reduces, the value of the core product. For example, even when Internet service is offered by all hotels, the quality of the customer experience with the Internet service is still a differentiator.

One hotel may require you to get into a closet, fish out the cables and force you to shape yourself into a yoga pose to hook up those cables to your laptop, while another hotel may offer wireless Internet access from anywhere on the property. All airlines provide seating and, depending on distance and class, also provide meals and entertainment while transporting you from point A to point B. Differentiation in seating can come in legroom and comfort. First-class services can offer six and a half feet of seat length, single seats, pajamas, and privacy partitions between seats. The quality of the entire customer experience is most definitely a source of differentiation.

Brand Image

Brand image is a supplementary feature of the product in that it adds to customer value. Brand image is the sum total of all the perceptions and attitudes about a brand. The image of the firm in the general media as well as for each individual customer provides a measure of the perceived quality of the product. The reputation of a firm is usually a result of the firm's product and actions. Where there is very little tangible evidence of the product, as in the case of Web-based services, an entire industry of so-called "reputation managers" has emerged. These reputation managers are Web sites that rate the reputation of others! A firm's image is an implicit source of differentiation in the market. Brand image is the ultimate differentiator. When all else can be seen as equal, the brand image captures the essence of the difference in customer value among the alternatives available to the customer.

Firms have to determine what their total product offering is and what it should be. The value bundle of core and supplementary product needs to be designed based on what the customers expect as standard from all providers of a solution in a product category. The supplementary product might also contain features that are sources of differentiation among solution providers reflecting the positioning strategy of the firm. Firms must constantly watch the various solutions that are being offered. Sometimes the threat of competition comes from newer business models.

For example, online broker ETrade surprised the banking business when it began to open ATMs with new services. A deep and broad analysis of customer needs could reveal value-creating opportunities.

Matching Product to Customer Value Chain

To determine how best to match the total product as the superior solution to fit customer need, the firm must understand the customer's value chain. This is an integral part of the product concept development of the customer-focused firm. A thorough understanding of the customer needs and the customer value chain will help the firm conceive its product from the customer's point of view. Firms that best relate their own value chain to the buyer's value chain, said Michael Porter, will enjoy a sustainable differentiation strategy.

The value chain is essentially a chain of value-creating and value-consuming activities, where the value created as output from one activity becomes the input to another value-creating activity that in turn creates value as input for another activity, and so on. Thus, any activity can be assessed by the value it creates versus the value it consumes. This is why activity-based costing practices make a lot of sense. As, the value creating activities *within a firm* are those that contribute to the creation of either the core product or the supplementary product.

The value created by these activities is derived by the processing of the productive factors of the firm—its people, facilities, and equipment. There may be assets or value components sourced from external suppliers or intermediaries that contribute toward producing either the core or the supplementary product. Some outsourced services may even be delivered directly to the customer.

When any value component of the total product is outsourced, as in the case of a retailer offering customers outsourced financing options for purchases, or airlines outsourcing catering services, there is the obvious issue of quality assurance in the value creation that is outside the control of the firm. Externally (to the firm) when you relate other firms' value-creation activities into a value chain, you see that the value created by one entity contributes to the value created by the next entity in the value chain.

The same idea is referred to by economists, in the context of forecasting, as "derived demand." The demand for a product is dependent on the market for another product, such as aluminum and aircraft sales for example. A homeowner who gets a home improvement job done receives (customer) value from the home contractor who in turn is receiving value from the retailer who in turn receives value in the form of products and services from the supplier or manufacturer.

THE VALUE CREATION AND DELIVERY PROCESS

As, the execution of the product concept as the delivery of the product involves a process, a sequence of activities. Therefore, designing the product must necessarily include a design of the delivery process. Lynn Shostack proposed a technique called "blueprinting" to detail the process design in the delivery of services. The service blueprint is a map or flowchart as a visual representation of the process of service delivery.

Essentially, the blueprint design is diagramed in three steps. In the first step, all types of customer interactions with the firm are listed. Next, these interactions are arranged in sequence of occurrence. In the final step, processes within the firm that are required to create and provide each customer interaction are mapped. How and what information, materials, facilities and equipment, and people are processed must be included in the service blueprint.

The customer-focused blueprint is one that is designed with the customer in mind. With the activities in the customer's consumption cycle in mind, processes within the firm need to be designed in such a way that the desired value added in the solution is reflected at each and every encounter with the customer. Commerce Bancorp, for example, encourages its employees to make suggestions in streamlining the service delivery process. Commerce Bancorp employees receive a fifty-dollar reward for finding something about a process that does not contribute to customer value and instead is an impediment to serving the customer; the bank immediately adjusts its operations.

Even as a simple representation of the value creation and delivery process, the service blueprint has a variety of important strategic, analytical, and diagnostic uses. In designing the delivery of the product, it can be used to determine the uniqueness of the service process. When compared with competitive blueprints, where and at which points in the process the firm derives its competitive advantage and superiority in customer value become evident.

Thus, the service blueprint can be used in a strategic analysis of the differentiating features and benefits of the service delivered by the firm. Only with such comparative analysis of the service blueprint is it possible to ensure that the value creation and delivery processes are commensurate with the superior customer value planned in the product concept and operations design.

The service blueprint has two major dimensions that characterize the nature and scope of the service delivery process: complexity and divergence. The complexity dimension reflects the number of steps or activities in the process. A highly complex service process has a great variety of activities during the series of customer interactions. Some of these activities occur in the front stage and some in the back stage, away from the customer's view.

A so-called line of visibility determines what the customer sees or does not see. The customer-focused firm will need to examine everything that the customer sees and experiences to determine whether the service delivery at the service encounter is contributing to or detracting from customer value.

The divergence dimension reflects the degree of flexibility at each customer interaction. The greater the divergence, the greater the customization built into the service—the greater the number of options the customer is given to choose from at each interaction. Therefore, supplementary product benefits such as customization must be mapped into the service delivery process.

Complexity and divergence decisions will determine the position of the firm's offering compared to competitive offerings. Competitive blueprints can be compared to determine how competitive value bundles differ from each other. It becomes clear that the positioning of each competitive offering is reflected in the service blueprints.

The patient experience is very carefully orchestrated to support the entire concept of the "Shouldice Method." The surgical procedure itself is probably the least sophisticated element of the whole process. The recovery process is more important than the surgery. Every step in the blueprint is designed for a speedy recovery and an overall "enjoyable" experience—despite the anxiety and pain of the surgery. The method is known for a very low recurrence rate and high customer satisfaction. The hospital even has patient reunion parties each year that are sometimes attended by as many as a thousand former patients.

For this service, its critical steps are not in the surgical procedure but in in the recovery process and the total customer experience. All customer interactions depicted in the blueprint are not of equal importance in terms of criticality toward customer value—some are more important to the customer than others. It is imperative that the firm employ its knowledge of customer expectations so that the critical interactions are highlighted for priority when allocating resources of the firm.

This is the primary application of the blueprint technique. Jan Carlson, CEO of the SAS airline, popularized the notion of the "moment of truth" in services.

While each customer interaction is a moment of truth, those product features and customer encounters with the firm that are considered critical to the satisfaction of the customer are considered *critical incidents.* The critical incident technique has been applied in the managing of services to understand what can make or break the customer's experience. The method was initially developed for the U.S. Air Force in simulations to help in cockpit design and pilot training.

A simple question to the customer soliciting a verbal description ofmct is stocked and well displayed and that the floor salespeople are presenting the product to the customer in the way Handspring had instructed them to do. Microsoft hands out a free Casio pocketPC to every sales rep who completes its training. These examples show an awareness that customer interactions at these intermediaries are failpoints and need to be monitored.

Critical incidents help in assigning the appropriate level of resources within the firm. Thus, the service blueprint is useful from a quality control perspective. Customer evaluations of a firm's service can be linked to specific customer encounters in the blueprints and all processes directly affecting or affected by the critical incidents must be monitored for quality. Customer-focused quality control efforts can be focused on critical variables that can be controlled. Service recovery procedures must be designed into the process at these points.

Interactive technologies provided by the information age revolution are now an integral part of the design of the value creation and delivery process. These technologies work through the three primary productive components of customer value—the people, the infrastructure in facilities and equipment, and processes and systems of value creation and delivery. Consider all the ways in which the customer can interact with a firm. Each touch-point can be made by the converging technologies of today. For example, in some interactions the location of either buyer or seller becomes irrelevant.

Customers can interact by wireless or wired means, which can be by voice, video, or text, initiated by either party; they are constantly getting cheaper and better in features and functionality. The basic difficulty with any of this newer interactive technology is that the objective and role of the technology can be lost sight of and the technology itself become the focus. The final measure is whether the technology is contributing toward sustainable profits for the firm by improving customer value.

The benefits of interactive technology come in the form of efficiency and efficacy. Efficiency is reflected in increasing productivity and efficacy is reflected in improved customer value. Both of these outcomes contribute to the bottom line of the firm. For a firm competing on service, interactive technology is critical to sustain profits because of what it can do to customer value.

Maximize the return from interactive technologies by deploying it at the critical points; prioritized by its customer value-creating power. For example, a common source of dissatisfaction and irritation to the customer is the length of waiting time before being served. Any point in the process where there is likely to be a wait is a potential critical incident requiring the firm's express attention. If there are interactive technologies that can be used to effectively manage the customer in these situations, customer value is not threatened.

The Problem of Waiting Time

All the service components in the total product, being susceptible to the inherent characteristic of being produced and consumed in real time, force customers to the experience of "wait." As, demand and supply need to be matched as closely as possible. To avoid idle capacity, services adopt the queuing (and scheduling) approach to processing customers, resulting in a certain amount of wait before the process begins. In multi-stage processes, which many services are, in-process waits are common as well. The problem of course is that no one wants to wait.

Customers will wait for a certain amount of time that is reasonable to them as per their expectations. What is reasonable is a very subjective judgment, of course—one that requires analysis of the factors that determine the perception of waits.

Maister's work on the psychological cause and effects of wait suggests a way to reduce the negative consequences where wait is a given.

- Preprocess waits feel longer than in-process waits. Allow the customer to begin the process by completing the first step in the value delivery process.
- Unoccupied waits feel longer. Keep the customer in wait occupied with activities, preferably related to the product or service.
- Uncertain waits feel longer. Keep the customer informed about how long the expected wait is to likely to be.
- Unexplained waits feel longer. Keep the customer informed about why they are having to wait.
- Inequitable waits feel longer. Serve customer based on priority, determined by what is considered just in the ambient society.
- Value of the service. Ensure that the customer value you are providing is clearly superior to any alternative.

The most important common thread through all of these suggestions is that they all have to do with managing the customer perceptions. The firm is better placed if the customer perceptions can be influenced favourably by managing customer role and expectations in the value creation and delivery.

The Customer-focused Firm

To varying degrees, customers play a role in the production of products and not just in the consumption. Firms that realize this have paid serious attention to how the customer fits in the organization. In services, the role of the customer is abundantly evident. Customers engage in a coproduction role. In services or in the service component of the product, customers are coproducers in self-service configurations.

All services as we saw earlier involve some kind of customer participation, as in the case of providing required information to the tax preparer, for example. Even when placing the order with the provider, the customer is essentially contributing to the production of the product by providing input into product specifications.

When the customer is interacting with the firm and this interaction has some relevance to the production of the product, by definition we have the customer engaging in coproducing the product. Service firms instinctively manage the role of the customers in their participation in the service.

Restaurants have menus, professors have syllabi, airlines have their method of emplaning passengers according to a certain priority, etc. Sometimes managing customer roles may be in the form of a complementary service. For example, Universal is experimenting with a calming zone adjunct to its roller-coaster rides, for people who need help with coaster-phobia before they get on the ride.

UPS and other package delivery firms instinctively accommodate special customer requests as to where their packages should be deposited if the customer is not at the location of delivery. It is a matter of perspective. If we take the notion of value creation a step further, we could argue that even in the case of packaged goods, the value hasn't really been created to the customer until the customer actually begins to use the product.

Value creation and value consumption are both inextricably interwoven into a continuous and overlapping set of activities. This is an important issue in a service orientation. In the case of services, customer interaction is a given. And the firm must include the customer in the design of its operations.

The customer-focused firm by always keeping the customer in central view manages the role of the customer in the value creation and the value consumption activities. For example, providing excellent product assembly instructions improves the value created for the customer in an "easy to assemble yourself" product.

Conversely, even with a well-engineered product, poor instructions reduce customer value. Recent product innovation studies have shown that some firms are equipping customers with the tools to design and develop their own products, ranging from minor modifications to major new innovations. PTC (formerly Parametric Technology) is a world leader in computer-assisted-design (CAD) technology, whose software solutions bring suppliers and customers together so that a client can use the software during product development to virtually interface with upstream and downstream players.

Ultimately, anything that the firm can do to manage the customer's role in the value creation as well as value consumption process is an imperative for the customer-focused firm. As mentioned earlier, Procter & Gamble is recruiting families to allow a team of their ethnographer-filmmakers to observe their daily routines to get a better sense for how their customers use household products.

The actual use situation says a lot about how a product should be designed. It would also be a way to learn how the customers should be instructed in the appropriate use of the product. How does a firm take a systematic approach to managing the customer? First, the firm identifies all the activities that the customer enacts in the value creation as well as value consumption blueprint.

Next, the firm scripts the role for the customer at each activity. Firms then have to determine how best to communicate and educate the customer in playing the appropriate role. Customers' performance of their roles will depend on their ability and inclination to perform those roles. The consumer's ability will depend on consumption skills that the customer's past experience may have provided.

The customer's inclination will depend on the personal characteristics of the customer. Familiarity with the service and service provider could affect the ability and the inclination of the customer in the role performance. In the case of services and the service components of a product, customer role is managed by the service provider. The service provider's production skills and motivation could affect the way in which the service provider manages the customer's role.

The service provider's familiarity with the segment and the specific customer will influence the service provider's skills and motivation in managing the customer's role performance. The service provider's production skills are reflected in its operations and customer interaction skills. The personal characteristics of the service provider can affect the service provider's motivation. When designing the service delivery process, it is important that the firm incorporate these factors on the customer's role performance.

Staging the Customer Interaction

The essence of customer-focused design of the value delivery process is in the design of the customer interactions that make up the blueprint. Customer interactions have gone by various names in research on services—service encounters and moments of truth, for example. Designing the customer interaction requires analysis and decisions regarding three of the structural dimensions of the value delivery process: the process itself, the participants, and the physical facilities and equipment. Customer roles have to be defined so that customer participation can be designed into the delivery process as appropriate.

One useful framework that has utility in managing customer interactions is to view service encounters metaphorically as "drama." When firms and customers interact, firms try to put on the best performance—like theater. The firm's *actors* perform their roles for the *audience,* the customer. In any service, there are actors and audiences involved in producing *performances* in a *setting.*

For example, restaurant customers are audiences with hosts and waitstaff as actors in the physical setting of the restaurant. Just as in theatrical production, there is a stage (the dining area) and a backstage (the kitchen); there are acts (welcome and seating, appetizers, main course, and dessert), scripts (menu and specials), props (menu card and table setting), and costumes.

Each element is carefully choreographed to produce the intended impression on the audience. Any service provider can examine each of these elements and determine the exact impression that would be appropriate for each customer segment. The "drive-thru" or take-out type of fast-food restaurant confronts different impression management challenges compared to the sit-down type of restaurant.

Different types of services would require a different combination of these theatrical elements for the desired impression. Services rendered at arm's length over the telephone or by mail, such as in investment brokerage services or credit card services, would see these elements differently from the face-to-face setting of hotels or airlines.

Internet "clicks" retailers would find a different set of issues compared to the "bricks" retailers. Hybrid retailers have to approach the issues differently for the two different settings. In some cases, the performance is shared by a number of customers, as in a restaurant or a hotel or airline where customers share many aspects of the firm's productive factors—employees, facilities, and equipment.

The setting dictates a shared product, and some aspects of the setting are visible (onstage) to the customer and some are invisible (backstage). Performers or actors (frontline employees) utilize scripts, costumes, and props in their performances. Every feature or theatrical element is carefully choreographed for the intended impression.

Therefore, just as in theater, managers can focus on impression management for customer-focused business activities. World-class service firms like Disney employ a service orientation profile (personality and skills) in their hiring; they call their employees the cast and carefully train them in both operations and customer interaction skills. Disney's "guests" are treated in a customer-focused manner evident in the culture, in the way the cast is empowered and motivated to provide customer-focused performances.

What is the type of setting where the customer value is delivered? There could be no interaction necessary with the value provider at certain phases in the consumption cycle, and there could be phases of physical, face-to-face interaction, or electronics-mediated interactions. At each interaction, the value provider must determine the line of visibility between onstage and backstage, what is or should be visible to the customer.

What is the process and duration of the various steps in the interaction, and what kinds of orientation must there be for the participants? What is the customer role in each setting, and are there other customers in shared experience? Ultimately, all of the theatrical elements need to be carefully directed and choreographed to provide the appropriate impression. *Servicescape* is a term that refers to the immediate physical and social environments containing a service experience, transaction, or event.

The servicescape plays a number of different roles such as packaging the value bundle, facilitating the value delivery activities, socializing the employee and the customer, and differentiating the product. Managers must understand which servicescape elements can be controlled for the desired behaviours from both employees and customers.

The process of delivering the product must be analyzed, using techniques such as blueprinting and choreographing impressions on the customer.

What is the role of each process in the value creation and delivery as seen by a firm with a customer focus? What should the structure and content of the process include by way of design?

What are the critical points in the process for its meeting customer needs and preferences? The firm should have in place metrics and customer-determined benchmarks that will trigger recovery procedures, anticipating that the firm will sometimes fail the customer. A boutique hotel set in the heart of downtown will win the race for new and repeat business with the help of customer-relationship management. Beating the competition is not an easy task in the highly competitive world. The Hotel Customer service always has been king at the room property known for unique amenities.

Using the theatrical metaphor, any impression that the actor, the audience, the setting, or the performance imparts must be examined and managed by the firm. The focus is on the effect each customer interaction or service encounter has on customer value from the customer's point of view. Customer-focused firms design the value creation and delivery process with the customer in mind.

7

Customer Relationships

THE RIGHT CUSTOMER

Markets consist of customers with diverse needs and differences in customer profitability. When serving multiple groups of customers, the goal must be to maximize the profitability of the combination of segments. When different segments are targeted, the firm essentially has a portfolio of customer segments—just as investors have an investment portfolio that maximizes returns at a certain level of risk, firms manage customer portfolios for maximum profits. As standard, hotels are fitted with an integral magnetic stripe reader for credit and debit cards and our EFT system is approved by all the major banks and clearing houses.

However, in an age when credit card fraud is on the increase, hotels can protect you and your customers from fraud with the addition of Chip and PIN devices. Chip and PIN solution can be integrated to operate with your Hotel billing system's configurable client credit limit. In other words, this is the selection of customers at any point in time, compared to other segments, from which the firm can generate maximum profits. Firms must attract these most profitable customers and then must establish systems and procedures to retain them.

Most firms serve different segments depending on how the definition of segment is aggregated. The "segment-of-one" used in common business parlance to refer to customization at the individual level is really a maximum disaggregation of a market segment. As we saw, most firms facing fluctuating demand and experiencing peak, shoulder and low periods of demand find it inevitable that, at different times, different segments must be served.

Of course, each of these segments must have a compatible fit with the overall corporate image as well as a compatible fit with the products, services, employees and other customers. The question is, are they selected based on their combined long term value to the firm? Most firms forecast the volume and revenues from various segments at certain price points at different times in the purchase cycle. In the typical firm, sales and communications efforts follow these underlying assumptions in pricing and in messages targeting sales prospects. The typical firm then attempts to formalize advertising campaigns to reach as many people as possible in the case of packaged goods. In the case of business-to-business services, the salespeople focus on making a sale.

Most firms then struggle to orchestrate all these messages for acquisition of the customer in a coordinated fashion. Much less attention is paid to the retention of the customer. Barring the well-run operation, common business practice for many firms is short-term oriented. On the contrary, a customer-focused firm begins by approaching sales as acquiring the right customer. The customer-focused firm also approaches the acquisition of customers as only the first step in managing the relationships with its customers. Once acquired, the customer must be retained. But, not always retained at any cost—a necessary condition is that the benefits outweigh the costs of acquiring *and* retaining that customer.

Customer-focused firms align all their activities and processes in acquiring and retaining the right customer. They see their value-creating assets as most profitably leveraged by focusing on the most valuable customers. In principle, the value of the customer is determined by contribution to the firm's objectives over the lifetime of the customer. The right customer is that customer whose inclusion in the firm's target market helps maximize returns on the firm's assets.

Customer Equity

Ask a manager, "What is your firm's most valuable asset?" Chances are that you will not get the response, "my customers." You will find even fewer firms that actually make an assessment of this value in any real sense. The valuation of the customer is implicit in sales figures—essentially, the revenues generated by customers of the firm. What is the flaw in using sales as a proxy in valuing a firm's customers? Consider this.

Two customers with the same cash value of purchases may not be of the same value to the firm. There may be differences in the cost of serving these two customers. The true value of the customer to the firm, or the equity that the firm has in that customer, must include all revenues and also all costs related to that customer, as in financial investments. A recent framework by a team of researchers defines customer equity as the "total of the discounted lifetime value of all the firm's customers."

They articulate three drivers of customer equity: value equity, brand equity, and relationship equity. They define value equity as the objective assessment of the utility of the brand, and value equity is driven by quality, price, and convenience; brand equity as the subjective assessment of the brand above and beyond the perceived value, and brand equity is driven by brand awareness, attitude toward the brand, and corporate ethics; and relationship equity as the tendency of the customer to stick with the brand, and relationship equity is driven by loyalty programmes, special recognition and treatment, affinity programmes, community-building programmes, and knowledge-building programmes.

Their framework—the customer equity diagnostic—is offered as a way to determine which customers to acquire as well as what will enable their retention. If we define customer value as the value of the firm or a product as perceived by the customer, customer equity is the converse and refers to the value of the customer to the firm. If the objective is to maximize the returns from your investments—the customer portfolio—you must maximize customer equity. This makes sense because you can maximize sustainable return on assets by maximizing customer equity for the long term.

To maximize customer equity, we must be able to measure it. If customer equity is simply the value of a customer to the firm, we can articulate that value in the same way that customers articulate our value to them. Just as customer value is the difference between benefits and costs to the customer, conversely, customer equity is the difference between the benefits and costs to the firm in serving a customer.

One team of researchers describes their method of measuring customer equity as follows: "[we] first measure each customer's expected contributions toward offsetting the company's fixed costs over the expected life of that customer. Then we discount the expected contributions to a net present value at the company's target rate of return for marketing investments. Finally, we add together the discounted expected contributions of all current customers." Evident in their metric are the following important points about customer equity:

- It is the sum of the equity of all of a firm's customers.
- It summates the gross contribution of each customer, taking into account benefits as well as costs of serving a customer.
- It includes consideration of future revenues and variable costs from each customer.
- It is a time-discounted present value of future benefits to the firm.

It becomes evident that the customer equity concept when disaggregated to the individual customer level allows us to look at the revenues and costs of serving an individual customer. It helps answer the question, which customer should we serve? The ideal customer to the firm is the one that gives it the maximum long-term customer equity, which theoretically you want as a brand-loyal customer. However, as we will see in the next section, the converse is not true, because not all brandloyal customers provide maximum customer equity.

Who Is The Right Customer?

The concept of brand loyalty is a well-researched topic. The notion of a customer having a lifetime value and the prominence of database systems in managing customers have spawned a renewed interest in relationship marketing. Just making repurchases doesn't make a customer brand loyal. There must be some commitment by the customer to the firm for relational continuity reflecting a positive patronage bias. Not all brand-loyal customers have a positive disposition to the provider—some relationships may be forced because of a lack of choice.

Brand loyalty reflects a financial, social, or structural bonding with the customer. Relationship marketing seeks to enhance the mutual benefits from the relationship with the right customer—seeking brand loyalty from the right customer. To determine who the right customer is, we need to understand what benefits the firm expects from an ideal customer. Management system is designed with you in mind. Knowing the needs of modern hotels, simplifies the communication between the waiting and kitchen staff.

Customer's orders are communicated automatically to the kitchen for display on a kitchen management system or for printing on a kitchen printer. This minimises wait times and eradicates ordering mistakes that can irritate customers and cost your restaurant unearned revenue. When combined with handheld terminals, orders can be taken directly from tables, speeding up the ordering experience further.

At the outset, it is clear that the stream of purchases from the brandloyal customer is the primary benefit. In truth, the value of a brand-loyal customer to the firm must go beyond the purchases made over the lifetime of the relationship with that customer. As shown, revenues can be direct and indirect. Direct revenues are all of the customer's purchases, and indirect revenues are the cash value of all of the other benefits the customer accrues to the firm, in the form of direct revenues from referred customers. Costs to serve are drastically reduced, as brand-loyal customers are generally easier to serve. The argument is that as customers get familiar with the firm, its processes and products, customers will require less costly assistance from the firm in purchasing and using the product.

Loyal customers may even be able to open up ways in which to reduce the costs of serving the customer. Other benefits of brand loyalty would include product improvement contributions, new product opportunities, ideal sources for market information, and favourable word of mouth. At an overall level, all these benefits add up to a degree of stability and potential growth for the firms. Those brand-loyal customers who are committed in their patronage recognize their benefits from the firm and show commitment in the provider firm.

To select the right customer, the firm must be able to measure the value of the loyal customer from all these benefits as well as the costs of acquiring and retaining that customer. It is not easy to quantify all of these benefits. But it is possible to calculate the direct and indirect revenues from each customer. It is also possible to calculate the acquisition costs and relationship maintenance costs. Information technology has allowed us to obtain that data and made it easy to calculate the lifetime value of a customer.

The Calculus of Lifetime Value

A commonly used practice inherited from the direct marketing industry experience is called RFM (referring to "recency, frequency, and monetary data")—a method to determine whom to send promotions from among your customers. It takes into account the value of a customer's purchases, how recent they were, and how often they were purchased. As with the danger of any one approach, RFM has been used without much consideration for other important dimensions of the most valuable customer, such as how profitable the customer really is. RFM is therefore not a proxy measure for the lifetime value of a customer.

Indeed, if the costs of serving different customers show a variance, then the RFM method could attract the wrong customer. As, there are three main factors in calculating the lifetime value of a customer.

It is not just a simple product of the value of each purchase and the number of times the customer will purchase the product over that customer's lifetime. The lifetime value of a customer should also include referral value. And, it should include the lifetime costs as well. CRM technology has made it possible to do this, but, how many firms actually use this understanding in how they design and implement their CRM solutions?

Lifetime Revenues

Lifetime revenues are the sum of all purchases that the customer will make. An assessment of the progression of purchases over the lifecycle of the customer is a key point to be made here. For instance, consider what a college student's financial lifecycle would mean to a bank. First, it is a savings or checking account with a debit card and perhaps even a credit card. The college student may also be a good candidate for an education loan. Once graduated, this ex-student is now in the market for a car loan, and quite soon a home mortgage.

Once other life events such as marriage and children occur, there are more car loans, mortgages, home equity loans, trusts, custody accounts, education loans for children, and associated financial products that a typical family would need. USAA, the life insurance and financial services company, follows marriages, births, and other life events so that it can advise customers on changing needs.

Every firm should attempt to develop such a long-term consumption profile for the typical customer in each segment, charting their potential purchases over a lifetime to take into account the life events of the customer—a customer lifecycle analysis. A similar case may be made for business customers based on an assessment of growth potential, so that any B2B firm has to project the growth of its customers and factor that into a lifetime value calculation.

Not all customers become brand loyal. We have seen that superior customer value is a prerequisite for brand loyalty. What percentages of new customers find the firm's customer value to be superior? The lifetime value of a customer must also factor the probability of the acquired customer becoming brand loyal. Thus, the lifetime value of a customer is the first purchase, plus the probability of repeat purchases for the duration of the relationship with the firm. The probability consideration takes into account that a customer may not be a good fit, that a competitor may have been able to provide a better fit, or that the need situation changed for the customer, such as in the case of relocation of the consuming unit.

Lifetime Costs

An activity-based costing approach allows a firm to account for direct costs that the firm incurs in the relationship with a specific customer. Once again, with information technology it is possible, where it makes sense, to attribute marketing and operating costs to individual customers. To obtain the full benefit from CRM investments, it is important to track costs at the individual customer level as well. Costs include acquiring and remarketing to the customer over the lifetime of the customer. Costs also include value creation and delivery costs of serving the customer. Thus, the costs after acquisition include not only the costs of serving the customer, but also relationship maintenance and development costs such as the costs of cross-selling or upselling, called remarketing costs. Once again, the costs related to the first purchase are separated from that of lifetime purchases so that the probability of repeat purchase is taken into account when calculating lifetime costs.

Referral Value

The indirect revenue of referrals from a loyal customer is an often overlooked aspect of customer equity. The typical CRM solution and database marketing approaches ignore the referral power of a customer in calculating the lifetime value of a customer. Most firms do not even capture this data, partly because it is difficult to obtain information when knowledge systems in a firm are not configured to obtain it. The other reason may be that firms are not proactively looking for referrals from their loyal customers in any systematic way.

How is the value of referrals from a customer calculated? To answer this question requires looking at the process and mechanics of how referrals work. Who provides a referral? Customers who are satisfied and who have a certain degree of loyalty are the ones who are likely to convey favourable messages about a firm and its products and services. A key piece of information needed here is what level of satisfaction a brand-loyal customer needs to have before being likely to refer a customer. The next obvious question is, who receives the referral? Customers are likely to convey this information to family, friends, and colleagues.

However, not all who receive the referrals are appropriate customers for the firm. What proportion of the customers who received the referral are good candidates for the firm? Out of the ones that are appropriate for the firm, not all are likely to be suitably influenced by the referral to make the first purchase. Finally, if a purchase is actually made, what proportion of referred customers makes repeat purchases? Those that are moved to try the product may not all turn into loyal customers, but if they do, then their lifetime purchases add to the value of the customer making the initial referral.

SELECTING AND ATTRACTING THE RIGHT CUSTOMERS

The task of creating and delivering superior customer value must be complemented with the selection of the appropriate customers and the effective management of relationships with those customers. The hospitality industry is a fascinating one from a CRM perspective, because of the quality and quantity of customer touchpoints. In the world of servicing guests, there are as many challenges as there are, well... challenging customers, but in the current age of "branding" one of the biggest ones is ensuring a consistent customer service experience. Today's hotels offer a multitude of lucrative services, all of which need to be recorded immediately against the right customer's bill.

Zonal can integrate any third party billing program to ensure that all room-charged items can be cross-checked quickly and easily at the point-of-sale for matching name against a stated room number. Commonly, hotels have a number of different sales areas for patrons to drink, eat and enjoy services.

Hotel management has the ability to define different products and prices for each of these sales areas, allowing them to apply premium price bands for exclusive areas. This challenge is three-pronged: First, managers must be able to manage consistency in the face of interchanging slow and busy times and seasons. Second, consistency needs to be ensured across job titles, roles, and pay ranges.

Third (or perhaps First, if you'd like), the marketing message must be in tune with a plan to set guest expectations according to the season and customer tier considerations. Customer retention leading to more custom and bigger profit is easier if you can keep your customers happy. This can be achieved in your restaurants with minimal wait times for food orders and accurate service delivery - every time.

The fully integrated kitchen management system communicates all food orders, with special instructions if necessary, automatically from the PoS in your sales areas directly to the kitchen to minimise customer wait times. Real-time awareness of current stock holding and usage gives you the power to manage supply and monitor profit margins more effectively. The stock control system is one of the most powerful in the industry and gives you the flexibility to monitor movements of products of all divisions between the different zones in your site. Emergency transfers of champagne cases from the cocktail bar to the function room can now be recorded easily.

As with any strategy, the goal is to help meet the corporate objectives, which often begin with defining the customer segments that can help move the enterprise in the right direction, and then approach them with the right marketing message, via the right marketing channels. On the subject of job roles, while some job roles had specific training on interacting with customers, others did not, or worse, were trained in an inconsistent way.

So the first order of things in this area is to establish a clear procedure for greeting, servicing, and addressing guest issues across various situations. All employees which come in direct contact with guests need to be in tune with this common standard. A set of behaviour and service standards also provides clear guidelines which can empower employees to provide special, or "magical" moments to their guests. The guest servicing standards themselves should focus on not just consistent responses, but also should prevent consecutive negative experiences.

In other words, if a guest has experienced a negative event (i.e. complained that the room wasn't clean upon check in), this fact needs to be captured and made available to customer-facing employees so that they can put an extra effort into making sure that the remainder of the hotel stay or restaurant experience is as positive as possible. A further back-end benefit to capturing the negative event information is that it will enable analysis of customer experience shortcomings. This in turn allows for active methods for managing, monitoring, and predicting customer satisfaction, which can then lead to fine-tuning the marketing message, interaction standards, and employee training.

Predictive analytics can be used to understand latent pain or dissatisfaction before it percolates and impacts customer loyalty.Managing customer relationships should be guided by an understanding of what the customer's equity is to the firm. Customer equity, the value of customer to the firm, improves as superiority in customer value improves. Since customer equity is perhaps the firm's most valuable asset, the firm must continually seek to improve customer value for it best customers. A firm's potential return on customer equity should determine the investment it makes in customers. For its most valuable customers, the firm must guarantee superior service quality and customer service, with special attention to recovering from inevitable product failures when they occur.

Maximizing long-term profitability comes from maximizing customer equity—firms must maximize the lifetime value of the customer, including revenues, referrals as well as costs of serving the customer. Customer acquisition and retention efforts must be guided by the worth of the customer to the firm.

Maytag provides premium service to its premium customers—those who purchase the Neptune line of laundry machines. Neptune customers get a dedicated staff, a separate toll-free number and fast response on service calls. This is an example of the common business practice where firms allocate resources by the profitability and value of the customer. They utilize the opportunity in directly interacting with individual customers to determine customer profitability and allocate assets accordingly. And what are the benefits of the practice of differentiating among your customers?

Broadly referring to the practice as CRM can sometimes defeat its purpose by losing sight of the basic meaning of the term: managing customer relationships. Managing customer relationships would mean actively planning, organizing, directing, and controlling a firm's business relationships with its customers. The term might be "new" in its current usage, but the business practice of managing relationships with customers is certainly not new.

What has prompted the increased attention to CRM is new technology: how well firms can practice CRM has been advanced by information technology in the new economy. Technology brings with it the risk of missing the benefits of huge investment costs if used inappropriately, however. The benefits can seem so attractive that the costs are rationalized until the technology fails to deliver.

The American Customer Satisfaction Index, a measure of customer attitudes toward about 200 companies from over 30 different industries, has actually shown a decline, while at the same time CRM technology investments had grown about five times. When used with a fundamental understanding of CRM's purpose, the benefits of CRM technology enabling the business practice of managing customer relationships are clearly powerful. Siebel, Peoplesoft, Oracle, and other CRM technologies are really customer information management or customer knowledge management systems. These systems gather data and convert it to knowledge that will help firms in their customer relationship management activities.

The most significant contribution of CRM technology to the practice of business is not the technology itself, of course. It is in what the technology does to the practice of managing customer relationships. Because technology has now made it easy to do all the tasks of gathering and analyzing customer information, firms have been able to discover and realize the incredible benefits in proactively managing customer relationships. For example, Continental Airlines' customer information system allows its staff to mine data on passenger profitability and is also able to suggest remedies and perks for special requests or complaining customers.

Customer benefits from relationships with firms have been conceptualized under three categories: social, psychological, and customization benefits, in a two-part study using interviews and surveys. Financial services such as brokerage and banking are heavy users of CRM technology. Deregulation and information technology have effectively blurred the boundaries between those two once-different financial institutions.

They have had a heavy reliance on information because these are primarily knowledge businesses. "Signature"-level customers at Charles Schwab wait no longer than fifteen seconds to reach a customer service person, whereas other customers can wait ten minutes or more. Some banks have coded their customers so that customer service reps can decide on rates and fees depending on the customer's profitability code. Centura Banks rates its customers on a profitability scale of 1 to 5.

The most profitable customers get service calls from staff and an annual call from the CEO. Attrition rate at the bank is down 50 percent in four years, and—more interesting—the percentage of unprofitable customers has gone down from 27 percent to 21 percent. The hospitality industry was able to slash 50 percent of its promotion programmes and increase response rates by 20 percent with a good database of response behaviour from its mailing list. CRM systems have provided firms with the data they need to determine the revenues and costs to serve at the individual customer level, allowing firms to prioritize their allocations of value-creating assets and resources to the more profitable customers.

According to AMR research, the CRM market grew from $200 milllion to $1.1 billion between 1994 and 1997, and is expected to reach as much as $16 billion—an indication of how much firms want this technology to manage customer relationships. A firm's knowledge about its customers has allowed it to adjust customer value based on the profitability of the individual customer.

Just as with power, information technology has to be used judiciously. Discriminating against less profitable customers can seem unreasonable to all paying customers and could backfire with publicity. AT&T withdrew its minimum usage charges for its basic-plan customers who were unprofitable. GE Capital tried to charge credit-card users who were not accruing a minimum level of interest charges and ended up having to sell its credit card business. When used appropriately at the individual level, information technology can be very rewarding. Capital One's senior vice-president for domestic card operations, Marge Connelly, says, "We look at every single customer contact as an opportunity to make an unprofitable customer more profitable."

CRM systems are not just about profiling customers and loyalty programmes. To derive maximum benefits, one must broaden the thinking about CRM technology. The technology should be viewed as knowledge-based systems that seek to prioritize commitment of a firm's assets and resources to the more profitable customers while enhancing the relationships with ALL (right) customers. Pricing may not be the appropriate means to deal with the unprofitable customer. CRM systems give the firm access to information that may reveal other ways to manage the unprofitable customer. *Enabling* the managing of customer relationships is the goal of the CRM system.

Managing customer relationships is about selecting, acquiring, retaining, and enhancing relationships with customers by using an intimate knowledge of the customer's consumption domain to maximize the return on the firm's assets. With CRM systems, firms have the knowledge and the technological capability to identify, retain and enhance more desirable customer relationships.

This covers issues regarding which customers to acquire and retain for maximum sustainable profits. How do you assign value to customers and what is involved in that evaluation? Who is the right customer? Who should be in your customer portfolio? Firms look at customers as investments. How do you value these investments? Or, What is the equity of your customers?

MAXIMIZING LIFETIME VALUE

Maximizing the collective lifetime value of its customers should be the goal in managing customer relations. Head office Managers can analyse the performance of the business via the extensive reporting options on all aspects of your business and make product and price decisions for the whole organisation. Head office can either assume complete control of all matters (suitable for new sites or sites with inexperienced managers) or devolve varying amounts of control to site managers. At the furthest end of the spectrum you can reduce head office to a merely supervisory role where you only view global reports and produce financial audits. By increasing the number of customers *and* by increasing the lifetime value of each customer, firms can maximize their long-term profitability. To maximize the lifetime value of customers, you need to:

- Maximize lifetime revenues
- Maximize lifetime referrals
- Minimize lifetime costs

Maximizing Lifetime Revenues

Potential customers in a target market are by definition not yet customers. They may or may not be aware of or inclined to purchase from the firm. Firms have to nurture customers' dispositions to the firm through a number of stages before they can benefit from the loyalty of those customers. The acquisition process of customers could begin at any of the different stages on the road to loyalty. Customers may or not be aware or have an understanding of the features and benefits of the product. If the knowledge of the product is favourable, customers may have a liking or preference for the product.

Some customers may even have purchased the product but may not be repeat purchasers, may not be loyal to the product, or may have switched to a competitor. The right customers from any stage need to be moved toward a state of loyalty to the firm and its products. Can CRM technology be configured to capture information about the customer's stage in this process?

Once the appropriate customers are acquired, firms must look for increased usage and frequency, cross-selling opportunities, and trading up to premium versions. Retaining customers requires proactive customer management. If not, customers are likely to be indifferent to the firm, and a heavy user may become impatient and switch to the competition. Proactive customer management seeks to increase interest in the light user and treat the heavy user with appreciation and respect. Thus, the goal of maximizing lifetime revenues is achieved by maximizing the average purchase per year as well as the duration of the customer's relationship with the firm.

Maximizing Lifetime Referral Value

Referral customers have very low acquisition costs, since your brandloyal customers did the marketing for you. Following the mechanics of the process of word of mouth, maximizing lifetime referral value requires maximizing the number of referrals from each customer and maximizing the lifetime value of each referred customer. To maximize the number of referrals, one must maximize the drivers of referrals from a customer. In other words, firms must attempt to increase the probability of a customer making a referral of profitable customers. Firms must move loyal customers to become advocates of the firm.

When word of mouth is seen as a powerful customer acquisition tool, firms will find a way to stimulate referrals. Many firms are not proactive in stimulating referrals, assuming simply that "good word of mouth will happen if we do a good job." What must firms do to increase the value from referrals?

First, firms must identify the current and potential advocates of the firm. Firms must proactively look for individuals and organizations that are likely sources of referrals and stimulate and reward them for the right kind of referrals. Satisfied and loyal customers are not the only ones who can stimulate positive word of mouth. There are opinion leaders: such individuals and organizations as consumer reports, firms such as Gartner and Forrester, who might be considered experts in the field, and most important, the general and trade media.

Other ambassadors for the firm include players in often overlooked sources such as suppliers, resellers, employees, and other stakeholders such as investors. Community chat rooms on the Web are rich sources of information for the firm about what word of mouth is transpiring among its stakeholders.

Second, firms must attempt to stimulate referrals. Any new customer acquisition activity should record information on how the customer was moved to deal with the firm. When the firm obtains and records this information in the consumption profile of any customer, it is able to use it to calculate the average number of customer referrals made by each current customer of the firm.

Customers and advocates with similar profiles need to be approached about playing a referral role. Since some customers may be amenable and others not, firms must explore what it would take to move suitable customers to play an advocate role.

Finally, from Equation C it is also clear that the better the fit between the referred customer and the firm's products, the greater the lifetime referral value. Research has also shown that the customers referred to by satisfied customers tend to be a particularly good fit with the firm and its products and services.

The fit is better than with those customers attracted and acquired through marketing messages such as advertisements and coupon mailers. Brand-loyal advocates bring in like-minded customers. To get referrals to actually make a purchase or try the firm's offerings, it is necessary to get some incentives into the hands of the referred customers.

Minimizing Lifetime Costs

Reducing the costs of acquisition, costs of serving, and the cost of remarketing per customer can increase the lifetime value of a customer. Reducing costs to serve means that you need to be more efficient in the yield from your value-creating assets. We are drawn back to the yield management. Costs to serve per customer are reduced when you increase the cost efficiency or the capacity utilization efficiency. To reduce costs of acquisition and remarketing you need to be more effective in your marketing, both to new and to current customers. CRM technology can be used to continually learn from experience and utilize knowledge to reduce operating and marketing costs at the individual level.

Remarketing To The Right Customers

To maximize the total lifetime value of their customers, firms must proactively manage customer relationships. As, proactive customer relationship management should seek customer appreciation from the heavy user and attract more interest from light users with better value bundles if they can contribute more in their lifetime value to the firm. This is in contrast to the firm that may have good customer service, for example, but in its reactive mode will leave the light user relatively indifferent to the firm and the heavy user susceptible to a competitor.

Most loyalty programmes involve some kind of reward for the continued patronage of their customers. Referred to as frequency marketing, continuity programmes, awards or points programmes, or simply loyalty a programme, the goal of these programmes is to market and manage relationships with customers. First instituted by American Airlines in the 1970s to get around government regulation that prevented price competition, now many firms' programmes attempt to solidify their relationships with its customers. The rewards or awards, as they are called, may come in the form of free products and services at the firm, or sometimes even free products from other firms.

The smart firms impose restrictions on the use of these rewards, so that they are used to increase demand when and where needed. For example, the hospitality industry blocks out certain dates so that the promotions are targeted at different segments to entice customer utilization at low demand periods. The problem is that many of these programmes are misguided in design and implementation. One obvious omission is evident when the lifetime calculus is compared to the criteria for the rewards. The rewards focus on revenues for the most part. That costs are taken into account is not clear at all.

A recent *Harvard Business Review* article offers data that would be a surprise for managers who have not considered costs of serving the customer. Brand-loyal customers are not necessarily profitable customers. In their knowledge of their own value and indispensability to the firm, the brand-loyal customer could make costly demands of the firm.

The firm, in doling out the goodies along with the product and other business favours, may actually be spending more than it recognizes as costs of serving that customer. The only criterion for these (brand) loyalty programmes should be that they should maximize the customer equity for each customer, based on the calculus of lifetime value that we have discussed. To be meaningful and powerful in managing relationships with the right customers, these customer acquisition and loyalty programmes must specify the following:

- Objectives of the programme
- Market and customer scope of the programme
- Value for customer scope of the programme
- Impact scope (costs, timing, impact on people, process, physical assets, other customers, publicity opportunities, etc.)

The objectives of the programme need to be stated in the context of customer relationship management. What is the expected value of the programme to the firm? What specifically must the programme accomplish? Perhaps it is to shift demand from peak to low periods, to attract new segments, to get light users to become heavy users, to promote a new product offering, or some other specific objective. Without a known objective, no programme can be assessed on merit.

The next specific decision for customer relationship programmes is to specify the customer that the programme is intended for. Often, frequency programmes are so loosely formulated that the rewards are earned by the wrong customer. Consider this example of the unfortunate consequence of a poorly guided programme. One Mr. Phillips logged 1.25 million frequent flier miles—about $25,000 worth of airline travel—with an investment of 50 hours of his time and $3,140. Mr. Phillips took advantage of an offer he found on the package of a Healthy Choice frozen entrée: 500 American Airlines miles for every 10 UPCs, with early birds receiving a double count of miles! A Mr. Fisher participated in the same programme and got 12,000 Northwest Airlines Miles.

Even if the airlines got an awfully good financial deal with Healthy Choice, one must ask who the loyalty programme attracts—whether the airlines are in the grocery business or in the airline business. How do their returns from this investment compare with the returns that they would have achieved with programmes that targeted the frequent flier instead of the frequent grocery shopper? The objectives of the programme should determine the appropriate segment or customer for the programme.

The problem with most programmes is that they don't take into account the profitability of the customer. Who should be the target of the programme? Not every customer is right for the firm, as we have seen, nor is every customer right for every programme. The best programme is one that tailors the award to the target customer. Thus, giant supermarket retailer

UK-based Tesco mails 100,000 variations of promotions to its loyal customers.

Further, some customers may be more costly to retain, while others may be increasing their profitability to the firm. As, it is evident that firms need to look at the acquisition costs and retention costs of its customer base when determining the focus of their retention efforts. The calculus of the lifetime value of a customer is clear in its indication of what needs to be factored into deciding to which customer to target the promotion. Low acquisition costs and low retention costs are realized from your most profitable customers.

At the other end are your customers who were costly to acquire and cost you a lot to serve. Given the acquisition costs, the firm must keep a close eye on the customer's cost of retention. If the firm misjudged a customer's lifetime value or committed more resources to the acquisition of the customer than the revenue stream would justify, the firm has to either reduce retention costs or stop serving the customer if possible.

For the chosen customers, the firm needs to decide what they would do to motivate the customer to act. Customer knowledge should indicate what the customer is sensitive to, so that the value of the promotion can be appropriate for the specific customer or segment. The value of the promotion may be in the form of additional product, a complementary service, a straightforward price-break, or a discount for future purchases or a gift, among other things. Software firms are able to use lead customers in beta-tests and other benefits about new and innovative offerings before the rest of the market will find out, giving these B2B customers early mover advantage in their value chains in their industry.

Of course, a projected cost/benefit analysis is a must—what additional revenues have been realized and at what cost? For service firms, and where the programme is about service components, it is imperative that the promotion take into account what it would do to the demand patterns of customers. The last thing you want is for customers to strain your operation if your programme ends up drawing more customers during peak times when you are already at optimum levels of served customers. Any programme must consider the impact on other customers, on the staff, physical assets, and the delivery system or process.

For example, a shortage of airline seats infuriates frequent fliers who, as brand-loyal customers, having diligently set aside miles for use on family vacations, find they are not able to use the miles because use of awards is limited to a certain proportion of the volume on each flight and are restricted to certain times and dates. Estimates are that about 10 percent of all miles flown on a carrier can be from people cashing in on these rewards.

Does it make sense for frequent flier awards to range from personal digital assistants to designer watches? Are the costs and impact of these awards assessed? Another less obvious criterion is the potential for publicity in a promotion. A promotion that is newsworthy could attract the attention of a large number of potential customers and other stakeholders.

Firms must prioritize the management of customer relationships as a firm-wide imperative. Dell Computer, for example, has a "customer experience council" consisting of senior executives from each division or business line and major function that reports to a corporate vice chairman, no less. The council oversees measurement of several aspects of customer behaviour, including the effectiveness of its loyalty programmes. Dell even measures all the costs its customers incur in purchasing and using their products, including such things as shopping, ordering, installing, operating, servicing, and disposing of products.

The real value of tracking these revenues and costs over the lifetime value of the customer is that it allows firms to understand their brandloyal customers and anticipate their future needs. Such management practices will be able to deliver benefits to the heavy user to maximize their lifetime value. The lifetime value of the customer must be calculated for each customer—an assessment of revenues and costs over the lifetime of the customer's relationship with the firm. The investment in acquiring and retaining a customer must be made based on the customer's lifetime value to the firm.

A continuous monitoring of up-sell and cross-sell opportunities could increase the lifetime value of the customer. The potential customer equity from each segment or customer should determine the extent of value-creating adjustments to be made in terms of delivery process or product outcome customization in terms of value or other benefits to the customer or in terms of adjusting the price and other costs to the customer.

These changes in promotion offerings to acquire a new customer or remarket to a current or inactive customer will impact both costs and revenues and their effect on the lifetime value of the customer will determine subsequent investments in acquiring and retaining customers.

Guaranteeing Customer Value

Maximizing customer equity requires maximizing customer satisfaction by providing superior customer value. Ensuring product quality as the key driver of customer satisfaction requires checking the links between the firm's assessment of customer expectations and its ability to translate that assessment into product concept, operations design, and execution.

The doorman greeted the guest as the taxi pulled up to the Windsor Court Hotel, a 324-room hotel in downtown New Orleans, one of 120 independent luxury hotels of Preferred Hotels and Resorts Worldwide. Later, the waiter at the restaurant in the hotel accommodated off-the-menu orders—but the waiters did not make eye-contact with the diners. The guest room did not have the current edition of the Yellow Pages. This guest was one of Richey International's hotel spies, who had just conducted the Preferred test for the hotel. He has determined based on his experience as a customer that this hotel had met 88.5 percent of the Preferred standards, passing the 80 percent minimum. Firms such as Preferred want an unbiased assessment of the quality of their product and hire independent quality assessment firms such as Richey International to do the benchmarking of its hotels.

Firms also want to hear from you directly if you are a heavy user of their product. For instance, if you have over 1 million miles on your Sky Miles frequent flier account, or you fly 100,000 miles, or 100 trip segments, or 20 transoceanic segments in a year, you are a most-valued "platinum member" of Delta Air Lines and may be called to dinner in a private dining room in a luxurious setting. Delta wants to know what you think about the quality of their service.

Customers, especially the most profitable and valuable ones, are being called on for their perceptions of quality of the product received. Deliver a quality product and you are likely to have satisfied and loyal customers. The logic is pretty straightforward, and yet most firms struggle with at least some of the links in the chain: What is quality from the customer's perspective and how can the firm ensure the design and delivery of that quality?

Beginning in the late 1980s and continuing into the early 1990s, there was a groundswell of attention and interest in quality, primarily as a result of falling competitiveness of U.S. firms in the wake of Japan's advances. Quality gurus like Deming, Juran, and Crosby preached the gospel of quality. The Total Quality Management (TQM) movement's cornerstone, the prestigious Baldrige award programme administered by the National Institute of Standards and Technology, was a coveted prize for a great deal of effort by companies large and small. *Business Week* ran a number of articles profiling such winners as L.L. Bean, FedEx, Xerox, Motorola, Disney, and others.

As established and emphasized throughout this book, an understanding of customer value is a fundamental element of customer focus and service orientation. This provides a model for delivering customer value by focusing on the quality of the product, as judged according to how it meets customer expectations. To maximize profitability, the firm must maximize the lifetime value of the customer.

A key driver of this goal is customer loyalty, which is dependent on customer satisfaction. To achieve customer loyalty, it is imperative that firms create and deliver a quality product—as defined by the customer. What does the customer evaluate in determining the quality of a product? And, what actions of the firm can be linked to that customer perception of quality?

Perhaps the most significant research on perceived quality in services was conducted by Parasuraman, Zeithaml, and Berry and sponsored by the Marketing Science Institute in Cambridge, Massachusetts. Their contribution was timely and thorough, and revealed a number of important facets of customer perceptions of service quality. These researchers defined service quality as the difference or gap between customer expectations and customer perceptions of service. Their systematic study of customer evaluations across a variety of services revealed that customers evaluate services along certain key dimensions grouped under the acronym RATER: the R eliability of the firm's products, the A ssurance customers feel that their needs and expectations will be met, the T angibles associated with the service, the E mpathy displayed by the firm, and the R esponsiveness of the firm to their specific and individual needs.

Further, they found that there were four principal factors that contributed to the difference between what customers expect and what the firm delivers:

- How accurate is the firm's understanding and interpretation of customer expectations?
- Is this understanding of customer expectations effectively translated into product design?
- What is the gap between what is envisioned and what is delivered?
- How good is the match between what is delivered and what is advertised?

Quality translates customer experience with the product to customer value. Quality of customer experience is framed with the costs of access to and use of the product. Customer value is what customers ultimately evaluate in making the decision on future patronage. Their loyalty to a solutions provider depends on their comparison of actual customer value with expected customer value. What determines how well a firm meets a customer's expected value?

THE MECHANICS AND MANAGEMENT

The model presented here is based on Parasuraman, Zeithaml, and Berry's work on service quality. It uses the same logic to incorporate more directly the notion of costs to the customer. *Quality* may not fully convey the point that it is customer value that drives the relationship with the customer. Analysis of quality without the associated costs will not completely capture the customer's frame of reference. The crux of the model is that there are an ideal and an actual for both the customer and the firm:

- The customer's ideal—expected customer value
- The customer's actual—experienced customer value
- The firm's ideal—product concept
- The firm's actual—operations design

The ideal and the actual of the customer's expectations and perceptions and the firm's product concept and operations design are placed in the context of the competition, the technology, the economy, and the legal and social environment within which they operate.

For example, competitive forces and the social environment can shape customer expectations and affect their comparative evaluation of customer value. The firm's ability to hire the appropriate personnel to deliver the product as conceived and designed can also be affected. Firms design a product concept based on their understanding of the customer's expectations, and then configure their value-creating assets accordingly in an operations design, which for the most part determines what they actually deliver as customer experience.

Thus, customer expectations, product concept, operations design, and customer experience are all linked. Customer value is dependent on this *expectations* link, the *design* link, and the *execution* link. The product concept needs to be closely aligned with customer expectations—the expectations link into the firm. The firm interprets and converts the customer's ideal—expected customer value—into what becomes the firm's ideal—product concept. The firm's actual—the operations design—is the firm's implementation of the firm's ideal—the product concept.

The design link is how well the firm has been able to implement the firm's concept of customer expectations with its productive assets. The design or configuration of a firm's assets executes the product concept, which is what the customer experiences. The execution link reflects how well the customer's actual experience is aligned to the intent of the operations design. Thus, firms must align the customer's ideal expectations to the product concept with a strong expectations link, which in turn is linked to the operations design by a strong design link, followed by an execution link, which determines the customer's experience.

Customer expectations management, studied with a sample of about 100 managers at the leading service firms in the U.K., was found to be composed of three key dimensions: keeping promises, marketing orientation, and employee skills. Another study in a small electric utility company in the United States found that frontline employees had a good understanding of customer expectations. If we assume that customer's expectations were perfectly understood, reflected in the product concept and translated into operations design and therefore customer experience, we should find that customer value is high.

However, in practice this is an invalid assumption. Customer expectations play a very critical role in shaping customers' perceptions of quality. When customer expectations are met, we find perceived quality is high, and when not met, we find perceived quality is low.

A closer look at the model will reveal that it is a good vehicle to frame all that can be done to improve customer value by increasing benefits and decreasing costs to the customer. It is a safe assumption to make that improving quality will improve customer value. Creators of the University of Michigan's American Customer Satisfaction Index have shown that customer expectations are linked to perceived value and customer satisfaction over time. Improving quality relative to costs to the customer requires strengthening all the links in the model. Tracking the logic from expectations to product concept, to operations design, to customer experience are a number of management actions that must be taken to ensure the desired customer value.

As, firms can make several check to ensure that the customer-focus and service orientation helps keep the value created and delivered closely aligned with customer expectations. Firms devote most of their attention to the value creation and delivery that affect the perceptions of the customer. However, if service quality is defined as the comparison between expectations and perceptions, shouldn't firms be focusing attention on shaping customer expectations as well?

Managing the Expectations Link

How closely the firm's conception of the product resembles the customer's expectations is a key conceptual link. This link is a function of how well the firm understands customer expectations and how well that understanding is translated into product concept and design. Evaluating the quality of products, especially that of services and service components of products, is difficult for the customer. To understand the implications of this difficulty, think of services as being dependent on search, experience, and credence dimensions. Some services are higher in search qualities that can be evaluated before the purchase. Experience qualities are those that can only be assessed during or after consumption, whereas credence qualities are hard to evaluate even after the service.

Similarly, customer expectations are just as complicated as customer evaluations. Research has shown that there is a zone of tolerance in customer expectations. The zone of tolerance is the range of expectations on any of the attributes that are important to the customer. The low end of the range is the minimum level of service that determines what is adequate. The high end of the range is the maximum level of service, referred to as what is desired. Customers will accept anything below the desired, as long it is above the adequate level.

To be able to manage expectations, firms need to understand how customer expectations are shaped. Firms need not only to understand customer expectations but to help shape them so that they are realistic. Customers form expectations from their own past experience with the firm's product as well as with similar products from competitors. In the absence of such experience, customers draw from their experience with the firm's other products or from similar products in general. The firm's own communications, both explicit and implicit, shape customer expectations.

Explicit communications come from all overt marketing messages. Implicitly, all visible actions and evidence of the firm—its prices, its location, its culture reflected in the way it conducts business—could communicate something about the firm. Customers are also influenced by others regarding consumption need situations and the solutions appropriate for those needs. This product-related information can come from messages they receive from the media, family, and friends. Firms are generally focused on their own overt communications and ignore the effect that other sources have on customers and their expectations.

It should become clear now that customer knowledge management is a critical starting point for any firm. The firm's effective use of CRM technology can enable the firm to have a more thorough understanding of customer expectations. Based on customer knowledge, we can see that a failure in this regard could be the result of ineffective use of available sources of information on the market segment and individual customer information. Are all the touch-points set up to capture and record customer information? Is there a process for sharing customer information across the firm? For example, is there bottom-up communication from frontline employees to managers who participate in product design? Recognizing that customer expectations are dynamic, market research and customer research should be a continuous exercise. Instruments used to gather customer information should be evaluated for validity and reliability and should be easy to use. Inappropriate or inaccurate market research could result in management designing the product concept based on poor information from the marketplace about expected customer value.

An effective customer information system is critical in designing a product concept that would deliver the expected customer value. Management could perceive market needs and customer expectations inaccurately or make poor use of information in defining the service concept. How good is the information on the customer? How complete is it? How well has the information been analyzed, interpreted, and assessed by the product designers? Information regarding the market needs to be disseminated and shared among individuals who are responsible for the service design. Is the information current, and is there adequate indication of how these expectations are likely to change in the near and long-term future? Corresponding changes in product design should be prompt and responsive.

Linking the product concept to the needs/expectations of the customer is dependent on how well information has been obtained on customer expectations and how well they have been utilized in the product concept. The irony is that sometimes the information is about the wrong customer! The value and validity of the information for product design depends on whose expectations are obtained and used in developing the product concept. The heaviest users or, more precisely, the ones with the most lifetime value should be the priority. In other words, the weight given to the information should be prioritized by the lifetime value of the customer. There is also the possibility that the customer not being the right customer could simply be a result of poor segmentation methods or targeting the inappropriate segment(s) or customer(s).

As we have seen, it is important that the right customer be drawn to the firm. Marketing communications could be attracting customers who are not intended for the service. This might be manifested in poor media or message strategy, setting up inappropriate customer expectations for the product concept. The question here, of course, is whose expectations were obtained and who is actually using the product. Thus, if the firm has not attracted the customer whose needs it can best satisfy at sustainable profits, then at the outset, the firm is at a disadvantage. Customer expectations are hard to measure. As we saw on customer knowledge management, firms may not have good information on the critical aspects of what customers expect. Research can be flawed and the data not valid, or the means of ascertaining the information is not reliable. Frequently the information is stale and customer expectations, being dynamic, have changed. If you have an inappropriate or inaccurate account of customer expectations, the product concept is not going to be aligned with what customers actually expect.

The Design Link

The link in the chain between what is conceived and what is designed into the firm and its value-creating processes depends on how effectively the firm's resources (people, raw materials, supplies, and systems) have been configured to create and deliver the product as per the product concept. The link could be broken with inaccurate configuration of a firm's resources, for instance, in poor selection of employees. In other words, the fit between job description (responsibility and tasks) and employee profile (skills, education, experience, and personality) represents a significant factor in how well the design is linked with the concept.

Poor empowerment of the frontline employee could fail the product concept in design. This could result from inadequate technical and customer service training, information systems, backroom efficiency, and other support structures. To be able to deliver the product as conceived or designed, internal marketing should be effective. For example, lack of clear communication of such things as the product concept, customer expectations, the marketing strategy, etc., to the frontline employee reflects poor internal marketing—and similarly in reverse, when the product concept decisions have not incorporated the frontline employee, the product is not conceived and operations not designed with that valuable input from the frontline. In any firm, there is an inevitable disconnect between what the customers expect and what the frontline perceives that the customer wants or what the managers think that the customer wants. For the frontline personnel to be empowered, they require the knowledge and the tools as well as the authority and motivation to use them. If not, the firm will find a disconnect between product concept and execution.

The Execution Link

If the product concept is not supported by the appropriate corporate culture, frontline employees are at a disadvantage in executing the product concept. Backroom employees should see frontline employees as internal customers and the entire corporate culture focused on customer satisfaction. A number of things must happen for the firm to ensure that the product concept can be delivered. All productive factors must execute the design to deliver the product as conceived.

Employees need to be selected, hired, trained, and motivated to execute the design. They need to be empowered so that they have the ability and the inclination to provide the service as designed. Employees need to be allowed the discretion to accommodate and customize to each customer as far as possible. With the right kind of training, frontline employees in services other than just professional services can also make the right decisions. What was actually delivered and the customer's perception of the product experience need to be continually monitored by the firm, so that the firm understands whether customer expectations were met. Perhaps, during customer interactions, the provider was ineffective in obtaining customer-specific information or in interpreting and using it in customizing the experience for each customer. In many services, customization is a key determinant in how well each customer is satisfied with the product experience.

For example, customers use tangibles (service provider's smile and other nonverbal cues) differently. Some customers need more assurance regarding the product than others. Some customers' information needs are different from others, and their evaluation of the service provider's responsiveness depends on how well the service provider is able to accommodate them. The service provider's ability to empathize with the customer reflects the ability of the service provider to understand the individual customer so that the actual delivery is closer to the individual customer. Customer perceptions are just as critical as customer expectations. Customer experience may in reality be different from the intial concept. One way firms reduce the disparity between perceptions and reality is to encourage or require managers to work in the front line. By the same token, an argument can be made for allowing the frontline to work backstage, so that they are knowledgeable about how the backstage works to support the frontline.

Bibliography

Aruna Zachariah: *Print Media Communication and Management : Elements, Dimensions and Images*, Kanishka, Delhi, 2006.

Baran, Paul A.: *The Political Economy of Growth,* New York, Modern Reader Paperbacks, 1975.

Benería, Lourdes. *Gender, Development, and Globalization, Economics as if All People Mattered,* New York and London, Routledge, 2003.

Borcherding, K., : *Contemporary Issues in Decision Making,* Amsterdam, North-Holland, 1990.

Burke, Frank M., *Valuation and Valuation Planning for Closely Held Businesses,* Englewood Cliffs, NJ, Prentice Hall, 1981.

Carroll, A. : *Business and Society: Managing Corporate Social Performance,* Boston: Little, Brown & Company, 1981.

Caviglioni O. : *Mapwise: Accelerated Learning Through Visible Thinking,* Network Educational Press, 2000.

Cootner, Paul : *The Random Character of Public Finance,* MIT Press, 1964.

Copeland, Tom, Tim Koller, and Jack Murrin, *Valuation: Measuring and Managing the Value of Companies,* New York, Wiley, 1994.

Desmond, Glenn, and John A, Marcell, *Handbook of Small Business Valuation Formulas and Rules of Thumb,* Valuation Press, 1993.

Dimson, Elroy: *Stock Market Anomalies,* Cambridge University Press, 1988.

Fraser, Steven, *Labor Will Rule, Sidney Hillman and the Rise of American Labor,* Reprint ed. Ithaca, N.Y.: Cornell University Press, 1993.

Fruhan, W. E.: *Financial Strategy, Studies in the Creation, Transfer and Destruction of Shareholder Value.* Homewood, 1979.

Goleman D.: *Emotional Intelligence,* New York: Bantam, 1995.

Guala, F.: *The Methodology of Experimental Economics,* New York, Cambridge University Press, 2005.

Guarti, Luigi, *The Valuation of Entrepreneurship,* Blackwell Publishing, 1994.

Harrigan, K. R.: *Strategies for Declining Businesses.* Lexington, MA: Heath, 1980

Hausman, D. M.: *The Inexact and Separate Science of Economics,* Cambridge, Cambridge University Press, 1992.

Hayek, F. A. *Individualism and Economic Order,* The University of Chicago Press, Chicago, 1948.

Howard, P.: *Business Finance,* Roseville, 1990

Jagbir Sharma: *Advanced Environment Chemistry*, RBSA Pub, Delhi, 2006.

Janis, I. L., & Mann, L.: *Decision Making, A Psychological Analysis of Conflict, Choice and Commitment.* New York, Free Press, 1977.

John A, Marcell, *Handbook of Small Business Valuation Formulas and Rules of Thumb,* Valuation Press, 1993.

Lindblom, C. E.: *A Strategy of Decision: Policy Evaluation as a Social Process*, New York, The Free Press, 1970.

Loomes, G.: *Current Issues in Microeconomics*, New York: St. Martin's Press, 1989.

Magnussen, L., *Evolutionary and Neo-Schumpeterian Approaches to Economics*, Kluwer, Boston, 1994.

Manuel, G. Velasquez : *Business Ethics Concepts and Cases,* Delhi, Pearson Education, 2002.

Marris, R. L., and Wood, A.: *The Corporate Economy*, London: Macmillan, 1971.

Peirson, G., Bird, R., Brown, R., & Howard, P.: *Business Finance*, Roseville, 1990

Pennings, J. M.: *Decision Making, An Organizational Behaviour Approach,* New York, Markus Wiener Publishing, 1983.

Pfeffer, J., and Salancik, G. R.: *The External Control of Organizations, A Resource Dependence Perspective*, New York, 1978.

Porter, M.E. : *The Competitive Advantage of Nations,* London, Macmillan, 1998.

Roth, A. E.: *The Handbook of Experimental Economics*, Princeton, Princeton University Press, 1995.

Shrivastava V.K. : *Environments and Social Concerns*, Concept, Delhi, 2011.

Sims, Ronald R. : *Ethics and Corporate Social Responsibility: Why Giants Fall,* New York, Praeger Publishers, 2003.

Som Nath Tiwari : *Global Warming and Its Effects on Environment*, Adhyayan, Delhi, 2007.

Taylor, F. W.: *The Principles of Scientific Management*, New York, 1917.

Tinbergen, Jan.: *On the Theory of Economic Policy*; Amsterdam, North-Holland 1952.

Trugman, Gary R., *Guide to Conducting a Valuation of a Closely Held Business*, New York, American Institute of Certified Public Accountants, 1993.

Weber, M.: *The Theory of Social and Economic Organizations*, New York, Oxford University Press, 1947.

Wood, A.: *The Corporate Economy*, London: Macmillan, 1971.

Woodward, J.: *The Oxford Handbook of Philosophy of Economics*, New York, Oxford University Press, 2009.

Yegge, Wilbur M., *A Basic Guide for Valuing a Company*, New York, Wiley, 1996.

Zipp, Alan S., *Business Valuation Methods* New York, American Institute of Certified Public Accountants, 1990.

Index

K

M

O

P

R

S

V

❑❑❑

www.ingramcontent.com/pod-product-compliance
Lightning Source LLC
Chambersburg PA
CBHW050524240926
51846CB00003B/685
* 9 7 8 9 3 8 3 2 6 3 5 1 6 *